JOHN D. BLEDSOE

THE GOSPEL OF ROTH

THE GOOD NEWS ABOUT ROTH IRA CONVERSIONS
(AND THE CHANGES THAT CAN MAKE YOU MONEY!)

LandMarc
PRESS

This book is dedicated to my mother Aggie Jenkins
who is the life of every party!

Cover Design: Publications Development Company

Produced by LandMarc Press

For general information on our other products and services of for technical support, please contact LandMarc Press at (936) 544-5137x224, fax (936) 544-2270, or on the web at www.LandMarcPress.com.

ISBN 978-0-9797184-8-9

Printed in the United States of America.

10 9 8 7 6 5 4 3 2 1

CONTENTS

INTRODUCTION

THIS BOOK IS AN ATTEMPT to provide some clear guidelines about a very confusing topic: Roth IRA conversions. There have been many articles concerning Roth IRA conversions in both the general and financial press that have been filled with errors, inaccuracies, incorrect innuendo, and just downright bad advice. I have received many phone calls from people who discussed Roth IRAs with their stockbroker, butcher, banker, accountant, neighbor, the clerk at the brokerage house, or some other Roth "expert" who has given them some misinformation. I would like to take this opportunity to clear the air on the most common misconceptions about Roth IRA conversions.

MYTH NUMBER 1

"You should run the numbers and look at your situation before you decide if you should convert to a Roth IRA. Maybe even run your figures through one of those Roth IRA conversion calculators."

WRONG.

Because you can undo Roth conversions in the future, you should convert first and run the numbers later. This is what I call the Roth Conversion Option or RCO. RCO is a strategy for converting all regular IRAs into Roth IRAs first and not deciding to actually commit to any of the Roth IRA conversions until later. Convert all regular IRAs (and available retirement plans) into several separate new Roth IRAs divided by asset class as early in the year as possible. Think January 4, 2010. Decide before the recharacterization deadline of October 15 the year after the conversion in which Roth accounts are to remain converted. For 2010 conversions, the deadline to unconvert is October 17, 2011. This decision that you will make before the 2011 deadline is based on all of the information known before the deadline, including the Roth account performance after conversion and other important factors. This would be a good time to run the numbers and use a Roth conversion calculator. The RCO is repeated every year you have regular IRAs or available retirement plans.

You do not have enough facts to make a good decision until you know the RCO results. If some of your converted Roth accounts go up by 40 percent before the deadline, it will result in a different answer than the accounts that stayed the same or went down in value. Deciding to convert to Roth IRAs now is like a doctor deciding to perform surgery without any x-rays or without even taking your temperature. Convert all of your regular IRAs and available retirement accounts to Roth IRAs on January 4, 2010, and wait until mid-2011. Then run the numbers and decide before the October 17, 2011, recharacterization deadline. And you can even pick and chose which Roth conversions to undo and which ones to keep before the deadline.

MYTH NUMBER 2

"You cannot use any of the money converted to a Roth IRA for five years without additional taxes and penalties."

WRONG.

You may use up to 100 percent of the amount converted and contributed to a Roth even the day after you convert without any additional taxes (and no penalties if you are over 59½). The reason for this is that Roth IRAs use a very favorable accounting method called first in, first out or FIFO. What this means is that any withdrawals from a Roth will first be considered from the principal or basis, which is tax-free. After 100 percent of the amount of your conversions and contributions have been withdrawn then taxes or penalties may apply, but only if the five-year rule has not been met. People who are under 59½ will still be subject to the old 10 percent early withdrawal penalty on converted IRAs. That is exactly as it was before these people under age 59½ converted to a Roth. So to those of you who are under age 59½ and who have complained about this, I say GROW UP!

MYTH NUMBER 3

"It is better to convert to a Roth in 2010 and use the one-time government income tax deferral special to pay the tax in 2011 and 2012."

MAYBE AND PROBABLY NOT.

2010 is a special year indeed, but mainly because the income restriction for Roth IRA conversions has been lifted starting then, which allows everyone to make the conversion. Also, for Roth conversions in 2010 only, you do not have to pay any income tax triggered by the conversion in the year 2010, but you may wait and recognize half the income from the 2010 conversion in 2011 and the other half in 2012. You do not have to defer payment of income tax on 2010 Roth conversions if you elect not to. Paying the taxes on 2010 Roth conversions in 2010 might actually be more appealing than the deferral to 2011 and 2012 because tax rates may go up. The way you hedge your bet here is to use the RCO (see myth number 1) and wait until 2010 is over and see what income tax rates are announced for 2011. You actually have until the same October 17, 2011, deadline to commit to which year(s) you elect to pay the tax for 2010 Roth conversions. You should consult with a tax professional before April 2010 to make sure you pay enough in withholding or estimated payments to the IRS to avoid any penalties, no matter which option you end up taking.

MYTH NUMBER 4

"I don't want to convert to a Roth IRA because Congress is going to change the law and start taxing Roth IRAs in the future."

NOT LIKELY.

Congress can be unpredictable and certainly can make law changes at will, but taxing Roth IRAs would be unlikely for a couple of reasons. The accounting method that Roth IRAs use is FIFO (see myth number 2), and the gain from Roth IRAs would be hard to get to from a tax standpoint. In the past, when changes of this magnitude occurred, the existing participants have been "grandfathered" and protected from these changes. Also, it would be far easier for the politicians to raise more revenue simply by increasing tax rates across the board. Finally, it would create a huge uproar if the tax-free nature of Roth IRAs were ever threatened. I talked to many people who were fearful of this over a decade ago when the Roth IRA was first introduced who now are very glad they made the switch and conversion to a tax-free Roth IRA.

MYTH NUMBER 5

"It will take years for me to earn back the money in my Roth IRA to recover the loss that I would sustain from the income tax payment triggered by the Roth conversion."

WRONG.

Many people who convert from a regular IRA to a Roth IRA have more spendable (after-tax) money from the very first day that they convert. If the conversion temporarily pushes you into a higher tax bracket, you may have less spendable money for a time (typically a very short time). The amount of excess spendable money created by the Roth conversion then usually grows even greater over time. No pain no gain clearly does not apply to the Roth IRA conversion. The Roth IRA conversion can be advantageous even for people with short-time horizons and even for people who need income from their IRAs right away.

MYTH NUMBER 6

"My regular IRA is my money, and it is worth what the brokerage statement says that it is worth."

WRONG.

The regular IRA or retirement is always worth less than the account statement says that it is. That is because you have a partner in the IRA on every penny—the IRS. You are actually carrying a debt or a mortgage on your regular IRA. By converting to a Roth IRA, you are paying off this debt or mortgage and dissolving your IRS partnership. You owed the taxes on the regular IRA or retirement plan all along and the cost of income tax at conversion is not a cost at all but the payment of a debt. When you run the analysis of a Roth IRA conversion in your situation (at the end of the RCO), you may discover that the Roth IRA conversion will provide much more in spendable dollars both now and in the future than any other alternative.

MYTH NUMBER 7

"My taxes will be lower in retirement so I would not want to convert to a Roth IRA now at a higher income tax rate."

MAYBE NOT.

Most of the clients that I have had through the years thought that this would be the case. However, for almost all of them, the older they get, even through retirement, the higher their income tax bracket. This is particularly true for the folks who have saved well. Even if you are in lower tax brackets down the road, the Roth IRA conversion still may produce superior results in your situation. Be sure to use the RCO and run your specific numbers toward the end of the conversion option period.

MYTH NUMBER 8

"The best way for me to convert to a Roth IRA is to convert all my retirement accounts and regular IRAs in the same year."

MAYBE NOT.

For many people, the most efficient way for them to convert to Roth IRAs is to convert over a few years to maximize the use of the lower income tax brackets if they can. For people who are not in the top income tax brackets (before they convert to a Roth), and who have some time before age 70½, converting over several years may make more sense. Use the RCO every year and run the numbers before the end of the RCO period to see which strategy works best in your case.

MYTH NUMBER 9

"Converting to a Roth IRA will not be advantageous in my case because I have no other money to pay the tax except from my retirement accounts and IRAs."

IT DEPENDS.

Converting to Roth IRAs just before you are age 70½ will often be beneficial even if you have to pay the tax from IRAs. This is due to the fact that regular IRAs have mandatory increasing annual withdrawals after age 70½. Roth IRAs have no lifetime mandatory withdrawals. If you are substantially younger than 70½ make sure that you have no other way to pay some of the tax on smaller conversions each year. With either situation, do the RCO and run your numbers toward the end of the recharacterization deadline.

MYTH NUMBER 10

"My regular IRA can be deferred for a long time after I turn age 70½, and when I die my spouse or heirs will be able to continue this deferral for a long time in the future."

WRONG.

Most IRA holders desire this so-called "stretch" or maximum deferral strategy for their IRAs. However, the mandatory taxable withdrawals are in reality much faster than desired. Did you know that in just 14 years after you turn age 70½ more than half of your regular IRA will be lost to mandatory distributions in almost every case? This is due to those incessant and increasing annual mandatory taxable IRA withdrawals. Keep in mind that Roth IRAs have no lifetime mandatory withdrawals. If maximum income tax deferral is your desire, then the Roth is a much better vehicle.

SUMMARY

The conversion of a regular IRA to a Roth will be very beneficial to many people. Before you dismiss the Roth IRA as a bad idea or run the numbers, you really must convert to Roth IRAs using the Roth Conversion Option to see what the results are toward the end of this option period. Remember that if you make the conversions on January 4, 2010, you will have until October 17, 2011, to undo any or all of these Roth IRA conversions just as if they had never occurred. Or you may pick and choose among these Roth IRA conversions and leave any or all of them converted. If you do not convert in 2010, you will not have any options to go back and convert in the past. The RCO strategy will provide you with every possible option to maximize your regular IRAs and available retirement accounts under the best possible scenario. The result can be a huge increase in after-tax spendable money for you, both now and in the future.

If this has stirred your interest, read on. The ten chapters that follow will give you all the information you need to make intelligent decisions about how to use the Roth IRA conversion to sustain your hard-earned dollars.

THE ROTH CONVERSION OPTION

IF YOU FOLLOW MY ADVICE in the next few pages, you may increase your retirement spendable assets by over 40 percent! *Everyone should convert all of his or her IRAs to Roth IRAs on January 4, 2010.*[1] Many articles have been written about the major law change for Roth IRA conversions beginning in 2010. I find most of these articles vague at best, and more often than not, incorrect. Some of these articles are far more confusing than helpful.

Since the inception of Roth IRAs in 1998, you could only convert your traditional or regular IRA to a Roth IRA if your income was $100,000 or less. But, starting in 2010, you can convert your regular IRAs and

---

[1]January 4, 2010, is the *first* date everyone is allowed to convert to a Roth IRA. If you are reading this after that date you should convert as soon as you can following the instructions in this book.

other retirement plans to Roth IRAs regardless of income. Yes, you read that right—everyone can now convert to a Roth starting in 2010. And everyone should.

FOLLOW THE YOGI BERRA PRINCIPLE

This change in the law has all of the CPAs, financial planners, and engineers scrambling for their calculators and spreadsheet programs debating the virtue of potential Roth conversion for each situation depending on a dizzying array of assumptions about future income tax rates and the maximum number of angels that can dance on the eraser of a number 2 pencil. It is human nature to want to figure out the best answer before taking action; but this intuition is incorrect when it comes to Roth conversions. What you should do is take action, then figure out the best answer. Or to quote the great intellectual Yogi Berra, "When you come to a fork in the road . . . take it." Convert first and calculate later.

The general repeating theme of almost every article about Roth conversions instructs and cautions people to calculate their Roth conversion "suitability" *before* they make the conversion, implying that a good decision can be made in this order (calculate before you convert). This premise is wrong. Dead wrong. Backwards.

Figuring out if you should convert to a Roth IRA before making the conversion is putting the cart before the horse. Convert first and ask questions later using the method outlined next. Do it exactly this way and I will explain all of the reasons later. The time line for the Roth Conversion Option is as follows:

STEP ONE: (January 4, 2010, 9:57 AM CST.) Convert all IRAs and available retirement plans into new Roth IRAs divided by asset class or investment type. Do not combine or mix with older Roth IRA accounts for now. Keep separate Roth IRAs for assets that were in retirement plans. No single Roth IRA account should exceed 20 percent of the total. If one asset class or investment type exceeds 20 percent of the total divide it into two IRAs or more as needed.

STEP TWO: (December 3, 2010 at lunchtime.) Recharacterize or unconvert any Roth accounts that lost substantial value from the conversion date of 1/4/2010. These accounts should be converted again to Roth IRAs on January 3, 2011 at 9:57 AM CST.

STEP THREE: (September–October 15, 2011.) Analyze and run your conversion numbers based on all known factors including increases in Roth accounts since the conversions.

STEP FOUR: (October 17, 2011, 8:30 AM CST.) Unconvert or recharacterize any accounts not selected to remain Roth IRA conversions back to regular IRAs.

CINDERELLA STORY

As you can see, you should convert to a Roth IRA first, then run the numbers later. This is because the IRS gives you until mid-October of the year *following* the year of a Roth conversion to undo the conversion. This "do over" is technically called a *recharacterization*. Your Roth IRA conversion is not final or complete until you pass this deadline for unconverting or recharacterizing. To advise a client properly on whether to convert to a Roth IRA is impossible in advance of learning this vital information. You must know about any increase in the Roth account after the conversion date but before the deadline for unconverting to be able to "run the numbers."

Even folks who otherwise would not ordinarily benefit from the Roth conversion may benefit greatly by converting if the value of the newly converted Roth goes up substantially during this option period. Like Cinderella and her pumpkin carriage, the Roth can be turned back into a regular IRA just as if nothing happened if you choose to do so before the deadline. The only way to have all the options and proper knowledge to make an informed Roth conversion choice is to convert first and ask questions later.

THE DETAILS

2010 is a special year. There is good news on the horizon for anyone with retirement accounts beginning in 2010. The title of this book is *The Gospel of Roth*. Gospel means good news. This good news or gospel is due to a tax law change that was enacted in 2006 called the Tax Increase Prevention and Reconciliation Act (TIPRA). What a catchy title from a clever Congress. I love it when taxes go on sale, no matter what they call it.

TIPRA changed Roth IRA conversions in two major ways for the year 2010. First this new law allows taxpayers at *any* income level to convert to a Roth IRA in 2010. In the past, Roth IRA conversions have been limited to folks with an income level of $100,000 or less. Beginning in 2010 and beyond, everyone can convert to a Roth IRA, regardless of income. Notice that this lifting of any income restriction for Roth conversions is not limited to 2010 but applies in the years afterward as well.

Second, for 2010 only, the conversion tax will not have to be paid in 2010, but can be postponed until 2011 and 2012. This law change will produce a remarkable opportunity that is unprecedented. TIPRA rocks.

SON OF A PREACHER MAN

Perhaps I was drawn to the Roth IRA because of all the religious overtones found in the Roth language. My father was a Church of Christ preacher, and I still vividly remember his teachings. When a regular IRA is changed to a Roth IRA, that process is called a Roth IRA conversion. So you have the opportunity to take your wicked tax-deferred IRA and convert it to a tax-free Roth IRA.

Conversions Happen

The Roth IRA conversion begins by having your IRA account renamed a Roth IRA. This happens when you instruct your bank, brokerage house, insurance company, or other IRA trustee to make this change. This is simply a paperwork transaction. The underlying assets remain the same, but the account is typically given a new account number along with the new Roth IRA name.

So, if you had 500 shares of ABC mutual fund in a regular IRA, you now have the same 500 shares of ABC mutual fund in a Roth IRA. You can even continue to make changes to the investments within that account as usual. The value on the date of that conversion sets the exact amount of potential future taxable income that may be incurred as a result of that conversion. However, your conversion decision is not firm or final at that point.

You actually have until October 15 of the year following the year of conversion to unconvert this transaction. I believe Baptists call this backsliding instead of unconverting. The IRS calls this unconverting a recharacterization. You might call it a "do over." What actually happens when you recharacterize or unconvert is that you instruct your trustee (bank, brokerage house, insurance company) to undo the Roth conversion. Then the same 500 shares of ABC mutual fund (or whatever funds the account is now invested in) are again titled in the name of a regular IRA. It is as if the transaction or conversion never took place.

The IRS is kind and reasonable in allowing you to do this. If your account value goes down after you make the conversion, it would be doubly sad to have to pay the tax at the higher amount and know your account has decreased in value. But you must make a Roth IRA conversion first, to enjoy this choice or option later. The option to keep or reject the Roth later is a great benefit to enjoy after you see what happens to your account value. If you make a Roth IRA conversion and the account goes up (sometimes substantially), you just might decide to leave it converted. This would be a doubly joyous occasion because you have seen your Roth IRA go up in value, yet the taxes due on this conversion would be based on a smaller amount.

This look-back window, that begins on the date you convert and extends to the date that you have to go firm on the conversion (October

15 of the next year), is what I call the *Roth Option Period.* This Roth Option Period can be as long as 22½ months, or shorter if you start the conversion later in the year. Great opportunities abound in what I have dubbed the Roth Conversion Option or RCO. Remember, Gospel means good news. And this is good news.

The government only allows you to recharacterize or unconvert one time per year per account. The number of accounts that you can have, however, is unlimited. So you can break up your IRAs into several Roth IRAs giving each a separate Roth Conversion Option. You will want to strategize with your own accounts in the way that you break these up to give yourself maximum future flexibility.

For example, if you have a large IRA rollover that has five different mutual funds in it, you will want to convert them into five separate Roth IRAs, with each Roth IRA holding one mutual fund. That way, you get to pick and choose the ones that stay converted and the ones that you unconvert in the future. Since these five different mutual funds may perform differently, you can select the ones with the best returns to remain converted. Remember your window of opportunity to recharacterize or unconvert is until October 15 of the year following this Roth conversion. So to maximize the time period for potential asset growth, you will want to convert as early in the year as possible.

It's Absolutely Certain; No Ifs, Ands, or Buts

Harry S. Truman said that he longed for a one-armed economist because any time he asked an economist a question, the economist would give him an answer that included "on one hand this, and on the other hand that." I feel the way old Harry must've felt every time I read one of these complicated articles about Roth IRA conversions. Advice that is good, *and* specific, is rare.

So I would like to repeat the good and specific advice from Step One. I recommend that you convert every dollar in every IRA or available retirement account that you have to a Roth IRA on January 4, 2010, at

9:57 AM Central Standard Time. Is that specific enough for you? I repeat, *every man, woman, and child should convert every dollar of every account in an IRA or other available retirement account to a Roth IRA on January 4, 2010, at 9:57 AM Central Standard Time.*

The obvious reason to do this is so that you will have the potential benefit of the Roth conversion option. Remember that you have not actually committed to this Roth conversion until October 15, 2011. Actually, October 15 falls on a Saturday in 2011, so you have until October 17. Your last day to unconvert or recharacterize Roth IRA conversions made in 2010 is October 17, 2011. January 4, 2010, is the first business day of that year. January 1 falls on a Friday, which will be a fine holiday (and a legal one as well). I recommend that you sober up over that long holiday weekend to prepare for your upcoming Roth conversion on Monday, January 4, 2010. I will explain the 9:57 AM part toward the end of this book.

Forget Roth calculators, projections about future tax rates, and other minutia that may just confuse you along the way. Some have accurately called this "paralysis by analysis."

The only way to take advantage of this great opportunity called the Roth Conversion Option is to actually convert your IRA accounts. I cannot think of any good reason why you would not participate in this Roth Conversion Option. By doing so, you hold all the cards. You may unconvert any and all accounts up until the deadline, but you don't get to convert in arrears. So if you do nothing and wait until 2011, you may have missed a great opportunity because the IRA conversion train may have left the station without you.

The No-Lose Situation

What if you convert a large IRA on January 4, 2010 (at 9:57 AM) that contains one mutual fund? Over the following one year and 10½ months the mutual fund goes up substantially—say 30 percent. Let's say the account was valued at $1 million on January 4, 2010. By October 15, 2011, it would be worth $1.3 million based on this assumption. You then could leave the account converted realizing a tremendous financial benefit. If you were subject to taxes at a rate of 35 percent, you would owe $350,000 in income tax on this conversion. You would have to pay $175,000 in 2011 and $175,000 in 2012. However, this might appear all the more compelling because at your decision point of October 15, 2011, your account was actually worth $1.3 million. So you have the option to decide whether to complete this Roth conversion committing to pay the taxes on $1 million with the knowledge that it's actually worth $1.3 million. This would save 35 percent of the $300,000 gain or $105,000 in taxes. You just profited $105,000 by using the RCO. That might be worth considering. I mean $105,000 here and $105,000 there and pretty soon we're talking about real money.

If you think that a 30 percent increase over a 22½ month period sounds extreme, please consider recent history. Over the past 30 years, the S&P 500 index has gone up by at least 30 percent nine times. That's almost one-third of the time. No one can predict the future, and I certainly don't know if your accounts will go up or down. However, there is a great likelihood that you will be very happy to have this RCO and to monitor your own account performance.

Maybe your IRAs are worth less now than they were a few years back by locking in a lower value for taxation, and watching the future come to you; this timing of the RCO seems really attractive.

This Roth Conversion Option does not cost you anything other than a little preparation. It is strictly a paperwork transaction handled by the IRA custodian or trustee. It is like a mulligan or a do over in golf. Some corporate executives have been under scrutiny lately for backdating their incentive stock options—an illegal practice where executives picked an advantageous lower price on their company stock that would profit them immensely in the future. The RCO is a legal way for you to backdate your own stock options. The Roth Conversion Option is like betting on a recorded football game that you have already seen.

You will have ample time to analyze and consider the many potential benefits that a Roth IRA conversion may have for you in your specific situation during the ensuing one year and 10½ months after you convert. That is 651 days. You will have time to finish reading this book and other books on the subject. You may even recommend *The Gospel of Roth* to others. You can run Roth calculators until your brain turns into mush. You will be able to employ professional advisors to help you with this decision. You will have time.

RCO THINKING: TO KEEP AS ROTH OR UNCONVERT—THAT IS THE QUESTION

Actually you should not decide on the Roth conversion specifics until you have used the RCO and seen the results. This way you are able to more accurately analyze how much and what accounts to keep converted to a Roth, if any, and you may know more about future proposed tax rate changes and your own situation. You will also be able to select—after the fact—which Roth accounts to keep converted and which ones to unconvert from each of your separate Roth IRAs. You can even choose to keep converted just a portion of a Roth conversion and unconvert the rest.

You have the chance with each converted Roth IRA to use the great line that Gilda Radner coined as the character Emily Litella on *Saturday Night Live*: "Never Mind!"

Anyone who would like to take advantage of this free one-time opportunity that will give you more financial options in the future should make this Roth conversion on January 4, 2010. The special 2010 deferral of tax to 2011 and 2012 makes it possible to take this Roth Conversion Option without even having to increase the amount of estimated tax that you pay to the IRS until after you have gone firm with any Roth conversions on October 17, 2011. When the IRS gives you a mulligan, I suggest you take it.

Jabez[2] has a large IRA rollover account that is worth $800,000. He is invested in eight different investments worth $100,000 each. He converts all eight investments into eight separate Roth IRA accounts on January 4, 2010 (first column). Then in early October 2011, the accounts have the values shown in the second column:

Roth IRA	1/4/2010	10/1/2011
1	$100,000	$106,000
2	$100,000	$118,000
3	$100,000	$111,000
4	$100,000	$104,000
5	$100,000	$134,000
6	$100,000	$101,000
7	$100,000	$128,000
8	$100,000	$113,000

Jabez is excited because all of his accounts increased in value. In his situation, we advise Jabez (in early October 2011) to leave his Roth IRAs number 5 and number 7 converted and recharacterize or unconvert the rest and he does just that by the October 17, 2011, deadline. You will better understand this recommendation after you read the remainder of this book. This is funny because all of the Roth conversion calculations that Jabez did back in 2009 told him not to convert. But we are able to give Jabez better and more accurate advice that has a very different outcome because he used the RCO and then ran the numbers after seeing the results 22 months later. By using the RCO, Jabez has all the options. He can leave all or any percentage of his IRAs converted or he can unconvert any or all of them before the October 17, 2011, deadline. With the RCO, Jabez has more than a prayer.

---

[2]All of the names of the folks in the examples are taken from the bible—it is the *gospel* of Roth, after all.

ROTH CONVERSION OPTION TIME LINE

| January 4, 2010 9:57 AM | Convert all regular IRAs and available retirement plans into several new Roth IRAs separated by asset class. This starts the 2010 RCO. |

| April 15, 2010 | Adjust income tax withholding for 2010 using 110% of 2009 total tax as safe harbor. If withholding not available, make 1st quarterly tax deposit for 2010. If using quarterly deposits, make again in July, October, and January. |

| December 3, 2010 | Recharacterize 2010 Roth IRAs that have lost substantial value since converting. Consider unconverting additional Roth IRAs that have marginal gains that you want to reconvert in 2011. |

| January 3, 2011 9:57 AM | Reconvert all regular IRAs and available retirement plans to Roth IRAs to start the RCO on them for 2011. Use separate new Roth IRA accounts divided by asset class. |

| April 15, 2011 | Pay balance of 2010 tax. Add payment for 2010 Roth conversion to preserve penalty-free option for 2010 rates until October 17. |

| October 17, 2011 | Deadline to keep or unconvert 2010 Roth IRAs (pick and choose). Deadline to select year(s) to pay tax for 2010 conversion (must use same choice for all 2010 conversions). |

| December 2, 2011 | Recharacterize 2011 Roth IRAs that have lost substantial value. Consider unconverting additional Roth IRAs that have marginal gains that you want to reconvert in 2012. |

| January 2, 2012 9:57 AM | Start RCO again on all regular IRAs and available retirement plans. |

This RCO opportunity reminds me of the great Will Rogers quote, "Don't gamble! Take all your savings and buy some good stock and hold it till it goes up, then sell it. If it don't go up, don't buy it..." The RCO allows you to do just that with your taxes.

In the chapters that follow, you will learn how converting to a Roth might yield 40 percent or more to your spendable retirement assets. You will understand the best methods for Roth conversion and how to figure out when to convert in every situation and when not to convert, as well as the potential Roth disadvantages. I will show you how to maximize the power of the Roth conversion and strategies for now and the future. You will learn the right questions to ask and get answers for your specific situation, and I might even show you how to be a Roth star. With the RCO, the IRS is not giving you just one "do over," like my golf buddies do; they are actually giving you a bucket of mulligans!

IN THE BEGINNING CONGRESS CREATED THE IRA (AND IT WAS GOOD)

TO UNDERSTAND THE ROTH INDIVIDUAL retirement account (IRA) adequately, it is important that you first understand regular IRAs so that you can determine the type of IRA that is best for you and the Roth IRA conversion opportunity. Since the introduction of the Roth IRA, it is important to specify to which type of IRA you are referring. In this book, Roth IRAs are always specified by Roth. Traditional or regular IRAs are called simply IRAs or regular IRAs.

ORIGIN

Although Congress began allowing regular IRAs in the 1970s, they became very popular in the 1980s. The thinking was that Social Security benefits were not going to be adequate for most Americans to retire on. For a nation of undersavers, Congress wanted to permit an individual retirement plan to serve as an incentive for taxpayers to save money for retirement. The IRA was particularly aimed at moderate-income folks who did not have a retirement plan at work. The rules were fairly simple. Subject to a few limitations, an individual could open an account with an insurance company, bank, or brokerage house and put up to $2000 for a working person and up to $250 for a nonworking spouse a year into this IRA. The amount contributed would be deductible from current income for income tax purposes. This money would be saved in these IRAs for folks until after they had reached age 59½ and then it could be withdrawn without penalty. The money would be taxed as ordinary income at the time it was withdrawn.

NO PAPERWORK

The IRA is very simple because the IRA holder does not have to supply any paperwork or additional reporting. The bank, insurance company, or brokerage house (called the trustee or custodian) does the reporting and compliance work behind-the-scenes, making the process very easy and simple to set up and maintain.

INVESTMENT CHOICES

The IRA itself is not an investment but a type of account. All money inside of these IRAs can be invested in a variety of ways, as directed by the account holder. This is what the IRS calls "self-directed." So the IRA holder may invest in stocks, bonds, mutual funds, CDs, annuities, public limited partnerships, or other types of investments. Note, though, that some investments are prohibited from IRAs. These prohibited investments include very speculative types of investments, life insurance, and investments that have a high probability of self-dealing (closely held businesses, artwork, loans, etc.). The IRA holder can pick and choose among the available investments and change investments at his or her discretion.

TAX-DEDUCTIBLE IRA CONTRIBUTIONS

The main feature of the regular IRA is its tax deductibility. This is very different from the Roth IRA, which is not tax deductible.

You could even wait until April 15 to make a tax-deductible contribution for the prior year. An annual tax discussion with your accountant was often the deciding factor in contributing to an IRA. If you were eligible, you could put up to $2,000 into an IRA and save up to $700 in taxes for that year depending on your tax bracket at the time.

That was very compelling to the folks who had the resources to save, but needed a little extra push. However, much to Congress's surprise, the people who took advantage of these IRAs were people who tended to save anyway, and the folks who Congress wanted to encourage to save money still did not. The deadline for IRA contributions is still April 15 of the year following the contribution year. You may contribute to an IRA as early as January 1 of the contribution year.

WHO CAN CONTRIBUTE TO A REGULAR IRA

The IRA contribution limits for 2009 and 2010 are generally $5,000 for people under 50 and $6,000 for those 50 and over. By the way, the increased limit that people age 50 and over can contribute is actually called a "catch-up provision." Age is the only qualifier, so that people closer to retirement age can save a little extra. After 2010, these limits are indexed for inflation in $500 increments but only until after inflation has passed the next $500 mark. Even if only one spouse has income, both spouses can contribute to IRAs up to their individual maximums. The income limits in the following discussion are for 2009 contributions.

If neither spouse has a retirement plan at work, then they can max out their deductible IRA contributions at no income limitation. Those maximums are $5,000 for those under 50 and $6,000 for others. If only one spouse is covered by a work retirement plan, they can still fully deduct their IRA contributions up to a modified adjusted gross income (MAGI) of $166,000. If their income is above that, then the deduction is phased out up to an income level of $175,999. At incomes at or above $176,000, no deductible IRAs are allowed.

If both spouses are covered by retirement plans at work, the maximum MAGI is $89,000 for full IRA contributions and full deductions. At incomes above $89,000 and up to $108,999, the deductibility is phased out. At $109,000 or above, no deductible IRAs are allowed.

Single people without a retirement plan at work have no income limit, and they can max out their IRA contributions ($5,000 or $6,000, depending on age). Single people with retirement plans at work can have a MAGI up to $55,000 and still have maximum and fully deductible IRAs. For single people, the deductible limit is reduced and phased out from $55,001 to $64,999 MAGI. At an income of $65,000 or above, no deductible IRAs are allowed.

For people who are married and filing separately, the phaseout is from the first dollar of income to $9,999. Above incomes of $10,000, the deductible IRA is not allowed for those who are married and filing separately.

MODIFIED ADJUSTED GROSS INCOME

This modified adjusted gross income is an example of how complicated Congress can make even the simplest things. MAGI is used in calculating your ability to contribute and deduct IRAs as well as some other things. Adjusted Gross Income (AGI) is a line on your tax return that generally is just that. You can look for it at the bottom of your IRS Form1040 page 1 or repeated at the top of your 1040 on page 2. Modified adjusted gross income then adds back any deductions taken for student loan interest, tuition and fees, domestic production activities, and foreign housing. It also adds back exclusions for foreign earned income, foreign housing, savings bond interest, and employer provided adoption benefits. For most people, their MAGI is the same as their AGI. MAGI always reminds me of Christmas!

The IRS comes out with a special instruction guide for IRAs each year called Publication 590. It covers all the IRA information for the current year concerning regular and Roth IRAs. Be sure to check the latest Publication 590 for the most up-to-date numbers concerning your situation each year. You can get a copy online from the IRS website at www.irs.gov.

If you are above the income limit, then no contributions can be deducted for IRA contributions. If you are in the "bubble" where the deductions for IRAs are being phased out, there is a worksheet found in Publication 590 to calculate the maximum you may deduct for an IRA that year. For single filers, the bubble or phase-out range from maximum to minimum deductibility is $10,000. For married folks, this bubble or range is usually $20,000. What this worksheet does is calculate where you hit in the bubble or phase-out range. So if you hit the range exactly in the middle, you are able to contribute and deduct up to half of the IRA maximum. If you hit the phase-out bubble at only 25 percent, you can use up to 75 percent of the deductible maximum IRA contribution of $5,000 or $6,000.

Everyone can contribute up to the maximum ($5,000 or $6,000) each year to an IRA but not everyone can deduct it. Actually, almost everyone can contribute with two exceptions or caveats. You must have earned income up to the amount contributed, and you must not be age 70½ or older during the tax year in question. Even if only one spouse works, both spouses may contribute up to the maximum, not to exceed their gross income. So for example, if both spouses are age 50, they could contribute to IRAs worth $6,000 each for a total of $12,000 if their earned income was at least $12,000. If their earned income was only $7,000, then they could contribute up to the $7,000 and allocate among the couple's IRAs in any way they see fit, not to exceed either one's individual maximum of $6,000.

NONDEDUCTIBLE IRAs

If your income is too high to be able to deduct some or all of an IRA contribution, you may still contribute each year up to the $5,000 ($6,000 for age 50 and older) maximum. The amount that is nondeductible is not unexpectedly called a nondeductible IRA, although it is not a separate IRA. If you make any contribution to a nondeductible IRA, you must declare it as such on your income tax return. You do this by completing Form 8606.

Let's say Dorcas is under age 50 and has a deductible IRA limit of $2,500 total in her situation. If Dorcas made IRA contributions totaling $5,000, she would report the nondeductible portion of $2,500 on Form 8606 with her tax return. Since the nondeductible portion is after tax (received no tax deduction), Dorcas would not have to pay income taxes on that nondeductible contribution when the money is withdrawn from her IRA or converted to a Roth. By the way, anyone can choose to make any IRA contribution nondeductible by noting it on Form 8606. So Dorcas would be allowed to elect to have her entire $5,000 IRA contribution nondeductible, if she wanted to.

However, when you have both regular and nondeductible IRAs, the calculation is a little more complex when you distribute or convert to a Roth. The IRS only lets you take out the nondeductible portion as a percentage of each IRA withdrawal or Roth IRA conversion. Even if you have multiple IRAs over the years and you only made a one-time nondeductible IRA contribution to one specific IRA, you must include all your IRAs, even the pure nondeductible ones, in the calculation when you withdraw or convert any IRA money. Over the years, the total of all nondeductible IRA contributions represents what is called the "basis" in the IRA. If the nondeductible amount or basis represents 10 percent of the IRA total then 10 percent of every IRA withdrawal or Roth conversion would not be subject to income tax. This is a moving target every year and ends when the entire IRA is withdrawn or converted to a Roth.

This added complexity has caused many people to steer clear of nondeductible IRAs. You will never receive any more than the total of your nondeductible contributions to your IRAs tax-free because any growth in the IRA will be subject to tax someday. For most people, it would be much simpler to have no money in nondeductible IRAs. If you want to avoid this nondeductible IRA calculation, simply contribute up to the maximum deductible IRA limit each year. If you have no nondeductible IRA contributions, Form 8606 is not required. However, nondeductible IRAs can have great benefits due to income tax deferral and should be considered now more than ever because of Roth conversions. We look at these nondeductible IRAs in a whole new light later in this book.

EARNED INCOME

You must have earned income to contribute to an IRA. Earned income is also called compensation and consists of wages, commissions, tips, salaries, and self-employed income. Compensation also includes alimony, nontaxable combat pay, and separate maintenance. Earned income does not include earnings and profits from property or partnerships unless that partnership provides services that are material to its income. Earned income is not interest, dividends, pensions, IRA distributions, deferred compensation, or annuity payments. Tax-free income or other payments excluded from tax are also not compensation. Finally disability income and Social Security payments are not compensation. You can never contribute more than your compensation or earned income to an IRA.

You are never required to contribute to an IRA even if you have in the past, so you make the choice whether to contribute to an IRA every year. You may have an unlimited number of IRAs, so you may make new contributions to new IRA accounts or even multiple IRA accounts if you wish, as long as the annual maximum is not exceeded.

TAX CREDIT IRA

Some people may receive additional income tax credits for a portion of their IRA contribution if they are not full-time students and their income is below a certain threshold. Check the most current IRS Publication 590 to find out if you qualify for these income tax credits.

SINGLE AND DIDN'T EVEN KNOW IT

For IRA purposes, if you and your spouse live apart for the entire year you are considered to be single for these qualification calculations.

REGULAR AND ROTH IRA CONTRIBUTIONS ARE COMBINED

Any contributions to a Roth IRA will lower the amount that you may contribute to a regular IRA and vice versa. The totals contributed each year for both Roth IRAs and regular IRAs are added together, for a maximum annual total IRA contribution of $5,000 or $6,000 for those age 50 and over.

Beginning in 2010, the IRA contribution limits of $5,000 and $6,000 will be adjusted for inflation. The current IRS Publication 590 will tell you exactly what that new limit is. This limit will come only in $500 increments and will be added to the IRA contribution maximum in the year after inflation has been calculated to grow to or past the next $500 bracket.

WATCHING YOUR IRA GROW

All the money in these regular IRAs grows tax-deferred. A person who has contributed to his or her IRA for several years will see the balance grow unfettered by income tax, making the total much larger than if the same investments had been made outside of an IRA. This tax-deferral is another compelling feature of the regular IRA.

TEACHING THE IRA TO ROLL OVER

Many people have retirement plans set up at work. These retirement plans include defined benefit plans, defined contribution plans, profit-sharing plans, Keogh plans, simplified employee pensions (SEPs), 401(k)s, 457s, 403(b)s, and others. When a person leaves an employer or retires, or when a retirement plan is terminated, that person can have the retirement monies or assets transferred to an IRA. This is known as an IRA rollover. Many people choose to roll over their retirement plans into IRAs so the income tax deferral can continue and so they can direct the way that the assets are invested. They also want to postpone the payment of income tax. The IRA rollover is the primary way that most really large IRAs got that big. I have seen many IRA rollovers that were the single largest asset that a person had. In fact, IRA rollovers worth millions are not that uncommon.

ARE YOU NUTS ... DO YOU HAVE NUA?

If you have a retirement plan and some of it invested in your company's stock, then special care is advised. This is called net unrealized appreciation (NUA) for that potential gain in the company stock. Special privileges apply for NUA stock and you may be able to distribute it directly out of your plan to a brokerage house and sell it with the income tax treatment being long-term capital gains. Long-term capital gains are generally taxed at substantially lower rates than regular income. If you have any of this NUA stock, be sure to run the numbers because it may be to your benefit to distribute and sell in this manner rather than the other choices. Once you roll the company stock over from a retirement plan into an IRA, it is too late to preserve this option.

IRS KEEPING TRACK

Each year the trustee of your IRA is required to report the value of every IRA to the IRS as of December 31 of the prior year. The IRA holder gets a copy of this information but so does the IRS. This information is used by the IRS and Congress to calculate the amount of eventual tax that it will someday collect on each IRA. This information is used to calculate growth information as well as to make sure that each taxpayer is following the strict IRA distribution rules.

As mentioned earlier, you can have an unlimited number of IRAs. If at all possible, rollover IRA accounts should always be kept separate from regular IRA accounts. These regular accounts that were always IRAs that you contribute to annually are called contributory IRAs. Because of the retirement plan origin of rollover IRAs, there may be some options that are available in the future for these rollover IRAs that are not available to contributory IRAs. If these rollover IRAs are mixed in the same account as a regular contributory IRA, these future options will be lost. However, there may be some savings associated in consolidating all of your contributory IRAs.

COMBINING IRAS

You may roll over a regular IRA to another regular IRA. Typically this is done by filling out the paperwork at the institution where the IRA is held to transfer it to another IRA account. This is done without the IRA holder touching the money in between. This is called a trustee-to-trustee transfer or a direct rollover. The advantage of this type of transfer is that no taxes are withheld and no report of this transaction needs to be made by the IRA holder.

Many people use this trustee-to-trustee transfer to consolidate multiple IRA accounts down to one or two. There is also no limit to the number of trustee-to-trustee transfers that you can make. Alternatively, you can remove the assets from an IRA and take possession of these funds in your individual name. This usually results in the IRA trustee withholding taxes on the amount removed. Once the money has been removed from an IRA in this fashion, the individual has 60 days to roll the money back into another IRA. Any amount that has not been put back into an IRA within this 60-day window will be subject to income tax and any applicable penalties. To avoid any shortfall using this method, you must pay out of pocket to make up any tax withholding that the first trustee deducted to come up with the same deposit amount for the new IRA account before the 60-day window is up. Any taxes withheld by the first trustee will be credited to you when you file your income tax return the next year. Unlike the trustee-to trustee transfer, you can only use this method one time per 12-month period for each IRA. In general, as you will soon see, the trustee-to-trustee transfer is the safest and preferred method for moving IRAs.

MANDATORY WITHHOLDING

A major disadvantage of not using the trustee-to-trustee transfer from qualified retirement plans to IRAs is that the IRS requires trustees of qualified retirement plans to withhold 20 percent of any plan distribution. The trustee then applies that 20 percent toward that individual's tax liability. If you only intended to roll over the retirement plan account into an IRA, you would have to come up with money out of pocket to avoid any unintended taxes.

When David left his employer of 25 years, he asked that his $500,000 retirement account be sent to him. David knew that he wanted to roll over the entire $500,000 into an IRA rollover account. When he received a check for $400,000, he knew that something was wrong. He looked on the statement attached and saw that the missing $100,000 was for tax withholding. However, the 60-day clock on David's distribution started when the retirement plan of his former employer sent him the check. He only has 60 days to roll over the money into an IRA rollover account. If he deposits only the $400,000 into an IRA rollover, he will owe taxes and possible penalties on the $100,000. This certainly is an unintended result. If David has the resources, he can come up with the $100,000 from another place and roll over the entire $500,000.

By the way, the $100,000 that was withheld has not vanished. The IRS has held it for David without interest, and he can get a refund of any amount not due for taxes. The problem is that the refund cannot be made until after January 1 of the following year and David must apply for the refund by completing his Form 1040 or individual income tax return. This 20 percent mandatory withholding only applies to distributions from qualified plans. Distributions from IRAs have a 10 percent withholding provision, and unlike distributions from qualified plans, you can opt for no withholding if so desired. In hindsight, David should have chosen the trustee-to-trustee transfer method.

THE DAY OF RECKONING
—TAKING MONEY OUT

Every dollar that has been contributed to regular IRAs plus any growth will be subject to eventual income taxation. That is the essence of tax deferral. You received a tax deduction when the money was put into these IRA accounts. That is why the money in regular IRAs is called pretax dollars. They have not been subject to income taxes—yet.

All of the assets put into IRAs are allowed to grow without current income tax. After what is usually many years of income tax deferral and when the IRA account is the largest that it has ever been, then comes the income tax. Eventually the IRS will be paid taxes on every dollar as it is withdrawn.

WAIT UNTIL AGE 59½ TO WITHDRAW MONEY

Because the money in the IRA was supposed to be used for retirement, the IRS demands that you wait until retirement age for you to get any money out. The age of appropriate retirement has been deemed by Congress to be age 59½. Withdrawals before that age are called early withdrawals and incur penalties.

I don't know what genius came up with age 59½ instead of age 59 or 60 but it is likely that it was a government worker whose years of public service had left him bitter. Maybe it was a frustrated former math teacher who wanted to make his prediction come true that you would need to learn fractions in school because you will need to know them in real life. I mean what logical person would use 59½ as the appropriate age to begin withdrawing funds for retirement without any penalty? What was wrong with age 59 or 60? This must be the same guy who came up with 3.4 ounces being the safe amount of liquids that can be carried inside a one-quart baggie aboard an airplane. No matter what its origin, we are stuck with age 59½ as an important milestone.

This age—59½ to begin penalty-free withdrawals from IRAs—is not an impairment for those folks who save money because they want to keep the money growing as long as possible before being subject to the tax.

As an incentive to keep the money in the IRA at least until retirement age, the IRS imposes a penalty of 10 percent on any IRA withdrawals before age 59½. This penalty for any amount withdrawn from IRAs is in addition to regular income taxation of these withdrawals.

Mary retired at age 57. She has a fairly large IRA that is to be the sole source of her retirement income. Because she has not reached the age of 59½, every dollar that she takes out of her IRA will be subject to the 10 percent penalty until she reaches that age.

EXCEPTIONS TO THE EARLY WITHDRAWAL PENALTY

There are a few exceptions to this 10 percent penalty for early withdrawal. You can withdraw IRA money prior to age 59½ without penalty for the following reasons:

- Death
- Disability
- Annuity payments (Substantially equal periodic payments)
- Medical expenses above a certain amount
- Medical insurance if you are recently unemployed
- Qualified higher education expenses
- First home costs and expenses
- IRS levy on your IRA
- Qualified reservist distribution

Death

This is a hard way to get around a penalty. If the owner of an IRA dies prior to age 59½, any distributions by the beneficiaries after the IRA owner's death are exempt from the early withdrawal penalty.

Disability

If you are disabled before age 59½, you are exempt from the early withdrawal penalty. Disabled is defined as not being able to perform any income-earning activity as a result of a physical or mental condition. A physician must determine that your condition is expected to result in death or to be of long, continued, and indefinite duration.

Annuity Payments

This is the main loophole for people who want to take early distributions from their IRA without penalty. This is what the IRS calls "substantially equal and periodic payments for life." This is sort of a manual or do-it-yourself annuity. What this means for Mary is that we calculate a life annuity amount using a variety of life expectancy tables to match the income that she requires. Mary must continue withdrawing this exact same amount for five years and she must also be over age 59½ before she can stop or alter this withdrawal amount. These withdrawals must be made at least once per year, and she has the option of using her life expectancy alone or her life expectancy combined with that of her beneficiary for this calculation.

Caution is required to ensure that Mary fulfills both of these conditions. She must continue these exact same withdrawals for at least the five-year minimum and not cease until she reaches age 59½ (whichever takes longer). She cannot change the annual withdrawal amount until both conditions are met. If Mary were to stop taking the distributions or even alter the amount after less than five years, she will owe penalties for the entire period of withdrawals prior to 59½! The IRS lets you choose from three different methods for this complex calculation. You now get a one-time change in the calculation method without triggering the penalty. Even if penalties are successfully avoided, you will still owe income taxes on each distribution as you take it. 72(t) is another name for this annuity loophole, and it refers to the section in the Internal Revenue Code where this exception is found. If you want to take money out using this method, I suggest you consult a professional to assist you with this important and complex calculation.

Medical Expenses above a Certain Amount

If you have unreimbursed medical expenses above 7.5 percent of your adjusted gross income (AGI), you can withdraw penalty free from your IRA up to that amount above the 7.5 percent.

Medical Insurance if You Are Recently Unemployed

Medical insurance paid for you, your spouse, and dependants after you lost a job may qualify as an amount you can take from your IRA before age 59½ without penalty. You must have drawn unemployment compensation (state or federal) for at least 12 consecutive weeks because you lost your job and can only use this exception in the year that the unemployment benefits were received and the year after. The distribution without penalty is limited to the amount of insurance paid and distributions made no later than 60 days after you are reemployed.

Qualified Higher Education Expenses

You may qualify for an exception for the early distribution penalty if you paid for qualified education expenses at eligible institutions for you, your spouse, your children, or your grandchildren's education.

First Home Costs and Expenses

This exception comes with a $10,000 maximum and can be used for a first-time home for you, your spouse, your parents, your children, or your grandchildren. You may buy, build, or rebuild a first home. First-time homeowners are defined as homeowners who have not owned a home for the prior two years.

IRS Levy on Your IRA

If the IRS puts a levy on your IRA, you need some good news. Here it is: The amount that the IRS takes under the levy still triggers income tax, but the early withdrawal penalty tax is waived.

Qualified Reservist Distribution

If you are in the reserves of a branch of military service and get called to active duty for at least 179 days, you may qualify for this exception. You have to have made the distribution while on active duty to qualify for this exception to the early withdrawal penalty.

BE CAREFUL OF THE EXCEPTIONS

These are all of the exceptions to the early withdrawal rules. Strong caution in using these exceptions is advised. You will learn later in this book why these exceptions are usually sought by people who will likely be broke someday and outlive their retirement assets.

BUBBLE PERIOD

People who are older than 59½ and younger than 70½ are in an IRA phase called the bubble period. Here choices abound with regard to your IRA. You can choose to take money out of your IRA or leave it in to grow tax deferred. You do not have to take any money out of your IRA or retirement plans until the magical age of 70½.

Unlimited Withdrawals

You can take an unlimited amount of your IRA without penalty once you turn 59½. You still have to pay income tax on any withdrawals, but there is no cap on the maximum. In the 1990s, there was a maximum amount that you could withdraw from an IRA without penalty and even an extra penalty for dying with too much in your IRA. Those penalties are now gone.

Simple-Minded People

The Simple IRA has an extra penalty of 25 percent instead of 10 percent if you should distribute the money within two years of your first contribution to the Simple IRA plan. This 25 percent would apply even to what normally would be a penalty free-roll over or conversion. So be sure to wait the two years from your first contribution before doing anything with these Simple IRA funds. There is no 25 percent penalty when you roll assets over from your Simple IRA into another Simple IRA plan; so, waiting out the two years is usually the best solution.

READY OR NOT, IRA WITHDRAWALS MUST START BY AGE 70½

The IRS mandates that you start taking money out of your IRA by age 70½. Again, we have the same inexplicable half year. Age 70½ is considered the appropriate age, and the IRS forces people to start removing money from their IRAs then. If this were a horror movie, it would be called *The Incredible Shrinking IRA!* After reaching age 70½, you must withdrawal a certain amount each year from your IRAs. The penalty for not doing so is 50 percent of the required withdrawal amount plus income taxes. With that draconian penalty, it is easy to understand why you should comply with these mandatory IRA distribution rules. It is not as easy to understand the rules themselves.

THE UNRAVELING BEGINS ... REQUIRED BEGINNING DATE

A milestone date for having to take money out of your IRA is April 1 of the year after a person turns 70½. This April 1 date is called the required beginning date or RBD. The half year is calculated as six calendar months after your birthday.

James and John are both age 70 on their birthdays in the year 2010. James' birthday is June 30 and John's birthday is July 1. These men are only one day different in age but they have very different IRA rules. James' RBD is April 1, 2011. This is found by adding six months to his 70th birthday of June 30, 2010. James' age of 70½ is reached on December 30, 2010 (June 30 plus six calendar months). Therefore James' RBD is April 1, 2011. For John, it is a different story. Because he is age 70 on July 1, 2010, his age 70½ milestone is January 1, 2011. Lucky John has an RBD of April 1, 2012. John and James have RBDs that are 1 year apart. Please note that this RBD date is April 1 or April Fool's Day and not the more common other important April tax date of April 15.

This required beginning date is actually meant to be an extension and relief from subsequent years' mandatory withdrawals after the year that you turn 70½. After the year in which you turn 70½, the mandatory withdrawals must be made by December 31 for each year.

LIFE EXPECTANCY CALCULATION

The IRS publishes three life expectancy tables in the back of every year's Publication 590. These are smartly identified as Tables I, II, and III. (Don't you just love Roman numerals?) Table I is only for beneficiaries of IRAs. Table II is only for married people who have turned 70½, who have spouses that are more that 10 years younger than them, and whose younger spouse is the sole beneficiary of their IRAs. Table III is the table for everyone else. Table III is used for single people, married people whose spouses are not more than 10 years younger, or for married people with a spouse who is 10 years younger or more and who is not the sole beneficiary of the IRAs.

IRA VALUATION DATE

The IRA value for all IRAs is determined as of December 31 the year before the required distribution. For example, 2010 mandatory distributions will use the total value of all IRAs on December 31, 2009. IRA custodians or trustees are required to send out a statement each year reflecting the IRA account value as of this important date. A word of caution however, the IRA custodian not only sends an annual statement to the IRA account holder, they also send a copy to the IRS.

Divide and Conquer (or at Least Distribute)

For the exact amount that must be distributed during the year, you must divide the value of your total IRAs as of December 31 of the prior year by the life expectancy of your age that distribution year using Table III or Table II (for those with the sole beneficiary spouses who are more that 10 years younger). Once required minimum distributions are started, they continue every year including the year of your death.

James, who will be 70½ during 2010, has a December 2009 IRA balance of $1,000,000 when you add up the value of all his combined IRAs. James' spouse is seven years younger than he is, so he must use Table III. His Table III life expectancy is 27.4 years at age 70, which was his age as of his June 30 birthday in 2010. James must divide $1,000,000 by 27.4 to arrive at his required distribution of $36,496.35. He actually may wait until April 1, 2011 (his RBD) because he just turned 70½ the year before. However, James must also take a second mandatory distribution for the year 2011 by December 31, 2011. Let's assume his combined IRA balance on December 31, 2010 was $1,100,000. James turned 71 during 2011 so his Table III life expectancy is 26.5. His required distribution for the year 2011 is $41,509.43 ($1,100,000/26.5 = $41,509.43). So if James waits until early 2011 to withdraw his first required distribution of $36,496.35, he will have that plus the $41,509.43 distributed the same tax year. He may want to consider taking his first distribution of $35,496.35 in 2010 if that results in lower overall income tax due to his tax bracket in the years 2010 and 2011. James actually would have a lower mandatory distribution in 2011 because the IRA balance would be lower on December 31, 2010, if he made the first required distribution of $36,496.35 before that date. Every year after the year James turns 70½ he will do the same calculation to take distributions from his IRAs.

Remember John who turned 70 on July 1, 2010? He is fortunate because his 70½ date is January 1, 2011, and thus his RBD is April 1, 2012. He will use age 71 for his first year of required minimum distributions because he was born in the later part of the year (after June 30). This is the case for approximately half of the population that are born after June 30 who will begin their required IRA distributions using age 71. This is the case because their 71st birthday occurs in the same year that they are 70½.

NO CREDIT FOR EXCESS WITHDRAWALS IN PRIOR YEARS

You may always take out more than the required amount, but never less. If you take out more than what is required in any given year, you do not receive any credit for the next year. Every year you must take out at least the minimum. Not counting the RBD year, all IRA required minimum distributions must be taken between January 1 and December 31 for that year. You must always use the December 31 IRA value of the year before to calculate your distributions.

MARITAL STATUS

Your marital status for IRA required minimum distributions only comes into play if you have a spouse who is more than 10 years younger and who is the sole beneficiary of your IRA. If this is the case, Table II is used, which is more favorable because it has a longer life expectancy (resulting in smaller mandatory withdrawals) because of the decade-plus younger spouse. If this is the case, and your spouse dies after January 1, you may still use Table II for the year of your spouse's death. However, if you are divorced during the year and change the beneficiary (usually a good idea), then you must use Table III. If you qualify to use Table II by having a spouse who is more than 10 years younger, you are not required to have this spouse as the sole beneficiary of all of your IRAs—just the ones on which you wish to use Table II. You can have some IRAs using Table II with your spouse (who is more than 10 years younger) as the sole beneficiary, and you can have other IRAs where other beneficiaries are named and you must use Table III. Now wouldn't it have been easier if you had married someone around your own age so that you could use Table III like the rest of us?

PICK AND CHOOSE

You can aggregate or combine the total value of all your IRAs for this required minimum IRA distribution calculation or you may withdraw from any IRA that you choose as long as you meet the minimum withdrawal requirement. You do not have to withdraw from each of your IRAs.

THE 50 PERCENT PENALTY

If you have a required distribution of $40,000 and wait until after the deadline to make this distribution, the penalty is $20,000 or 50 percent! You still have to distribute and pay the income tax on the full $40,000, but you will be sharing it with the IRS. The $20,000 or 50 percent penalty is not tax deductible either. It is obvious that the IRS is serious about you taking the money out of your IRA at least as fast as the rule requires. If you make a mistake, there may be some chance of one-time forgiveness for the penalty, but it must be a better excuse than "I am old and confused!" These minimum distributions have to continue every year including the year that you die.

ONE TIME MORATORIUM

In 2009, the mandatory required minimum distribution IRA rules were suspended *for one year only*. No distributions from IRAs were required in 2009. In 2010, the mandatory distribution rules will apply as well as in all future years. This was great news for savers over age 70½ who did not want to take the money out anyway. For spenders, most of their IRA money (if not all) has already been depleted so it was not such big news for them. Maybe there is another lesson here?

A WORD ABOUT LIFE EXPECTANCY

It is helpful to understand a little bit about life expectancy at this point. Life expectancy is a number that boring statisticians called actuaries use to express the expected length of life of a very large group of people. Life expectancy is actually the statistical midpoint of the occurrence of everyone's death in the entire group. The IRS Tables II and III are actually joint life expectancy tables where two lives are put together and the expectancy number is the death of the second person to die. This is intended to put everyone on an even playing field with regard to minimum IRA required distributions. Table I is a single life expectancy table and you can see how much shorter it is as a result of having only one life in the calculation. We will learn how Table I is used when we discuss inherited IRAs. IRS Tables II and III are also recalculating. That means that you get to look up a new life expectancy every year. The actuarial phenomenon here is that you do not lose one year of life expectancy with every year of life. Maybe those boring actuaries aren't so boring after all!

HIS AND HER IRAS

IRAs are in the name of only one person that the IRS calls the participant or account holder. Even in a community property state where it may be clear that both spouses own all assets equally, the IRA is only listed in one person's name. Generally, the IRA can never be taken out of that person's name without triggering income tax. The control of the IRA in estate planning is via the beneficiary designation that every IRA has. In a divorce situation, through what is called a Qualified Domestic Relations Order (QDRO), the IRA may be transferred from a divorced spouse to the other spouse who is renamed as the IRA holder. This is done directly by the IRA custodian or trustee without touching the money.

SPOUSAL ROLLOVER

If an IRA holder dies and his or her spouse is the beneficiary, the surviving spouse has the choice to roll the IRA over into their own name or leave it in the name of the (now deceased) original IRA holder. If spousal rollover is elected, then the spouse beneficiary will be treated as the account holder. This means that the spouse may treat the inherited IRA as his or her own and must follow the IRA distribution rules accordingly. Being able to roll over the inherited IRA into your own name is a privilege available only to the spouse beneficiary. Most spouses who are beneficiaries will choose to roll the IRA over into their own name. All nonspouse beneficiaries must leave the inherited IRA in the name of the original owner until the money is withdrawn. You must draw out the money in an inherited IRA according to the IRS's rules.

INHERITED IRAs

The beneficiary of an IRA must pay income tax on the inherited IRA as money is taken out. The inherited IRA stays in the name of the original IRA owner. To preserve and maximize income tax deferral, beneficiaries often delay the removal of money from an inherited IRA as long as possible. However, although a beneficiary may remove the IRA proceeds without penalty as fast as he or she wants, there are minimum required distributions from the inherited IRA that have to be met to avoid the 50 percent penalty. After the death of the IRA owner, the beneficiaries generally must separate and divide up the IRAs (by beneficiary) before September 30 of the year after the IRA owner's death.

Eunice died in May 2010 leaving her two IRAs equally to her two children, Ester and Ruth. Eunice had named both children as the beneficiaries on each IRA because she wanted each child to inherit exactly the same amount. After Eunice's death, the two IRAs are split down the middle and divided into four IRAs by beneficiary, with two for Ruth and two for Ester. Ruth and Ester must begin to distribute from the inherited IRAs the year after their mother died. Using the account balance from the IRAs as of December 31, 2010, Ruth and Ester must distribute their inherited IRAs using their own Table I life expectancy based on their age in 2011. Ruth turns 57 during 2011, so she looks up age 57 on the life expectancy Table I and finds her life expectancy number is 27.9. Ruth then has to divide her inherited IRA balance as of December 31, 2010, by 27.9 to come up with her required minimum distribution for 2011. Assuming the balance was $400,000 on December 31, 2010, the required distribution for 2011 would be $14,336.92 ($400,000/27.9 = $14,336.92). Ruth must remove at least $14,336.92 from the inherited IRA before the end of 2011.

Ruth does not need to recalculate or look up her Table I life expectancy for future years' distribution calculations, she simply has to subtract 1 for each year from her starting life expectancy number of 27.9. So she can use 26.9 for 2012, and 25.9 for 2013, and so on.

Distribution Year	Age	IRA Balance End of Year	Life Expectancy (Subtract 1 year)
2011	57	2010	27.9
2012	58	2011	26.9
2013	59	2012	25.9

So you can now see the finite nature of the regular IRA. The inherited IRA will be distributed in its entirety during the life expectancy of the beneficiary. For Ruth whose life expectancy was 27.9 when she inherited the IRA, it will be gone in 28 years. In actuality, due to the ever increasing and incessant annual withdrawal nature of the required distributions, most of the IRA will be withdrawn long before then. This concept is discussed in detail in Chapter 6.

NON-RECALCULATING

Remember, inherited IRAs are subject to the life expectancy of the beneficiary found in Table I *only* for the year after the original IRA holder's death, based on the beneficiary's age that year. Subsequent required minimum distributions are non-recalculating; meaning that life expectancy is computed by subtracting one year from the prior year's life expectancy. You are never allowed to recalculate this life expectancy or use the life expectancy tables for any year other than the first year you inherited the IRAs.

FIVE-YEAR RULE

Instead of taking the IRA distributions from an inherited IRA over the life expectancy of the beneficiary, you can alternatively elect to take everything out of the IRA by the end of the fifth year following the year of the IRA owner's death. This rule is primarily for beneficiaries who screwed up by not taking their mandatory first year distribution in time and who want to avoid the 50 percent penalty.

Gomer inherits an IRA from his father who died in 2012. Gomer takes nothing out of his inherited IRA for 2013. He then has two choices. He can take all the money in the inherited IRA out by the end of 2018 or he can pay a 50 percent penalty on the required distribution for 2013 and then distribute as normal for 2014 and beyond. This five-year rule is also for people who die and leave their IRA to nonspecific individuals or when it is not sorted out by September 30 of the year following the IRA owner's death.

If an inherited IRA is left to multiple heirs and for some reason the inherited IRAs are not split up by beneficiary before September 30 of the year following the IRA owner's death, the required distributions will be made using the life expectancy of the oldest beneficiary according to Table I. If you split the accounts up by beneficiary before the September 30 deadline, then you can use each beneficiary's age for calculating the respective distributions.

OLDER BENEFICIARIES

If the IRA owner dies on or after his required beginning date and the beneficiary is older than the IRA owner, then he or she can use the original owner's age for the mandatory IRA distributions starting the year after death. Look up the original owner's age as if they were alive the year following death using life expectancy Table I.

ESTATE IS THE BENEFICIARY

Naming the estate the beneficiary of an IRA is usually a mistake. If the beneficiary of an IRA is an estate, then distributions must be made using the deceased IRA owner's age if he died on or after his required beginning date. This uses the deceased age the year after death according to life expectancy Table I and does not recalculate. However, if an IRA owner who has named his estate as beneficiary dies before his required beginning date, then all of the IRA must be distributed before the end of five years following the year of his or her death.

TRUST ME

If the IRA is left to a trust then certain trust rules will apply. In general, the trust must be valid and irrevocable after the IRA owner's death. Copies of the trust must also be given to the IRA trustee or custodian, and the trust must identify the beneficiaries. IRA inheritance trusts can be very powerful and beneficial in preserving the maximum income tax deferral for IRAs as well as for asset protection of the beneficiaries. Make sure that you use a competent specialized professional to draft this IRA trust if you decide to use this method.

INHERITED IRAS AND ROTH IRA DISTRIBUTIONS ARE SEPARATE TRANSACTIONS

Both inherited regular IRAs and inherited Roth IRAs have separate mandatory distributions. Distributions from inherited IRAs do not count toward inherited Roth IRA distributions and vice versa. Both regular and Roth IRAs must distribute accordingly every year, each without regard to the other, after the owner's death.

STRETCH IRAs

Because of the powerful nature of tax deferral that I talk about in detail later, many people intuitively want to leave their IRA intact for as long as possible. The concept of the stretch IRA was to minimize the required IRA distributions after age 70½, but in reality it is very limited as you will learn in the following chapters. The Roth IRA has a great advantage over regular IRAs for stretching purposes because you never are forced to take any money out of a Roth IRA during your lifetime.

If you want to maximize the IRAs income tax deferral after your death, you might consider younger beneficiaries for your IRAs like grandchildren and even great grandchildren. By looking at Table I, you can see where that might be a very powerful technique to keep the remaining IRA intact over more years after the IRA owner's death.

CHARITY

You may list a charity as a beneficiary of your IRA. The advantage of this is that the charity does not have to pay income tax on the inherited IRA. The charity must be qualified according to the IRS rules. This is a very efficient way to give some money to a charity at death.

Phoebe wants to give a gift of $100,000 to her favorite charity at death. She has a large IRA and substantial other assets. Phoebe has three children who are her heirs to the balance of her estate. If she makes the charity a beneficiary of $100,000 of her IRA, the charity will receive a $100,000 distribution from the IRA at Phoebe's death. The charity can then use the entire $100,000 IRA distribution, undiluted by income tax. (Charities are income tax exempt.) If Phoebe had just given a non-IRA asset to her charity instead, then her children would have the ultimate tax burden on the extra $100,000 that they would receive in extra inherited IRA accounts. The non-IRA charitable gift of $100,000 would reduce her children's inheritance by exactly $100,000 assuming no estate tax. However, the IRA gift alternative would only cost the heirs a net $65,000 assuming Phoebe's children are in the 35 percent income tax bracket. This is a way of actually getting a subsidized charitable gift from the IRS.

For people who want to make charitable gifts at death, the regular IRA will often be the most tax-efficient source of these gifts. Read Chapter 6 on stretch IRAs to understand that if you live for a long time past 70½ you will have less money available because your IRA will ultimately be reduced by required distributions.

QUALIFIED CHARITABLE DISTRIBUTIONS

From 2005 through 2009, you could give to charity up to $100,000 directly from your IRA if you were over age 70½. This was called Qualified Charitable Distribution (QCD). The donor does not get an income tax deduction on a QCD, but the donor also does not have to count this IRA distribution as income. This would effectively be an income tax wash (no tax cost). This QCD outcome is actually much better than getting a tax deduction and being taxed on that IRA distribution. QCDs are better for the donor because of the way our income tax deductions work.

If the IRA holder alternatively took a regular IRA distribution and then immediately gave that same amount to a charity, the results would not be an income tax wash like the QCD. The actual tax deduction would usually be less than the IRA distribution due to the way that charitable deductions are diluted and reduced through the Form 1040 maze. Making gifts from IRAs in the traditional way (non-QCD) actually costs you some additional income tax plus the gift.

These QCDs were initially supposed to be available only for years 2005 through 2007 but were extended through 2009. This technique may be extended again depending on the whims of Congress and the charm of the charitable lobbyists.

If QCDs are allowed in the future and you are over age 70½, this is one of the most efficient ways to give money to charity.

DISCLAIMER

You can decide that you do not want an inheritance that is given to you by disclaiming the asset. With IRAs, a beneficiary may disclaim all or part of an IRA by making this disclaimer. The assets disclaimed would then go to the next-in-line beneficiary just as if the disclaiming beneficiary were not alive at the time. Note that the disclaiming beneficiary has no say as to who then gets the IRA, but it would go to the next beneficiary in line, also called the *contingent beneficiary.*

BENEFICIARY DESIGNATION IS IMPORTANT

When an IRA account is opened or started, you must name a beneficiary for the IRA. Often you also name a next-in-line or contingent beneficiary who would be the beneficiary if the primary beneficiary has died before you.

Great care must be given to choosing beneficiaries, and these choices should be regularly reviewed and updated. Often people made their beneficiary decisions many years ago without much thought and when the IRA assets were smaller. Some folks even have ex-spouses or other persons as beneficiaries of their now substantial IRAs. At the death of the IRA holder, the beneficiary designation is what controls and has authority over the IRA based on contract law no matter what your will or living trust says. The will or living trust has no say over the IRA except when the estate is named as the beneficiary. As discussed earlier, the estate should almost never be the beneficiary of IRAs because of the unfavorable distribution rules at death. Changing a will or living trust is important in estate planning, but you must be certain to harmonize and coordinate the beneficiary designations as well.

Check each of your IRA accounts regularly to make sure they are in harmony with your desires. There is a Supreme Court case that shows when there is a conflict in obvious intention versus a disparate beneficiary designation, the beneficiary designation wins. The facts of this case are simple: A man named William Kennedy forgot to change his retirement plan beneficiary after his divorce. When he died many years later, the ex-wife was still named the beneficiary. Kennedy's estate plan to the contrary and common sense did not prevail. The Supreme Court ruled that the ex-spouse got the retirement plan money because she was the designated beneficiary.

You might also remember to check your other beneficiary designations on your other retirement plans, life insurance, annuities, payable on death (POD) accounts, and other so-called nonprobate assets. These beneficiaries can be easily changed via a special form furnished for each account by the IRA trustee. Keep a copy of the completed beneficiary change forms with your important papers as a backup.

CONDUIT IRAs

If you roll over a distribution from a qualified retirement plan, like a 401(k), profit-sharing plan, or defined benefit to an IRA rollover, the source of the IRA can make a difference to your future options. Technically this is called a *conduit IRA* because the sole source of the funding of this IRA was qualified plan money. As long as no regular IRA annual contributions were ever made to this conduit IRA account, and it is not mixed or co-mingled with other contributory or nonconduit IRA accounts, it remains a conduit IRA.

Conduit IRAs have one special unique power and privilege in that they can be rolled over into qualified plans. Regular contributory IRAs cannot be rolled over into qualified plans. If you ever mix conduit IRA accounts with nonconduit accounts, the entire account is no longer a conduit account, and it cannot be restored to one.

The primary advantage that a qualified retirement account has over an IRA is that it may purchase life insurance, whereas IRAs may not purchase life insurance. If new life insurance is desired by an individual or a couple, they sometimes use a new qualified plan funded with conduit IRAs to acquire the new life insurance.

The moral of the conduit IRA story is to never mix IRAs that are conduit (from qualified plans) with nonconduit or contributory IRAs until after the RCO is over and they have stayed converted as Roth IRAs. After the rechacterization deadline for Roth conversions has passed, then all Roth IRAs can be organized together at will. Any unconverted Roth IRAs that came from IRA conduit accounts are returned to conduit accounts and vice versa.

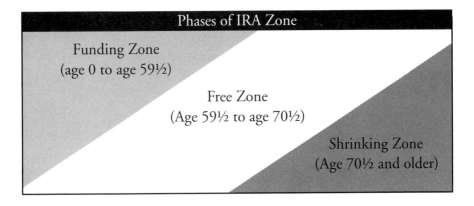

Phases of IRA Zone

Funding Zone
(age 0 to age 59½)

Free Zone
(Age 59½ to age 70½)

Shrinking Zone
(Age 70½ and older)

-------- This page unintentionally left blank. ---------

(Not really, just checking to make sure you were paying attention!)

THE ADVENT OF
THE ROTH IRA
(AND IT WAS EVEN BETTER)

THE ROTH IRA BEGAN WITH the Taxpayer Relief Act of 1997. It was named by and for the late Senator William Roth and was introduced as a way to expand individual retirement options by introducing a new and unique tax-free IRA that was unlike anything else available. The Roth IRA was first available January 1, 1998.

NO TAX DEDUCTION

A primary difference between the Roth IRA and the regular IRA is there is no income tax deduction for the Roth IRA. All Roth IRA contributions are made with after-tax dollars. In addition to Roth contributions, there is one other way to get money into a Roth IRA called a Roth conversion. Regular and rollover IRAs and other retirement plans may be converted or actually rolled over to Roth IRAs, subject to the rules and conditions you will learn about a little later in this book. Roth contributions are treated differently from Roth conversions in the Roth rules. Most of the time, you will want to keep these Roth IRAs separate for a while by using at least two different Roth accounts (or more), if you are doing both Roth conversions and contributions.

TAX-FREE GROWTH AND WITHDRAWALS

The Roth IRA grows without any income tax, and the distributions from the Roth are income tax free. Tax deferral as found in regular IRAs is good, but tax free is even better in most cases.

PUTTING MONEY IN

For 2009, single tax filers who have modified adjusted gross income (MAGI) of less than $105,000 may fully contribute to a Roth IRA up to the annual maximum of $5,000 or $6,000 (for those who are age 50 or more). Married people filing jointly can make these same maximum Roth IRA contributions for each spouse with MAGI up to $166,000. Like the regular IRA, these maximum contributions are phased out for married filing jointly for MAGIs from $166,001 to $175,999. For people who are single, the phaseout is from a MAGI of $105,001 to $119,999. If you are single or married, no Roth contributions are allowed with MAGIs of $120,000 or $176,000 (or more), respectively. For people who are married filing separately the phaseout is from the first dollar of income to $9,999. If you are married filing separately with income of $10,000 or more, you cannot contribute to a Roth IRA. However, like the regular IRA, if you lived apart from your spouse for the entire year, you are treated as if you were single for the Roth limitations. Check the new limits for years after 2009 in the IRS Publication 590.

DEFINING YOUR MODIFIED ADJUSTED GROSS INCOME

The modified adjusted gross income or MAGI for Roth IRAs is the same definition that we covered on the traditional IRA with a couple of extra exceptions. This MAGI is still essentially your adjusted gross income, and for the Roth it also subtracts any required IRA minimum distributions or any Roth conversions from your income. IRS Publication 590 contains a Roth phaseout worksheet if you find your MAGI in the phaseout or bubble bracket. This worksheet will help you calculate the exact maximum that you may contribute to a Roth IRA if you are in the phaseout status.

MUST HAVE COMPENSATION

Roth IRAs are like regular IRAs in that you must have earned income or compensation up to the amount of your contributions to the Roth. The definition of earned income or compensation is the same as well.

RETIREMENT PLANS DON'T COUNT

You may contribute to a Roth IRA based solely on the income limits regardless of whether you (or your spouse) have a retirement plan at work.

NO AGE DISCRIMINATION

Unlike the regular IRA, you may contribute to a Roth IRA regardless of your age. So if you are 80 and still working or you have a spouse that is, you may contribute to a Roth IRA as long as you are below the income maximums listed previously. For people age 50 and above, the maximum Roth contribution is $6,000 and for people younger than 50 the maximum Roth contribution is $5,000. Beginning in 2010, these levels are supposed to be increased with inflation, but in $500 increments *only after* inflation has passed the next $500 mark. Be sure to check out IRS Publication 590 to find out the latest numbers for any given year. This publication is on the IRS website: www.irs.gov.

PAPERWORK

The Roth IRA is very simple; the Roth IRA holder does not have to supply any paperwork or additional reporting. Like regular IRAs, the bank, insurance company, or brokerage house (called the trustee or custodian) has the reporting and compliance work done behind the scenes, making the process very easy and simple to set up and maintain. The Roth IRA must be so designated. Make sure the words Roth IRA appear on your investment statements that you receive from the Roth IRA trustee. Unlike the traditional IRA, you do not have to put down any information about your Roth IRA contributions on your income tax return. This is because you do not get a deduction for Roth IRA contributions because they are made with after-tax dollars.

WHEN TO ROTH

You may contribute to a Roth IRA for each year from January 1 at the earliest, to April 15 of the year afterward. Your Roth IRA trustee will note the year for which the Roth IRA contribution was made. Roth contributions made in the period from January 1 through April 15 could be either for the year before or the current year of the Roth contribution. If you did not make a contribution for the year before, and your income level for that year allows you to make a Roth contribution, you will always want to designate the earlier year for the contribution to have more future options.

COMBINED ROTH AND
REGULAR IRA CONTRIBUTIONS

Your combined total of both Roth IRAs and regular IRAs are counted against your $5,000 or $6,000 (for age 50 and over) limits. Theoretically if you are age 60, you could contribute some money to a regular IRA, nondeductible IRA, and a Roth IRA for the same year up to a combined total of $6,000. However, most people will select only one type of IRA (Roth or regular) that best suits their needs and contribute to it.

THE GREAT CONVERSION

You may be able to convert your regular IRA or retirement plan to a Roth IRA in 2009. Starting in 2010 and beyond, everyone may convert their regular IRAs and retirement accounts to a Roth IRA. Generally, when you convert a regular IRA or retirement plan to a Roth IRA, you have to pay taxes on the amount converted in the year that you convert.

ROTH CONVERSION TAX

When you roll over or convert from an regular IRA to a Roth IRA, all taxes become due on the regular IRA that same year. So if you were to convert or roll over an IRA to a Roth that is worth $500,000, all $500,000 would be added to your taxable income the year of the conversion. What a nerve-racking thought to pay taxes now so that we will not be taxed in the future! This seems to be counterintuitive and the opposite of traditional tax planning. But further analysis may prove that the seemingly premature payment of tax may be the wisest and best decision.

For 2009 and prior years, you can only convert from a regular IRA to a Roth IRA if you have a MAGI of $100,000 or less. This is true for both single filers and married filers. So if you are married filing jointly and your combined MAGI is over $100,000, you may not convert. Also for 2009 and prior years, if you are married filing separately, you cannot convert unless you and your spouse lived apart the entire year. Also, your MAGI would have to be $100,000 or less in the year that you converted to a Roth even with that exception. Beginning with 2010, anyone may convert regardless of income or filing status.

DIRECTLY CONVERT TO A ROTH
FROM YOUR RETIREMENT PLAN

Prior to 2008, you could only roll over or convert from IRAs to Roth IRAs. You had to roll other types of retirement plans into regular IRAs first, before subsequently converting the regular IRA into a Roth IRA. Now you can directly convert to a Roth IRA, either all or part of a distribution, from your:

Qualified pension

Profit-sharing plan

Stock bonus plan

401(k) plan

IRA annuity plan

Tax-sheltered annuity plan 403(b)

Governmental deferred compensation plan (457)

2010—A MOST SPECIAL YEAR

Beginning in 2010, everyone may convert regardless of his or her MAGI. This opens the door to even the high-income earners who have been shut out of this great opportunity all these years. This MAGI restriction is lifted for all future years as well, so everyone can convert to a Roth IRA in 2010 or thereafter.

The year 2010 also brings a one-time special to Roth IRA conversions. If you convert from a retirement plan or regular IRA to a Roth IRA in 2010, you may postpone the income tax due as a result of the conversion until 2011 and 2012.

Saul converts his $100,000 IRA to a Roth IRA in 2010. He does not have to include any of the income for this conversion in 2010, but adds $50,000 to his income in 2011 and $50,000 to his income in 2012. This postponement of tax payments on conversions is only available for Roth IRA conversions that occur in 2010. For all other years after 2010, the income tax triggered by Roth conversions would be added to the taxable income for the same year the conversion was made.

You are not forced to postpone the income tax payment on Roth conversions for 2010 until 2011 and 2012 if you do not want to. You may elect to pay the tax on Roth conversions in 2010 if you prefer. You simply opt out of the extended payment option on your 2010 tax return. You have to decide either to defer *all* the tax for all Roth conversions made in 2010 until 2011 and 2012 or to pay *all* of the conversion tax on your 2010 income tax return. You may not choose to defer the income tax for some of your 2010 Roth conversions and not to defer the tax on the rest. *It is all or nothing.*

However, if you are married, you may choose to defer the tax and your spouse may elect not to. Or vice versa. You will have until October 17, 2011, to finalize this and all your other 2010 Roth options. The income tax forms for 2010 have not yet been created as I write this, but I suspect that this election to pay the tax in 2010 will be made on IRS Form 8606. That is the same form used for reporting nondeductible IRAs. The automatic default position for 2010 Roth conversions is to divide that taxable conversion amount by 2 and include that amount for income on both 2011 and 2012 income tax returns. If you convert $100,000 in 2010 then you would simply include $50,000 of additional taxable income on each of your 2011 and 2012 income tax returns.

The reason that this election of paying the income tax on Roth conversions made in 2010 on the 2010 income tax return may be a very viable option is that income tax rates may increase in 2011 and or 2012. Also, a person's individual situation with regard to their total income projections during these years may make this option far superior to the alternative. The great thing about this 2010 IRS special is that you have until October 17, 2011, to "go firm" on all of your 2010 conversion decisions. Be sure to read the section of this book that discusses avoiding income tax underpayment penalties.

If you use the default option of paying the income tax on 2010 Roth conversions during 2011 and 2012, then you must not take any distributions from your newly converted Roth IRA until after the end of 2011 or you will trigger an acceleration of the income taxes that you postponed on the pro rata share that you distributed. This acceleration calculation of deferred tax will most likely be handled on IRS Form 8606 as well. The IRS wants to make sure that folks do not use this one-time special income tax deferral without keeping the converted Roth intact for the duration of that two-year period.

TAKING MONEY OUT OF A ROTH

Roth IRAs have *no* lifetime mandatory distributions. Age 70½ is not important to a Roth IRA holder because you are never forced to take any money out of your Roth IRA in your lifetime. You may take tax-free distributions from the Roth if you want to, but you do not have to. When you die and if your spouse is your Roth IRA beneficiary, he or she may roll over the Roth IRA as his or her own. Then the inheriting spouse will also have no lifetime mandatory distributions for the balance of his or her life, as well. This is a huge benefit for savers, as I illustrate in the chapters ahead.

THE FIVE-YEAR CLOCK

Generally speaking, you must both be over the age of 59½ and have had the money in the Roth IRA for five years from the first contribution or rollover before being able to take money out of the Roth IRA without penalty or income tax. The Roth was funded with after-tax dollars that will not be subject to income tax, but for the Roth earnings to also be tax-free you must meet both the five-year and age 59½ barriers. The IRS considers this five-year span to be met using what they call a *clock*. This clock is started by either a Roth contribution or a Roth conversion—whichever starts first.

Start Your Clock(s)!

The clock started by a Roth contribution begins on January 1 of the year the contribution is designated for, while the clock started by a Roth conversion begins on January 1 of the actual year of the Roth conversion. Subsequent Roth conversions and contributions do not reset the Roth clock. Contributions and conversions to a Roth can provide different clock results.

Paul makes both a Roth contribution and a Roth conversion on February 12, 2010. It is his first time to contribute or convert to a Roth. Paul's Roth clock started by the conversion begins on January 1, 2010, because that is the year of the conversion. His Roth contribution clock would actually start a year earlier on January 1, 2009, if he designated that contribution for the year 2009. Paul will only use the earlier and more favorable clock starting date of 1/1/2009. So using your fingers (only one hand needed), you can count off Paul's five-year clock—2009, 2010, 2011, 2012, and 2013. His Roth clock has tolled by the end of 2013. So Paul's Roth IRA five-year clock has run and completed for all Roth distributions by the end of 2013. Any future contributions or conversions to Paul's Roth IRA will not change or reset the clock that ends after 2013. His first qualification for qualified Roth distributions (the five-year clock) will be met beginning January 1, 2014.

The second requirement for complete penalty-free and tax-free Roth distributions is that the Roth IRA owner be age 59½ or older. This is probably something you do not want to rush—that day will come soon enough. Once the Roth five-year clock has completed and you are over age 59½, no income taxes or penalties will be accessed on any Roth IRA distributions. If you are short on either the five-year clock or age 59½, you may have to pay income tax on the gain, plus a 10 percent penalty for the early withdrawal if you are not yet 59½. This will not be a problem to most folks as you will learn when you read the ordering rules of Roth distributions a little later in this chapter.

As you can see by Paul's example, it may take less than five actual years for the five-year clock to run out. You may want to make a Roth contribution now if you qualify to start the five-year clock sooner, if you are at least age 54 or older. Also, for the Roth clock to be started by a Roth conversion, you will have to leave at least some part of one Roth converted at the end of the Roth Conversion Option (RCO). If you unconvert everything, that will not start the clock.

EXCEPTIONS TO AGE 59½ AND THE FIVE-YEAR RULE

Like the regular IRA, the Roth IRA has a few loopholes that you might be able to use to get the money from a Roth IRA earlier than normal without penalties or extra tax. Let me spend a moment here to discuss the potential folly of this. If the Roth IRA is income tax free when you take it out and it grows tax free until then, why would you want to rush taking money out of your Roth IRA? Because of the Roth's unique attributes, it should be the last money in the world that you ever touch. If you are spending down your Roth IRA before you are 59½, you are about to be seriously poor or even broke.

If you have read this stern warning and still have to get to your Roth IRA and pull it out before the five-year and age 59½ goals have been reached, then see if you qualify for an exception to the 10 percent penalty. These exceptions only get you out of the pre-age 59½ penalty. If you do not meet both the 5 year and age 59½ rules for withdrawals, any gains on the Roth will still be subject to income tax ... and there is no exception for this.

Jonah made a Roth conversion of $50,000 and left it in his Roth account for a few years. He never made any annual Roth contributions. After four years on the Roth conversion clock, he withdrew his entire Roth conversion account, which had grown to $70,000. He would have to include the $20,000 gain as taxable income, and there are **no exceptions** to this. Note that he never has to pay income tax twice on his $50,000 basis (after-tax amount invested). He will also have to pay 10 percent on the entire $70,000 unless he is over age 59½ or qualifies for another exception.

ROTH FIVE-YEAR AND AGE 59½ EXCEPTIONS

The exceptions to the 10 percent penalty for early Roth withdrawals include being over age 59½ plus all the other exceptions that regular IRAs have. These were defined in Chapter 2 but they are listed here again for your convenience. You may withdraw money from your Roth IRA before the five-year clock is up for the following exceptions:

Over age 59½

Death

Disability

Annuity payments (Substantially equal periodic payments)

Medical expenses above a certain amount

Medical insurance if you are recently unemployed

Qualified higher education expenses

First home costs and expenses

IRS levy on your IRA

Qualified reservist distribution

See Chapter 2 for more specific details for these exceptions as they are the same for regular IRAs as well.

ORDERING RULES FOR ROTH IRA DISTRIBUTIONS

The IRS lumps all of your Roth IRAs together for purposes of calculating if there is a penalty or income tax on your premature Roth distribution. The IRS calls this *aggregation*. It does not matter which Roth account you remove money from because these ordering rules will supersede reality. Any money that comes from your Roth IRAs will be considered taken out in the following order:

1. Roth contributions
2. Roth conversions in the order converted (taxable conversions first, then nontaxable originating from nondeductible IRAs, if any)
3. Roth earnings

Simon has made a few contributions to Roth IRAs over the years totaling $20,000. Simon converted a regular IRA to a Roth IRA worth $980,000. Due to earnings, his combined Roth balance is now $1,200,000. Simon can take out $20,000 from his Roth IRA without penalty or income tax no matter what his age is. The first $20,000 would represent his contributions to Roth IRAs and are never subject to the 10 percent penalty or additional taxes. If Simon is over age 59½, he can take $1,000,000 from his Roth with no penalties or additional taxes. This is the total of his Roth contributions and conversions. If he is wants to take out the final $200,000, he may want to wait until the age 59½ and five-year clocks have tolled so he can get even the last $200,000 tax and penalty free. If he cannot wait, then he should check for any exceptions that he may qualify for, to at least avoid the 10 percent penalty.

Roth contributions may be withdrawn at any time without regard to age or clocks, with no penalty or taxes. This makes Roth IRA contributions a great place to save money knowing emergency access is available without penalty. Conversions may be withdrawn at any time after Simon is over 59½, without regard to clocks, with no taxes or penalties.

There is another exception for the pre age 59½ 10 percent penalty for conversions. As long as the actual Roth conversion has met the five-year test independently (without regard to the other clock), that conversion may be removed before age 59½ and will not be subject to the 10 percent penalty. Any earnings in a Roth are not exempt from the penalty unless a different exception applies.

MY OLD DOG FIFO

Another wonderful truth about Roth IRAs is that they use a great old accounting methodology called first in, first out (FIFO). That means that until all the basis (after-tax contributions and tax-paid conversions) is withdrawn, there will be no tax on withdrawals because the money has already been taxed. It is true that age 59½ must be achieved before you can get the Roth conversions out without a penalty or exception, but that is the same deal with regular IRAs and most other retirement plans.

INHERITED ROTH IRAs

Roth IRAs are built to be income tax free with no lifetime mandatory distributions. With due care on the part of the beneficiaries, this tax-free status can be enjoyed and extended for a season even after the Roth IRA owner's death. When a Roth IRA is established, a beneficiary is named as part of the paperwork. When the Roth IRA holder dies, the beneficiary has some choices with regard to this inherited Roth IRA. If the beneficiary is also the spouse of the original Roth IRA holder, special privileges apply. The spouse/beneficiary may roll over the Roth IRA into his or her own name. This benefit is only available for spouse/beneficiaries. The spouse/beneficiary may also keep the inherited Roth IRA in the name of the original holder and must then take distributions starting when the original Roth holder would have been 70½. Perhaps the only reason why a person who inherits a Roth IRA from a spouse would not roll it over into his or her own name is if he or she is under age 59½ and wants to start taking distributions from the Roth before that age is attained without penalty. This spouse/beneficiary could always change the name of the inherited IRA into his or her own name later after they are past age 59½. It is nice to have options. If the spouse/beneficiary of a Roth IRA rolls the Roth into his or her own name, he or she will have no mandatory lifetime distributions.

If nonspouse beneficiaries, like children or grandchildren, inherit the Roth IRA, they have two choices on how to distribute the Roth IRA. Each separate beneficiary would split off his portion of the inherited Roth IRA and begin to take mandatory distributions over his life expectancy beginning the year after the original Roth holder's death. He can combine inherited Roth IRAs that came from the same person. Each beneficiary determines his or her life expectancy by looking up his or her age for the year after the original IRA holder's death on life expectancy Table I found in the back of IRS Publication 590.

Eve inherits a Roth IRA from her mother who died in 2009. Eve will turn 59 in 2010. She determines her life expectancy in Publication 590 to be 26.1 years. Eve looks at the value of her inherited Roth as of December 31, 2009, and finds that it is $300,000. Eve divides $300,000 by 26.1 to come up with $11,494.25. Eve must distribute from her inherited Roth IRA at least $11,494.25 during 2010. For the next year, she simply subtracts a year from the life expectancy of the year before and uses 25.1 for her 2011 mandatory inherited IRA distribution. This Table I life expectancy is non-recalculating, meaning that Eve only looks up her life expectancy when she begins this process and subtracts 1 for each subsequent year. The minimum required distribution must be taken out of the inherited Roth each year to avoid the 50 percent penalty.

FIVE-YEAR RULE ALTERNATIVE FOR DISTRIBUTIONS

If the nonspouse beneficiary distributes less than the required amount in the year after the original Roth holder's death, then that beneficiary must distribute 100 percent of the entire inherited Roth IRA by December 31 of the year that is five years after the death of the original Roth IRA holder. If Eve, in the previous example, made no distribution from the inherited Roth in 2010, she must make a complete distribution of the entire inherited Roth IRA by December 31, 2014. If Eve does this, she will avoid the 50 percent penalty. If total withdrawal of the inherited IRA is not made by the end of 2014, the five-year option is not possible and 50 percent penalties will apply to every one of the previous years that the distribution was short of the annual minimum.

Inherited Roth IRAs are still subject to the original five-year clock for the tax-free distributions of earnings. This should not be a problem because of the favorable ordering rules of money taken from a Roth. The 10 percent penalty will never come into play for inherited Roth IRAs because of the death exception, but care should be taken by the beneficiaries not to withdraw everything too quickly from the inherited Roth to ensure that all the proceeds will be income tax free.

If the beneficiaries fail to split up the Roth among separate beneficiaries by September 30 of the year after the death of the original Roth IRA holder, then the distributions must be taken according to the age and life expectancy of the oldest beneficiary. These same rules would apply for a beneficiary that is a trust and where the trust has more than one beneficiary.

ESTATE IS THE BENEFICIARY

Naming the estate the beneficiary of a Roth IRA is usually a mistake. If the beneficiary of a Roth IRA is an estate, distributions must be made using the deceased IRA owner's age if he died on or after his required beginning date. This process uses the deceased IRA holder's age the year after death (according to life expectancy Table I) and does not recalculate. However, if a Roth IRA owner who has named his estate as beneficiary dies before his required beginning date, then all of the Roth IRA must be distributed before the end of five years following the year of his or her death.

DISCLAIMER

You can decide that you do not want an inheritance that is given to you by disclaiming the asset. With Roth IRAs, a beneficiary may disclaim all or part of an Roth IRA by making this disclaimer. The assets disclaimed would then go to the next-in-line beneficiary just as if the disclaiming beneficiary were not alive at the time. Note that the disclaiming beneficiary has no say who gets the Roth IRA but it would go to the next beneficiary in line—also called the contingent beneficiary.

BENEFICIARY DESIGNATION IS IMPORTANT

When a Roth IRA account is started, you must name a beneficiary. Often you also name a next-in-line or contingent beneficiary who would be the beneficiary if the primary beneficiary dies before you. Great care must be given to choosing beneficiaries, and these choices should be regularly reviewed and updated. Often people made these beneficiary decisions many years ago without much thought and when the Roth IRA assets were smaller. Some folks even have ex-spouses or other unintended persons as beneficiaries of their now substantial Roth IRAs. At the death of the Roth IRA holder, the beneficiary designation is what controls and has authority over the Roth IRA based on contract law no matter what your will or living trust says. The will or living trust has no say over the Roth IRA except when the estate is named as the beneficiary. As discussed earlier, the estate should almost never be the beneficiary of Roth IRAs because of the unfavorable distribution rules at death. Changing a will or living trust is important in estate planning, but you must be certain to harmonize and coordinate the beneficiary designations as well.

Check each of your Roth IRA accounts regularly to make sure they are in harmony with your desires. As mentioned in Chapter 2, there is a Supreme Court case (Kennedy) that shows when there is a conflict in obvious intention versus a disparate beneficiary designation, the beneficiary designation wins. The facts of this case are simple. A man named William Kennedy forgot to change his retirement plan beneficiary after his divorce. When he died many years later, the ex-wife was still named as the beneficiary. Kennedy's estate plan to the contrary and common sense did not prevail. The Supremes (the court not the group) ruled that the ex-wife got the retirement plan money because she was the designated beneficiary.

You might also remember to check your other beneficiary designations while you are at it on your other regular IRAs, retirement plans, life insurance, annuities, payable on death (POD) accounts, and other so-called nonprobate assets. These beneficiaries can be easily changed via a special form furnished for each account by the financial institution. Keep a copy of the completed beneficiary change forms with your important papers.

RECHARACTERIZATION
AND UNCONVERT LIMIT

You are able to convert and unconvert to a Roth IRA only one time per year per account. You may do so with an unlimited number of different Roth IRA accounts, and these options apply to each independently. After you unconvert or recharacterize a Roth IRA, you have to wait to convert that same account again. You actually must wait from the date you unconverted the Roth, until the later of 30 days and the next calendar year before you again convert or reconvert. Therefore, if one or more of your Roth conversion accounts has lost value within the same calendar year that it was converted, you will probably want to unconvert it around December 1 so you can start the RCO process over again at the very beginning of the following year.

Jobab converted eight IRAs to eight Roth IRAs on January 4, 2010. By December 2010, two of his conversions were underwater (valued lower than they were on the conversion date). He would unconvert or recharacterize these two accounts around December 1, 2010, so he can begin a new RCO on them in the first week of 2011. He needs to unconvert them in early December so he can reconvert them in early January because of the 30-day minimum rule on reconverting the unconverted.

ASSET PROTECTION AND THE IRA

Regular IRAs and Roth IRAs have additional asset protection from the claims of creditors based on the state law where the IRA holder resides. This is often capped at a certain amount, but it can be an additional advantage of regular and Roth IRAs. Some states may protect regular IRAs differently from Roth IRAs. Check the laws for your specific state to see what level of protection exists for these accounts.

As you get past the age of 70½, the Roth IRA conversion may be superior as an asset protection tool since Roth has no mandatory distributions. (Also the Roth is superior in this context as a Roth IRA is after tax thus larger than a regular IRA which is smaller than it appears due to income taxes due on any distribution.)

Inherited IRAs and Roth IRAs typically have none of these asset protection attributes, making an IRA inheritance trust all the more important and valuable.

ROTH IRA MATH

MY DADDY USED TO TELL me when I was young, "Johnny boy, there are three kinds of people in this world," and then he would grin at me holding up three fingers. He would finish by saying, "those that are good at math and those that aren't!" Most people are not good at math. This is unfortunate because bad math leads to money problems, which make people stressed out financially and mentally. Being bad at math is very expensive. But no one is born with fully developed math skills. Money math skills can be learned. You can learn how to correctly calculate most money equations that can help you make better financial choices. Sometimes folks are so intimidated by the need to do a calculation that they freeze and go with their gut or intuition. Going with your gut or first impression may be a way to get the correct multiple-choice answer on a history pop quiz, but it is a terrible way to make an important money decision. Many people will spend hours shopping to buy a car or major appliance, meticulously making sure that the model, color, price, reliability, options, and features are perfect for them. After they've made their decision on their specific purchase, they seem so relieved that they let their guard down and make incredibly poor decisions about how they choose to pay for the items; choices involving financing, leasing (heaven forbid), and extended warranties. These poor decisions are often very expensive and generally more than offset any savings they may have hoped for on the purchase price. Intuition is not your friend when it comes to numbers, and it is easy to suffer from mathematical vertigo. However, almost anyone can learn to calculate better money decisions that will make a huge impact in their financial future.

Often the illusion that something is a good deal appears so logical that we do not even question it or calculate the alternatives. However, we can improve our lives greatly by making better financial choices. In this book, I want to show you how to figure out the best strategy for your situation so you can make an informed decision. In the examples ahead, I show you how to calculate all of the alternatives so you can see what is best for you. It would be helpful for you to run the numbers along with me so you can get a feel for the calculations.

Emotion is an important part of the financial decision-making process. Some people prefer stocks to bonds—others like CDs. Fear of the unknown is also an important part of this process. But fear can be overcome, especially when the unknown is better understood. Many people are afraid to fly on airplanes. Some people refuse to fly on an airplane for their entire life. That is their choice and prerogative. I still remember the first time I flew on an airplane, and I found it to be a terrifying experience. You may remember your first flying experience. However, I am grateful that I quickly overcame that fear of flying because my traveling tens of millions of miles has certainly been made easier by that method of travel. Keep an open mind as you read this book. Everyone is fearful of paying large amounts of tax especially when they feel like they could have deferred that payment. However, many things with math are counterintuitive. If you run the numbers, you may find that you are no longer so fearful especially if you find that it is in your best interest to do something that was contrary to your initial reaction. It is my hope that you will learn to make an informed decision—a decision that will benefit you and your family. So buckle up, get out your calculator and yellow pad and let's take off!

Saul has an regular IRA worth $1,000,000. He also has a money market account (non-IRA) worth $300,000. He does not need any income from his IRA account or money market account presently, but he enjoys knowing that he has these accounts "just in case" he needs them for income at some point. Let's presume that Saul is in an income tax bracket of 30 percent and could invest his money for income at a rate of 5 percent. Even if Saul does not want or need the income from these accounts, we are calculating the income potential as if he chose to maximize income each year to make our accurate comparison.

Let's do a before-and-after look at Saul's Roth conversion situation. If he were to invest the money market account worth $300,000 and the IRA account worth $1,000,000 for income at 5 percent, he would have the following net income results:

$1,000,000 in the IRA at 5 percent would yield $50,000 per year. At a tax rate of 30 percent, he would pay income tax of $15,000 each year. This means he would net $35,000 for the IRA with $50,000 gross income minus taxes of $15,000.

He could also invest the $300,000 for income at 5 percent. Saul would gross $15,000 per year on an investment with a 5 percent return. He would owe tax on this income of 30 percent or $4,500. His net income from the $300,000 would be $10,500 per year after tax. Saul's after-tax return from both his IRA and non-IRA account under this scenario would be $45,500.

You might say Saul has the "annual net income ability" from his regular IRA worth $1,000,000 and his $300,000 in outside IRA funds of $45,500 in their current form. He would net in spendable dollars $45,500 every year with no loss in principal forever with these assumptions.

Saul decides to convert to a Roth IRA. At $1,000,000, he would pay $300,000 to the IRS at a 30 percent income tax rate. He pays the tax from his money market (outside IRA) account leaving his newly converted and renamed Roth IRA worth $1,000,000. He would then be able to take income only from his Roth

IRA because his $300,000 non-IRA account has been spent to pay the tax on his Roth conversion. His Roth IRA of $1,000,000 would produce an income of $50,000 per year under this scenario. His income tax on the Roth is $0.

> Today, it takes more brains and effort to make out the income-tax form than it does to make the income.
>
> —**Alfred E. Neuman**

Wow, wait a minute. He was only able to receive $45,500 spendable money per year when he had gross assets of $1.3 million and now with gross assets of $1 million he gets spendable income of $50,000 per year. This Roth conversion results in substantially more money in available after-tax income. This is almost a 10 percent increase in available spendable income. Tax-free is better than tax-deferred any day.

Also, Saul did not just lose the $300,000. He owed it as a debt against the IRA, and he would never be able to get money out of his IRA without paying the tax. It is like he owed a mortgage of $300,000 on his $1,000,000 house. If he decides to pay off the house, he does not lose money. Saul may indeed feel poorer as a result of using his money market funds to pay off his $300,000 debt. This is a common feeling of loss, but it is actually a form of financial vertigo. By paying off the IRA debt, he will enjoy many more benefits starting now (and in the future) in the form of more available after-tax dollars.

By deferring the tax payment on his regular IRA, Saul would receive 10 percent less in potential income currently and be even worse off when income tax rates go up. If he currently needs no income, then the Roth conversion advantage is even greater for him to convert to a Roth IRA as soon as possible and enjoy a greater amount of assets after taxes in the future than he would have if he had not made the Roth conversion.

Also, waiting to convert is expensive because the amount of outside funds required goes up with increases in the regular IRA value. There may never be a better time for Saul to convert to a Roth IRA.

SUPERSIZE YOUR IRA

One way to look at the Roth IRA conversion is like you are supersizing your IRA by converting it to a Roth. Roth IRAs are worth more than regular IRAs of the same size because there is no tax due on the Roth when you spend the money—unlike regular IRAs that are always worth less than the gross amount due to taxes. When you convert to a Roth IRA and pay the income tax due as a result of the conversion with other non-IRA money, you are actually making an extra contribution to your tax-free future by paying off the taxes on your IRA early. In the previous example, Saul effectively is able to make another extra contribution to his tax-free retirement funds of $300,000. By paying off the tax with the $300,000, he has morphed these funds used to pay the tax from a very inefficient taxable state into the highest and best financial state—a tax-free Roth!

For years, many people have attempted to contribute the maximum to their retirement accounts each year as allowed by law. Using defined benefit plans or other pension plans, they have correctly and intuitively maxed out this important feature. When you convert to a Roth and make the tax payment from outside funds, you have effectively made a large retirement plan contribution to the amount of taxes paid.

THOUGHT EXPERIMENT WITH
MONEY IN A MASON JAR

Let's look at the future advantages that Saul might have if he makes the right decision. When you do this type of analysis, it is important to make the comparisons using the same parameters for each choice. Consider this to be a thought experiment where we want to contain all possible dollars in two imaginary mason jars and count the dollars in each jar year after year to determine which choice is best.

INTRODUCING THE SIDE FUND

Let's view Saul's situation over the long term and look at the effect of the Roth conversion, assuming that he has the $1,000,000 in an IRA and what I would call a side fund of $300,000. This side fund can be used to pay the income tax on his conversion, but if Saul does not convert to a Roth, we need to keep track of this $300,000 to compare the future results with or without the Roth conversion.

If Saul does not convert to a Roth IRA, he would invest the side fund as the previous example showed at a rate of 5 percent with an income tax drag of 30 percent. It is this income tax drag on the side fund that makes the Roth conversion more attractive. Let's presume he allows the money in these accounts to grow under this 5 percent earnings and 30 percent tax scenario. To get his 5 percent return, we can assume he is investing in CDs or bonds or mutual funds that have a fairly high turnover where the income tax would be ordinary income. Below I have run the numbers on this example showing the next 30 years. For simplicity, Saul is not taking any mandatory distributions from his IRA. The column headings from left to right show the important information.

The Year column starts at 0 and gives you the time frame beginning the day before the conversion. The Reg IRA column is his current regular IRA and has not been taxed yet. The Side Fund column shows his non-IRA funds growing after taxes are paid each year. The Net IRA+SF (side fund) column is his spendable IRA (after taxes) plus his side fund. The Roth IRA column shows the spendable Roth value he has available each year. His RCA is the increase that the Roth conversion has brought in spendable dollars. For example, if you had $100,000 in net spendable money with a regular IRA and $120,000 with a Roth conversion, your RCA would be $20,000. Finally, the RCA (%) column is the RCA as a percentage of spendable dollars increased as a result of the Roth. This is the most important number, and in the previous example, the $20,000 RCA is a RCA of 20 percent.

Year	Reg IRA	Side Fund	Net IRA+SF	Roth IRA	RCA	RCA (%)
0	$1,000,000	$300,000	$1,000,000	$1,000,000	$0	0.00%
1	$1,050,000	$310,500	$1,045,500	$1,050,000	$4,500	0.43%
2	$1,102,500	$321,368	$1,093,117	$1,102,500	$9,383	0.86%
3	$1,157,625	$332,615	$1,142,953	$1,157,625	$14,672	1.28%
4	$1,215,506	$344,257	$1,195,111	$1,215,506	$20,395	1.71%
5	$1,276,282	$356,306	$1,249,703	$1,276,282	$26,579	2.13%
6	$1,340,096	$368,777	$1,306,844	$1,340,096	$33,252	2.54%
7	$1,407,100	$381,684	$1,366,654	$1,407,100	$40,446	2.96%
8	$1,477,455	$395,043	$1,429,262	$1,477,455	$48,194	3.37%
9	$1,551,328	$408,869	$1,494,799	$1,551,328	$56,529	3.78%
10	$1,628,895	$423,180	$1,563,406	$1,628,895	$65,489	**4.19%**
11	$1,710,339	$437,991	$1,635,228	$1,710,339	$75,111	4.59%
12	$1,795,856	$453,321	$1,710,420	$1,795,856	$85,436	5.00%
13	$1,885,649	$469,187	$1,789,141	$1,885,649	$96,508	5.39%
14	$1,979,932	$485,608	$1,871,560	$1,979,932	$108,371	5.79%
15	$2,078,928	$502,605	$1,957,854	$2,078,928	$121,074	6.18%
16	$2,182,875	$520,196	$2,048,208	$2,182,875	$134,667	6.57%
17	$2,292,018	$538,403	$2,142,815	$2,292,018	$149,203	6.96%
18	$2,406,619	$557,247	$2,241,880	$2,406,619	$164,739	7.35%
19	$2,526,950	$576,750	$2,345,616	$2,526,950	$181,335	7.73%
20	$2,653,298	$596,937	$2,454,245	$2,653,298	$199,053	**8.11%**
21	$2,785,963	$617,829	$2,568,003	$2,785,963	$217,959	8.49%
22	$2,925,261	$639,453	$2,687,136	$2,925,261	$238,125	8.86%
23	$3,071,524	$661,834	$2,811,901	$3,071,524	$259,623	9.23%
24	$3,225,100	$684,999	$2,942,569	$3,225,100	$282,531	9.60%
25	$3,386,355	$708,973	$3,079,422	$3,386,355	$306,933	9.97%
26	$3,555,673	$733,788	$3,222,758	$3,555,673	$332,914	10.33%
27	$3,733,456	$759,470	$3,372,890	$3,733,456	$360,567	10.69%
28	$3,920,129	$786,052	$3,530,142	$3,920,129	$389,987	11.05%
29	$4,116,136	$813,563	$3,694,858	$4,116,136	$421,277	11.40%
30	$4,321,942	$842,038	$3,867,398	$4,321,942	$454,545	**11.75%**

Saul will always have more spendable money by converting to a Roth IRA. In fact he will have over $450,000 more by the 30th year. In percentages, Saul would be better off with an RCA of 4.19 percent, 8.11 percent, and 11.75 percent at years 10, 20, and 30, respectively.

If we were to recalculate Saul's example with a 10 percent earnings rate, the news would be even better as shown in the following chart. Again this example is without any mandatory IRA distributions:

Year	Reg IRA	Side Fund	Net IRA + SF	Roth IRA	RCA	RCA (%)
0	$1,000,000	$300,000	$1,000,000	$1,000,000	$0	0.00%
1	$1,100,000	$321,000	$1,091,000	$1,100,000	$9,000	0.82%
2	$1,210,000	$343,470	$1,190,470	$1,210,000	$19,530	1.64%
3	$1,331,000	$367,513	$1,299,213	$1,331,000	$31,787	2.45%
4	$1,464,100	$393,239	$1,418,109	$1,464,100	$45,991	3.24%
5	$1,610,510	$420,766	$1,548,123	$1,610,510	$62,387	4.03%
6	$1,771,561	$450,219	$1,690,312	$1,771,561	$81,249	4.81%
7	$1,948,717	$481,734	$1,845,836	$1,948,717	$102,881	5.57%
8	$2,143,589	$515,456	$2,015,968	$2,143,589	$127,621	6.33%
9	$2,357,948	$551,538	$2,202,101	$2,357,948	$155,847	7.08%
10	$2,593,742	$590,145	$2,405,765	$2,593,742	$187,977	**7.81%**
11	$2,853,117	$631,456	$2,628,637	$2,853,117	$224,479	8.54%
12	$3,138,428	$675,657	$2,872,557	$3,138,428	$265,871	9.26%
13	$3,452,271	$722,954	$3,139,543	$3,452,271	$312,728	9.96%
14	$3,797,498	$773,560	$3,431,809	$3,797,498	$365,689	10.66%
15	$4,177,248	$827,709	$3,751,783	$4,177,248	$425,465	11.34%
16	$4,594,973	$885,649	$4,102,130	$4,594,973	$492,843	12.01%
17	$5,054,470	$947,645	$4,485,774	$5,054,470	$568,697	12.68%
18	$5,559,917	$1,013,980	$4,905,922	$5,559,917	$653,996	13.33%
19	$6,115,909	$1,084,958	$5,366,095	$6,115,909	$749,814	13.97%
20	$6,727,500	$1,160,905	$5,870,155	$6,727,500	$857,345	**14.61%**
21	$7,400,250	$1,242,169	$6,422,344	$7,400,250	$977,906	15.23%
22	$8,140,275	$1,329,121	$7,027,313	$8,140,275	$1,112,962	15.84%
23	$8,954,302	$1,422,159	$7,690,171	$8,954,302	$1,264,132	16.44%

Year	Reg IRA	Side Fund	Net IRA + SF	Roth IRA	RCA	RCA (%)
24	$9,849,733	$1,521,710	$8,416,523	$9,849,733	$1,433,210	17.03%
25	$10,834,706	$1,628,230	$9,212,524	$10,834,706	$1,622,182	17.61%
26	$11,918,177	$1,742,206	$10,084,929	$11,918,177	$1,833,247	18.18%
27	$13,109,994	$1,864,160	$11,041,156	$13,109,994	$2,068,838	18.74%
28	$14,420,994	$1,994,652	$12,089,347	$14,420,994	$2,331,647	19.29%
29	$15,863,093	$2,134,277	$13,238,442	$15,863,093	$2,624,651	19.83%
30	$17,449,402	$2,283,677	$14,498,258	$17,449,402	$2,951,144	20.36%

At a 10 percent return, Saul's RCA jumped to 7.81 percent, 14.61 percent, and 20.36 percent for his 10-, 20- and 30-year projections. The benefit of the RCA is more spendable dollars for Saul, not his heirs. Sure, if he converts to a Roth and never spends the money, it will be beneficial to his heirs someday, but the primary outcome is more money for Saul both now and in the future.

But wait a minute. These two tables showed Saul to have no mandatory distributions over the next 30 years. For that to be the case, he would have to be age 40 or less. Let's now assume Saul is age 65 and will have to begin his mandatory IRA distributions af-

> The hardest thing in the world to understand is the income tax.
>
> **— Albert Einstein**

ter he turns 70½. Remember, he must take these distributions if he has a regular IRA whether he wants to or not. So the last examples would have been a great advantage and accurate for someone age 40 but for a 65-year-old it may get even better. We will run the numbers the same way with Saul at age 65 (born in January), having him turn 66 during year 1. He is earning 5 percent and being taxed at 30 percent. Any mandatory IRA distributions will be added to the side fund after tax each year for these calculations. The results are shown in the table that follows:

Age	Year	Reg IRA	Side Fund	IRA Net + SF	Roth IRA	RCA	RCA (%)
65	0	$1,000,000	$300,000	$1,000,000	$1,000,000	$0	0.00%
66	1	$1,050,000	$310,500	$1,045,500	$1,050,000	$4,500	0.43%
67	2	$1,102,500	$321,368	$1,093,117	$1,102,500	$9,383	0.86%
68	3	$1,157,625	$332,615	$1,142,953	$1,157,625	$14,672	1.28%
69	4	$1,215,506	$344,257	$1,195,111	$1,215,506	$20,395	1.71%
70	5	$1,231,920	$387,359	$1,249,703	$1,276,282	$26,579	2.13%
71	6	$1,247,028	$433,458	$1,306,378	$1,340,096	$33,718	2.58%
72	7	$1,260,668	$482,727	$1,365,195	$1,407,100	$41,906	3.07%
73	8	$1,272,662	$535,350	$1,426,214	$1,477,455	$51,242	3.59%
74	9	$1,282,822	$591,519	$1,489,494	$1,551,328	$61,834	4.15%
75	10	$1,290,945	$651,435	$1,555,096	$1,628,895	$73,799	**4.75%**
76	11	$1,296,813	$715,310	$1,623,079	$1,710,339	$87,260	5.38%
77	12	$1,300,483	$783,166	$1,693,504	$1,795,856	$102,353	6.04%
78	13	$1,301,444	$855,421	$1,766,431	$1,885,649	$119,218	6.75%
79	14	$1,299,775	$932,079	$1,841,921	$1,979,932	$138,010	7.49%
80	15	$1,295,257	$1,013,356	$1,920,036	$2,078,928	$158,892	8.28%
81	16	$1,287,659	$1,099,476	$2,000,838	$2,182,875	$182,037	9.10%
82	17	$1,276,741	$1,190,669	$2,084,388	$2,292,018	$207,631	9.96%
83	18	$1,262,250	$1,287,172	$2,170,747	$2,406,619	$235,872	10.87%
84	19	$1,243,927	$1,389,228	$2,259,977	$2,526,950	$266,973	11.81%
85	20	$1,222,074	$1,496,685	$2,352,137	$2,653,298	$301,161	**12.80%**
86	21	$1,196,506	$1,609,739	$2,447,294	$2,785,963	$338,669	13.84%
87	22	$1,167,040	$1,728,584	$2,545,512	$2,925,261	$379,748	14.92%
88	23	$1,133,499	$1,853,410	$2,646,859	$3,071,524	$424,665	16.04%
89	24	$1,095,716	$1,984,400	$2,751,401	$3,225,100	$473,699	17.22%
90	25	$1,054,386	$2,121,135	$2,859,205	$3,386,355	$527,150	18.44%
91	26	$1,009,477	$2,263,714	$2,970,348	$3,555,673	$585,324	19.71%
92	27	$960,983	$2,412,222	$3,084,910	$3,733,456	$648,546	21.02%
93	28	$908,929	$2,566,722	$3,202,972	$3,920,129	$717,157	22.39%
94	29	$854,493	$2,726,474	$3,324,620	$4,116,136	$791,516	23.81%
95	30	$797,858	$2,891,453	$3,449,954	$4,321,942	$871,989	**25.28%**

Saul now has an RCA of 4.75 percent, 12.80 percent, and 25.28 percent for years 10, 20, and 30. That is quite an improvement over the 4.19 percent, 8.11 percent, and 11.75 percent in the first example with no mandatory distributions using the same assumptions. Let's look at his situation at a 10 percent rate of return:

Age	Year	Reg IRA	Side Fund	IRA Net + SF	Roth IRA	RCA	RCA (%)
65	0	$1,000,000	$300,000	$1,000,000	$1,000,000	$0	0.00%
66	1	$1,100,000	$321,000	$1,091,000	$1,100,000	$9,000	0.82%
67	2	$1,210,000	$343,470	$1,190,470	$1,210,000	$19,530	1.64%
68	3	$1,331,000	$367,513	$1,299,213	$1,331,000	$31,787	2.45%
69	4	$1,464,100	$393,239	$1,418,109	$1,464,100	$45,991	3.24%
70	5	$1,557,076	$458,170	$1,548,123	$1,610,510	$62,387	4.03%
71	6	$1,654,026	$531,372	$1,689,190	$1,771,561	$82,371	4.88%
72	7	$1,754,818	$613,795	$1,842,168	$1,948,717	$106,550	5.78%
73	8	$1,859,254	$706,492	$2,007,970	$2,143,589	$135,618	6.75%
74	9	$1,967,060	$810,631	$2,187,573	$2,357,948	$170,375	7.79%
75	10	$2,077,868	$927,503	$2,382,011	$2,593,742	$211,731	8.89%
76	11	$2,191,206	$1,058,543	$2,592,387	$2,853,117	$260,730	10.06%
77	12	$2,306,968	$1,204,992	$2,819,869	$3,138,428	$318,559	11.30%
78	13	$2,424,021	$1,368,892	$3,065,707	$3,452,271	$386,565	12.61%
79	14	$2,542,115	$1,551,730	$3,331,211	$3,797,498	$466,288	14.00%
80	15	$2,660,384	$1,755,511	$3,617,780	$4,177,248	$559,468	15.46%
81	16	$2,777,798	$1,982,434	$3,926,892	$4,594,973	$668,081	17.01%
82	17	$2,893,133	$2,234,915	$4,260,109	$5,054,470	$794,362	18.65%
83	18	$3,004,954	$2,515,604	$4,619,072	$5,559,917	$940,845	20.37%
84	19	$3,111,581	$2,827,404	$5,005,511	$6,115,909	$1,110,398	22.18%
85	20	$3,212,497	$3,172,492	$5,421,240	$6,727,500	$1,306,260	24.10%
86	21	$3,305,910	$3,554,052	$5,868,189	$7,400,250	$1,532,061	26.11%
87	22	$3,389,792	$3,975,533	$6,348,387	$8,140,275	$1,791,888	28.23%
88	23	$3,461,858	$4,440,659	$6,863,959	$8,954,302	$2,090,343	30.45%
89	24	$3,519,556	$4,953,447	$7,417,135	$9,849,733	$2,432,597	32.80%

Age	Year	Reg IRA	Side Fund	IRA Net + SF	Roth IRA	RCA	RCA (%)
90	25	$3,562,778	$5,516,301	$8,010,246	$10,834,706	$2,824,460	35.26%
91	26	$3,589,169	$6,133,363	$8,645,781	$11,918,177	$3,272,395	37.85%
92	27	$3,596,207	$6,809,014	$9,326,358	$13,109,994	$3,783,636	40.57%
93	28	$3,581,223	$7,547,868	$10,054,724	$14,420,994	$4,366,270	43.43%
94	29	$3,545,804	$8,351,697	$10,833,760	$15,863,093	$5,029,333	46.42%
95	30	$3,488,081	$9,224,928	$11,666,585	$17,449,402	$5,782,817	49.57%

Now Saul has an RCA of 8.89 percent, 24.10 percent, and 49.57 percent in years 10, 20, and 30. That is a major improvement over the example using the same 10 percent earning rate and not having any mandatory distributions, which were 7.81 percent, 14.61 percent, and 20.36 percent. Having from 20 percent to almost 50 percent more spendable money would be a good thing.

CONCLUSIONS ON CONVERSIONS

For Saul or anyone who has the money outside their IRA with which to pay the income tax should they choose to convert to a Roth, several conclusions can be drawn based on these examples:

- The older, and thus closer to age 70½ you are, the greater the Roth conversion benefit is over the same number of years.
- The greater the investment return, the greater the RCA percent will be.

Also, as you will learn later, the higher a person's income tax bracket, the greater the RCA percent will be.

Look at the RCA percent tables in the RCA section of the Appendix to project your own situation.

WHAT IS YOUR ROTH TYPE?

Anyone who has non-IRA or outside (same-basis) assets with which to pay income tax due as a result of a Roth conversion is a Type 1 person. Remember that these same-basis outside assets are typically money market or CD type assets. If you have outside low-basis assets that would trigger an additional income tax on the sale of the assets (like appreciated stocks or real estate), then further calculations would be required. Often it is not advisable to sell assets that would trigger additional income tax to make the Roth conversion.

> Type 1 people have the money outside of their IRA with which to pay the income tax if they convert to a Roth IRA.

> Type 2 people have no other money with which to pay the income tax if they convert except from their IRA.

Before you decide which type you are, please consider all your options. How did you get your money in the retirement plan or IRAs in the first place? Are you still working, and do you have excess cash flow? Do you have other sources you can draw from? Are you still contributing to IRAs and retirement plans? Would this money be better used if you were to apply it to the income tax should you choose to convert? Do you have a low-cost loan source like a home refinance that should be considered?

TYPE 2 PEOPLE UNDER AGE 59½

If you are still a Type 2 that is okay and I still like you. Or as Jerry Seinfeld said about a closely related subject, "not that there's anything wrong with that!" Type 2 people just have to consider one very important factor: age. If you are under the age of 59½, you will not be able to pay the income tax from your newly converted Roth without a 10 percent penalty unless you qualify for an exception. I talked about the exceptions in Chapters 2 and 3 and presume that is not the case. I have already discussed how much I hate penalties, especially from the IRS! If you are an under-age 59½ Type 2, you need to examine your RCO advantage before you decide to pay the 10 percent. If one of your IRAs goes up by 40 percent during this RCO period, you may be able to justify it with mathematical ease. But I would rather you find the money almost anywhere else than pay the 10 percent penalty.

Let's run that math for fun. Say you converted an IRA containing a single asset class worth $100,000 on January 4, 2010, and observe that it is worth $140,000 on October 1, 2011. Let's presume you are in the 30 percent income tax bracket. So your cost to keep it converted would be:

Converted value of IRA	$100,000
Roth value at the end of RCO	$140,000
Income tax due for conversion	$30,000
10 percent penalty	$3,000
Net Roth value	$107,000
Regular IRA value	$140,000
Net regular IRA value	$ 98,000

As you can see, your net spendable current value of your converted Roth would be $107,000. You could use this amount without penalty after age 59½. The current value of your recharacterized or unconverted IRA that you could use without penalty after age 59½ would only be $98,000. Even though there is an advantage to the Roth in this situation, I would implore you to find another way to get the $30,000 to avoid the penalty.

Before you point it out to me, I am aware that I did not take out the penalty of 10 percent on the $3,000 withdrawn to pay the first penalty because this is a circular equation. If you took $34,000 out of your newly created and converted Roth, then you would have more than enough to pay the $3,400 penalty and $30,000 income tax. You might end up spending far more than the remaining $600 dollars for drugs or therapy to recover from this penalty. If you are under age 59½, please try everything in your power to avoid the 10 percent penalty by coming up with other sources to pay the tax even if your RCO results are 100 percent. There is no reason to give some of your hard-won gains back to the IRS by way of penalties if you can possibly avoid it.

TYPE 2 PEOPLE OVER AGE 59½

If you are a Type 2, having no outside money to pay the tax on the Roth conversion except from IRA funds, but are over age 59½, the math is very favorable for converting for two primary reasons. One, you may pick the very best IRAs to keep converted at the end of the RCO period every year. Two, you may enjoy lower income tax brackets by converting some of your IRAs each year up to an income tax bracket that you deem reasonable. Read the section later in this book carefully about maximizing your favorable income tax brackets.

You need to start this process as soon as you can so that optimally all your IRAs may be converted before you attain the age of 70½. Other than those two primary reasons, converting to a Roth before 70½ is neither an advantage nor disadvantage for Type 2s. The neutrality for Type 2s during this period between the ages of 59½ and 70½ is due to the commutative principal of math on this equation. If you are always in the 35 percent tax bracket and have no outside money with which to pay the tax, the RCA begins after age 70½. This is not counting any advantages the RCO might bring from year to year by keeping the big winners converted each year and unconverting the rest. For example, let's say that Saul is actually a Type 2 and at age 65 has $1,000,000 in a regular IRA, but has no outside funds with which to pay the income tax. Assuming a 5 percent earnings rate and a 30 percent income tax rate, here are the results:

Age	Year	Reg IRA	Side Fund	IRA Net + SF	Roth IRA	RCA	RCA (%)
65	0	$1,000,000	$0	$700,000	$700,000	$0	0.00%
66	1	$1,050,000	$0	$735,000	$735,000	$0	0.00%
67	2	$1,102,500	$0	$771,750	$771,750	$0	0.00%
68	3	$1,157,625	$0	$810,337	$810,338	$0	0.00%
69	4	$1,215,506	$0	$850,854	$850,854	$0	0.00%
70	5	$1,231,920	$31,053	$893,397	$893,397	$0	0.00%
71	6	$1,247,028	$64,681	$937,601	$938,067	$466	0.05%
72	7	$1,260,668	$101,043	$983,511	$984,970	$1,459	0.15%

Age	Year	Reg IRA	Side Fund	IRA Net + SF	Roth IRA	RCA	RCA (%)
73	8	$1,272,662	$140,307	$1,031,171	$1,034,219	$3,048	0.30%
74	9	$1,282,822	$182,649	$1,080,625	$1,085,930	$5,305	0.49%
75	10	$1,290,945	$228,255	$1,131,916	$1,140,226	$8,310	**0.73%**
76	11	$1,296,813	$277,320	$1,185,088	$1,197,238	$12,149	1.03%
77	12	$1,300,483	$329,845	$1,240,183	$1,257,099	$16,916	1.36%
78	13	$1,301,444	$386,234	$1,297,244	$1,319,954	$22,710	1.75%
79	14	$1,299,775	$446,470	$1,356,313	$1,385,952	$29,639	2.19%
80	15	$1,295,257	$510,752	$1,417,432	$1,455,250	$37,818	2.67%
81	16	$1,287,659	$579,280	$1,480,642	$1,528,012	$47,370	3.20%
82	17	$1,276,741	$652,266	$1,545,985	$1,604,413	$58,428	3.78%
83	18	$1,262,250	$729,925	$1,613,500	$1,684,633	$71,133	4.41%
84	19	$1,243,927	$812,477	$1,683,226	$1,768,865	$85,639	5.09%
85	20	$1,222,074	$899,748	$1,755,200	$1,857,308	$102,108	**5.82%**
86	21	$1,196,506	$991,910	$1,829,464	$1,950,174	$120,710	6.60%
87	22	$1,167,040	$1,089,131	$1,906,059	$2,047,683	$141,624	7.43%
88	23	$1,133,499	$1,191,576	$1,985,025	$2,150,067	$165,042	8.31%
89	24	$1,095,716	$1,299,401	$2,066,402	$2,257,570	$191,168	9.25%
90	25	$1,054,386	$1,412,161	$2,150,232	$2,370,448	$220,217	10.24%
91	26	$1,009,477	$1,529,927	$2,236,561	$2,488,971	$252,410	11.29%
92	27	$960,983	$1,652,752	$2,325,440	$2,613,419	$287,980	12.38%
93	28	$908,929	$1,780,670	$2,416,920	$2,744,090	$327,170	13.54%
94	29	$854,493	$1,912,911	$2,511,056	$2,881,295	$370,238	14.74%
95	30	$797,858	$2,049,415	$2,607,916	$3,025,360	$417,444	**16.01%**

Saul may still want to convert, but only enjoys an RCA after he is 70½. He still could be substantially ahead before age 70 depending on the RCO results each year. His RCA percentage is 0.73 percent, 5.82 percent, and 16.01 percent at years 10, 20, and 30. If he were to earn 10 percent, then the results would be as follows:

Age	Year	Reg IRA	Side Fund	IRA Net + SF	Roth IRA	RCA	RCA (%)
65	0	$1,000,000	$0	$700,000	$700,000	$0	0.00%
66	1	$1,100,000	$0	$770,000	$770,000	$0	0.00%
67	2	$1,210,000	$0	$847,000	$847,000	$0	0.00%
68	3	$1,331,000	$0	$931,700	$931,700	$0	0.00%
69	4	$1,464,100	$0	$1,024,870	$1,024,870	$0	0.00%
70	5	$1,557,076	$37,404	$1,127,357	$1,127,357	$0	0.00%
71	6	$1,654,026	$81,153	$1,238,971	$1,240,093	$1,122	0.09%
72	7	$1,754,818	$132,061	$1,360,433	$1,364,102	$3,669	0.27%
73	8	$1,859,254	$191,036	$1,492,515	$1,500,512	$7,998	0.54%
74	9	$1,967,060	$259,093	$1,636,035	$1,650,563	$14,528	0.89%
75	10	$2,077,868	$337,358	$1,791,866	$1,815,620	$23,754	**1.33%**
76	11	$2,191,206	$427,087	$1,960,931	$1,997,182	$36,250	1.85%
77	12	$2,306,968	$529,334	$2,144,212	$2,196,900	$52,688	2.46%
78	13	$2,424,021	$645,938	$2,342,753	$2,416,590	$73,837	3.15%
79	14	$2,542,115	$778,170	$2,557,650	$2,658,249	$100,599	3.93%
80	15	$2,660,384	$927,801	$2,790,070	$2,924,074	$134,003	4.80%
81	16	$2,777,798	$1,096,785	$3,041,243	$3,216,481	$175,238	5.76%
82	17	$2,893,133	$1,287,271	$3,312,464	$3,538,129	$225,665	6.81%
83	18	$3,004,954	$1,501,625	$3,605,092	$3,891,942	$286,850	7.96%
84	19	$3,111,581	$1,742,446	$3,920,553	$4,281,136	$360,584	9.20%
85	20	$3,212,497	$2,011,587	$4,260,335	$4,709,250	$448,915	**10.54%**
86	21	$3,305,910	$2,311,883	$4,626,021	$5,180,175	$554,154	11.98%
87	22	$3,389,792	$2,646,412	$5,019,266	$5,698,192	$678,926	13.53%
88	23	$3,461,858	$3,018,500	$5,441,800	$6,268,012	$826,211	15.18%
89	24	$3,519,556	$3,431,736	$5,895,425	$6,894,813	$999,388	16.95%
90	25	$3,562,778	$3,888,071	$6,382,016	$7,584,294	$1,202,278	18.84%
91	26	$3,589,169	$4,391,157	$6,903,575	$8,342,724	$1,439,148	20.85%
92	27	$3,596,207	$4,944,853	$7,462,198	$9,176,996	$1,714,798	22.98%
93	28	$3,581,223	$5,553,216	$8,060,072	$10,094,696	$2,034,623	25.24%
94	29	$3,545,804	$6,217,420	$8,699,483	$11,104,165	$2,404,682	27.64%
95	30	$3,488,081	$6,941,252	$9,382,909	$12,214,582	$2,831,673	**30.18%**

Saul now enjoys a better result at 10 percent earnings with an RCA at years 10, 20, and 30 of 1.33 percent, 10.54 percent, and 30.18 percent. He will still be compelled to do the Roth conversions to maximize his RCO each year. He may do this in balance with the potential to pay less tax by converting the account over several years to enjoy lower overall income tax brackets.

TAX HEDGE

For those of us who believe that income taxes may rise substantially over time, Roth conversions provide a great protection. The sooner you convert to Roth IRAs, the better prepared you will be against future income tax increases. In many ways, Roth conversions are an income tax hedge. If income taxes go up substantially in the future, then the Roth conversions that you make now will be even better.

ROTH CONVERSIONS AND THE SOCIAL SECURITY TAX

For many who are drawing social security, converting to a Roth IRA will trigger a higher amount of income tax for the year(s) that the conversion income tax is paid as a result of a larger amount of the Social Security benefit being taxed. Also Medicare Part B premiums could go up temporally as a result of the Roth conversion. For these people, it may actually be a great long-term benefit. Lower amounts of income tax in future years will be due for many Social Security recipients because any income or principal from the Roth will be tax free and no longer count against them, unlike regular IRA distributions.

Currently Social Security calculations do not include Roth IRA distributions as part of the "tax-exempt income" that counts against you when you figure the income tax on your Social Security benefits or Medicare Part B payments. Therefore, Roth conversions may save you substantial income tax in the future on Social Security benefits. Long term you may save on Medicare Part B premiums as well. However, if you are already drawing Social Security income, you may experience a higher income tax burden during the year or years you convert.

If you have not yet started receiving Social Security benefits, you may want to consider postponing them a few years to a later age for a larger amount of annual benefits in the future, which also gives you time to complete your Roth conversions.

SHOW TIME

For people who are near or over age 70½, there is an even greater urgency to convert to a Roth IRA.

Sharon is 69 this year, in the 25 percent tax bracket, and projects her earnings to be 7 percent in her IRA. Assuming her IRA balance is $500,000 and she is a Type 2, look at the results in the following table:

Age	Year	Reg IRA	Side Fund	IRA Net + SF	Roth IRA	RCA	RCA (%)
69	0	$500,000	$0	$375,000	$375,000	$0	0.00%
70	1	$516,752	$13,686	$401,250	$401,250	$0	0.00%
71	2	$533,424	$29,030	$429,098	$429,338	$240	0.06%
72	3	$549,927	$46,181	$458,627	$459,391	$764	0.17%
73	4	$566,158	$65,304	$489,923	$491,549	$1,626	0.33%
74	5	$582,001	$86,574	$523,074	$525,957	$2,883	0.55%
75	6	$597,326	$110,180	$558,174	$562,774	$4,599	0.82%
76	7	$611,988	$136,328	$595,319	$602,168	$6,850	1.15%
77	8	$625,959	$165,136	$634,605	$644,320	$9,715	1.53%

Age	Year	Reg IRA	Side Fund	IRA Net + SF	Roth IRA	RCA	RCA (%)
78	9	$638,941	$196,932	$676,138	$689,422	$13,285	1.96%
79	10	$650,901	$231,845	$720,021	$737,682	$17,661	**2.45%**
80	11	$661,656	$270,123	$766,365	$789,319	$22,954	3.00%
81	12	$671,008	$312,027	$815,283	$844,572	$29,288	3.59%
82	13	$678,738	$357,839	$866,893	$903,692	$36,799	4.24%
83	14	$684,610	$407,856	$921,313	$966,950	$45,637	4.95%
84	15	$688,364	$462,394	$978,668	$1,034,637	$55,969	5.72%
85	16	$690,038	$521,554	$1,039,082	$1,107,061	$67,979	6.54%
86	17	$689,402	$585,639	$1,102,691	$1,184,556	$81,865	7.42%
87	18	$686,213	$654,971	$1,169,631	$1,267,475	$97,844	8.37%
88	19	$680,215	$729,882	$1,240,043	$1,356,198	$116,155	9.37%
89	20	$671,145	$810,714	$1,314,073	$1,451,132	$137,059	**10.43%**
90	21	$659,253	$897,431	$1,391,870	$1,552,711	$160,840	11.56%
91	22	$644,359	$990,327	$1,473,596	$1,661,401	$187,804	12.74%
92	23	$626,292	$1,089,699	$1,559,417	$1,777,699	$218,281	14.00%
93	24	$604,893	$1,195,837	$1,649,507	$1,902,138	$252,631	15.32%
94	25	$580,764	$1,308,472	$1,744,045	$2,035,287	$291,242	16.70%
95	26	$553,887	$1,427,815	$1,843,230	$2,177,757	$334,527	18.15%
96	27	$524,278	$1,554,061	$1,947,269	$2,330,200	$382,931	19.67%
97	28	$491,993	$1,687,387	$2,056,382	$2,493,314	$436,932	21.25%
98	29	$457,138	$1,827,946	$2,170,800	$2,667,846	$497,047	22.90%
99	30	$420,908	$1,975,086	$2,290,767	$2,854,596	$563,829	**24.61%**

Sharon has many good reasons to convert. Her 10-, 20-, and 30-year RCA is 2.45 percent, 10.43 percent, and 24.61 percent. These numbers do not include any positive RCO results. Watch how these numbers increase if she had been in the 30 percent income tax bracket:

Age	Year	Reg IRA	Side Fund	IRA Net + SF	Roth IRA	RCA	RCA (%)
69	0	$500,000	$0	$350,000	$350,000	$0	0.00%
70	1	$516,752	$12,774	$374,500	$374,500	$0	0.00%
71	2	$533,424	$27,050	$400,447	$400,715	$268	0.07%

Age	Year	Reg IRA	Side Fund	IRA Net + SF	Roth IRA	RCA	RCA (%)
72	3	$549,927	$42,961	$427,910	$428,765	$855	0.20%
73	4	$566,158	$60,651	$456,962	$458,779	$1,817	0.40%
74	5	$582,001	$80,275	$487,675	$490,893	$3,218	0.66%
75	6	$597,326	$101,998	$520,127	$525,256	$5,129	0.99%
76	7	$611,988	$126,002	$554,394	$562,024	$7,630	1.38%
77	8	$625,959	$152,383	$590,555	$601,365	$10,810	1.83%
78	9	$638,941	$181,435	$628,694	$643,461	$14,767	2.35%
79	10	$650,901	$213,262	$668,892	$688,503	$19,611	**2.93%**
80	11	$661,656	$248,077	$711,236	$736,698	$25,462	3.58%
81	12	$671,008	$286,107	$755,813	$788,267	$32,454	4.29%
82	13	$678,738	$327,595	$802,712	$843,446	$40,734	5.07%
83	14	$684,610	$372,795	$852,022	$902,487	$50,465	5.92%
84	15	$688,364	$421,980	$903,835	$965,661	$61,826	6.84%
85	16	$690,038	$475,215	$958,242	$1,033,257	$75,015	7.83%
86	17	$689,402	$532,758	$1,015,339	$1,105,585	$90,246	8.89%
87	18	$686,213	$594,876	$1,075,225	$1,182,976	$107,751	10.02%
88	19	$680,215	$661,848	$1,137,998	$1,265,785	$127,786	11.23%
89	20	$671,145	$733,958	$1,203,760	$1,354,390	$150,630	**12.51%**
90	21	$659,253	$811,132	$1,272,610	$1,449,197	$176,587	13.88%
91	22	$644,359	$893,607	$1,344,658	$1,550,641	$205,982	15.32%
92	23	$626,292	$981,615	$1,420,019	$1,659,185	$239,167	16.84%
93	24	$604,893	$1,075,381	$1,498,806	$1,775,328	$276,522	18.45%
94	25	$580,764	$1,174,605	$1,581,140	$1,899,601	$318,462	20.14%
95	26	$553,887	$1,279,432	$1,667,153	$2,032,574	$365,421	21.92%
96	27	$524,278	$1,389,991	$1,756,985	$2,174,854	$417,868	23.78%
97	28	$491,993	$1,506,389	$1,850,785	$2,327,093	$476,309	25.74%
98	29	$457,138	$1,628,709	$1,948,705	$2,489,990	$541,285	27.78%
99	30	$420,908	$1,756,276	$2,050,912	$2,664,289	$613,377	**29.91%**

As you can see above, Sharon would have benefited more if she had been in the 30 percent income tax rate. Let's keep all of the parameters the same but say that Sharon is a Type 1 and look at the results:

Age	Year	Reg IRA	Side Fund	IRA Net + SF	Roth IRA	RCA	RCA (%)
69	0	$500,000	$150,000	$500,000	$500,000	$0	0.00%
70	1	$516,752	$170,124	$531,850	$535,000	$3,150	0.59%
71	2	$533,424	$192,110	$565,507	$572,450	$6,943	1.23%
72	3	$549,927	$216,109	$601,058	$612,522	$11,463	1.91%
73	4	$566,158	$242,283	$638,594	$655,398	$16,804	2.63%
74	5	$582,001	$270,807	$678,207	$701,276	$23,068	3.40%
75	6	$597,326	$301,867	$719,995	$750,365	$30,370	4.22%
76	7	$611,988	$335,664	$764,055	$802,891	$38,835	5.08%
77	8	$625,959	$372,319	$810,490	$859,093	$48,603	6.00%
78	9	$638,941	$412,147	$859,406	$919,230	$59,824	6.96%
79	10	$650,901	$455,279	$910,909	$983,576	$72,666	**7.98%**
80	11	$661,656	$501,953	$965,112	$1,052,426	$87,314	9.05%
81	12	$671,008	$552,423	$1,022,129	$1,126,096	$103,967	10.17%
82	13	$678,738	$606,960	$1,082,077	$1,204,923	$122,845	11.35%
83	14	$684,610	$665,850	$1,145,076	$1,289,267	$144,191	12.59%
84	15	$688,364	$729,394	$1,211,249	$1,379,516	$168,267	13.89%
85	16	$690,038	$797,692	$1,280,719	$1,476,082	$195,363	15.25%
86	17	$689,402	$871,036	$1,353,618	$1,579,408	$225,790	16.68%
87	18	$686,213	$949,731	$1,430,079	$1,689,966	$259,887	18.17%
88	19	$680,215	$1,034,090	$1,510,241	$1,808,264	$298,023	19.73%
89	20	$671,145	$1,124,440	$1,594,242	$1,934,842	$340,601	**21.36%**
90	21	$659,253	$1,220,748	$1,682,225	$2,070,281	$388,056	23.07%
91	22	$644,359	$1,323,294	$1,774,345	$2,215,201	$440,856	24.85%
92	23	$626,292	$1,432,356	$1,870,760	$2,370,265	$499,505	26.70%
93	24	$604,893	$1,548,209	$1,971,634	$2,536,183	$564,549	28.63%
94	25	$580,764	$1,670,601	$2,077,136	$2,713,716	$636,580	30.65%
95	26	$553,887	$1,799,732	$2,187,453	$2,903,676	$716,224	32.74%
96	27	$524,278	$1,935,786	$2,302,780	$3,106,934	$804,154	34.92%
97	28	$491,993	$2,078,928	$2,423,323	$3,324,419	$901,096	37.18%
98	29	$457,138	$2,229,302	$2,549,298	$3,557,129	$1,007,830	39.53%
99	30	$420,908	$2,386,298	$2,680,934	$3,806,128	$1,125,193	**41.97%**

Wow! With Sharon as a Type 1 with $150,000 with which to pay the income tax on the conversion, at a 7 percent earnings rate and a 30 percent tax rate, her RCA is 7.98 percent, 21.36 percent, and 41.97 percent in years 10, 20, and 30. And that does not include gains that she might have with positive RCO results.

ROTH VERSUS REGULAR FOR YOUNG SAVERS

Which is better, a Roth IRA or a regular IRA for young folks wanting to save money? The Roth is usually better for a few reasons.

Roth contributions are bigger. The amount that you can contribute to your Roth IRA is the same—$5,000—as what you are allowed to put in your regular IRA, assuming you qualify to max out either the IRA or Roth IRA. That $5,000 going into a Roth is worth $5,000 of real spendable money. You can buy $5,000 worth of hamburgers or other important stuff with a $5,000 Roth. A regular IRA is not so valuable. A $5,000 regular IRA can only buy you $3,500 worth of hamburgers if you are in the 30 percent tax bracket. The Roth is bigger and better because it is all *after tax.* It is denser from a money perspective. That reminds me of some of those high-level desserts like the key lime pie in a fancy restaurant versus the large, fluffy but cheap desserts I used to eat. The small dense, rich, flavor-packed piece often is the more satisfying choice and, ounce for ounce, just like a Roth, it packs more punch.

You may be thinking that if you put $5,000 into a Roth IRA you get no deduction but if you put $5,000 into a regular IRA you are only out of pocket for $3,500 (if you are in the 30 percent income bracket) because you will pay $1,500 less in income tax in the tax year that you make the regular IRA contribution. This theory is correct. However, for you to tangibly benefit from this $1,500 income tax savings for the regular IRA, you need to stash it somewhere you can actually access it in the future. This is very hard for most people who, despite their best intentions, fritter away their tax savings.

This reminds me of a great dinner I had years ago with a group of my guy friends. When the restaurant bill was presented, my buddy James figured out the damage. Now no self-respecting guy wants to be caught dead actually calculating who ordered what to divvy up a check. The protocol requires that the check be totaled including a generous tip and divided among all the men equally. By the way, if you did not eat or drink much, you should retaliate by ordering dessert—maybe key lime pie! My friend James determined that everyone owed $100 including tip. All of my nine buddies put $100 into the check folio that was passed around. When I receive the bill last, I paused for a second, and decided to pay the entire $1,000 with my credit card and pocket the $900 cash. Some game time brilliance must have occurred to me on my part involving airline miles or time value of money. At any rate, I figure I am only out $100 like everyone else for the meal and will pay the credit card bill in full at the end of the month, like always. After all, I have the $900 cash. Invariably, when I get the credit card bill with the $1,000 added at the end of the month, I no longer have the $900 in my wallet anymore to soften the blow.

People typically do the same thing with their tax savings. Whether they choose to max out the Roth IRA or the regular IRA during the year, it requires the same $5,000 at the time they write the check for their annual contribution. The Roth is most often the best choice because it is more money for the future, both in tangible dollars that they can locate in the Roth, and actually more spendable money as well. Even if you select the regular IRA maximum and contribute the corresponding tax savings in another savings vehicle, that non-IRA savings vehicle is less tax efficient than a Roth IRA in almost every case.

Also, the Roth IRA provides a better emergency cushion if you have to have funds before you turn 59½. The Roth can always be accessed without tax and penalty at any time up to the amount of total Roth contributions. You should not access the Roth early unless it is a bona fide emergency. To take money out of a Roth early is the same as stealing from your future funds. However, the decision to save money in this manner is made easier knowing that you can get to it if you absolutely, positively have to.

There are three primary factors involved with each money calculation concerning the Roth versus a regular IRA: earnings rate, taxation rate, and the time value of money.

EARNINGS RATE

It is difficult to predict the amount of return that your assets will receive in the future. Most people prefer to consider several possibilities in these calculations. I will typically use 5 percent and 10 percent in my examples just for the simplicity of the calculation. You should consider the type of investments that you chose and the historic returns that these investments have yielded in the past. Even if the ultimate return or earnings rate is higher or lower than these examples, the correct choice between a Roth IRA or regular IRA will still give the advantage to one or the other. In other words, if a Roth conversion provides an advantage at a 10 percent rate of earnings, the Roth conversion will still most likely be an advantage even if earnings are 2 percent or 20 percent.

Risk versus Reward

The relationship between what an investment will return based on its level of risk is called the *efficient frontier.* What that means is that the safest investments will have the lowest rate of return. Short-term government bonds and CDs have a low rate of return but little or no chance of loss (not counting inflation). Stocks over greater periods of time usually have better returns than CDs or government bonds, but present more risk especially for shorter lengths of time.

TAXATION RATE

Income tax is an important component in calculating the outcome of an investment or a retirement savings plan. When you earn money as a salary, wage, or bonus, you must pay taxes on the money earned in the same year. This is called *earned income* or *ordinary income* and is often taxed at the highest tax rate compared to certain types of investment earnings. At the time of this writing in 2009, the maximum tax for ordinary income is 35 percent. IRA and retirement plans are taxed at ordinary income rates when the money is distributed. Interest income from CDs and money market investments are also taxed at these ordinary rates.

Dividends are distributions from companies and are currently taxed in 2009 and 2010 at a maximum of 15 percent. Dividends are scheduled to be taxed at ordinary income tax rates beginning in 2011 (like they have been in the past).

Investments (stocks and real estate) that are held for a year or less are called short-term capital gains and are taxed at ordinary income tax rates. Investments held for more than a year are called long-term capital gains and are currently taxed in 2009 and 2010 at a maximum of 15 percent. In 2011, the tax rate for long-term capital gains is scheduled to be 20 percent. Chapter 5 has a more complete discussion of income tax.

TIME VALUE OF MONEY

Many people have a hard time with the concept that a dollar today is worth more than a dollar in the future. Intuitively, we understand this because most of us have experience with financial institutions—paying them back the principal plus additional interest on borrowed money. In this case, the financial institution enjoys money's time value, and we pay the interest. I learned this concept at a very early age by watching cartoons. Remember the Wimpy character on the Popeye cartoon? He was an expert in this concept. Wimpy was always trying to get a hamburger today and promising to gladly pay you back on Tuesday. Technically this is called the time value of a hamburger, but financially it makes good sense as well. If you gave me the loan of a dollar today, I would need to repay you more than a dollar in the future. Banks, credit card companies, and all other financial institutions utilize this concept.

As wealthy people know (because they've delayed gratification and had money to invest rather than immediately spending all the money they have), saved money presents an opportunity. If you can earn 5 percent per year on your money, then $100,000 today is worth $105,000 one year from now. In the following year, the $105,000 will earn interest of $5,250 and so on. The compounding of your money means you are actually earning interest (or investment gains) on interest. Einstein called compounding one of the wonders of the world. Mathematically, compounding it is a very important concept. It is very difficult to compute the effect of compounding without the use of a financial calculator, but you can do these calculations with a yellow pad or even in your head by using the rule of 72.

The Rule of 72

The rule of 72 states that if assets grow by 7.2 percent per year they will double in 10 years! For example if you have $100,000 invested at 7.2 percent annual interest, 10 years later you will have $200,000. That is $200,000 without having contributed any more than $100,000 (+10 years time) to this investment. This is a financial dream in that your money has begun to work for you instead of you working for it! We have 7.2 percent interest as the average for this example. In 20 years, you would have $400,000. In 30 years, you would have $800,000 and in 40 years, you would have $1.6 million dollars because you planted the seed of $100,000, watered it with 7.2 percent investment returns, and let it grow (without picking it or spending it) for 40 years. Yes, compound interest is magical, and the rule of 72 helps you figure out how magical.

The rule of 72 is commutative, meaning that if an asset grows by half the rate it will take twice the time to double. For example, if an asset grows by 3.6 percent, it will double in 20 years. Conversely if an asset grows by 14.4 percent, it would double in five years. This commutative rule means you can switch the 7.2 and the 10 for the same result. For example, if an asset grows by 10 percent it would double in 7.2 years. Time and money are a magical combination. With a little discipline and effort, you can use both for your maximum advantage.

THE MIRACLE OF INCOME TAX DEFERRAL

Tax deferral is a very powerful attribute because you do not pay income tax on the earnings in a tax-deferred account, like a regular IRA or retirement plan, until you remove the money from that account. Conversely, if you save money in a regular nondeferred account, you will have to pay income taxes as you go along. My mother used to tell me to never put off until tomorrow what you can do today. The exception to that rule is the payment of income tax. Procrastination can be a good thing when it comes to taxes. Income tax deferral in regular IRAs and retirement plans can make a significant difference in how much money you will have to spend due to the magic nature of combining tax deferral along with compounding.

By not paying current income tax on money that is reinvested, you are actually earning money from the time value of the government's portion that should have gone to tax. If you have $100,000 earning 5 percent, your annual earnings would be $5,000. If you are in the 30 percent tax bracket, then $1,500 would go to Uncle Sam and $3,500 would stay in your account. If you use income tax deferral, it changes the rules. If the same $100,000 was in a tax-deferred account instead, all of the $5,000 gain could stay in your account with a total of $105,000 earning 5 percent the following year. Under this magical tax strategy, you are profiting from the money that you were able to defer paying the IRS.

Focus only on the $1,500 portion that stays in your deferred account for the next year, remembering that it would have gone away already to taxes in a nondeferred account. Said another way, the $1,500 is not your money even though it is in your tax-deferred account. That $1,500 is effectively on loan from the government thanks to tax deferral. Let's presume that the $1,500 on loan from the government earns 5 percent or $75 in the following year. Now presume it is time to settle up. At a 30 percent tax bracket, the IRS gets $22.50 for the $75 earnings, which means that you get to pocket the balance or $52.50. Now you decide to pay back the government their $1,500 from last year and their $22.50 from this year leaving you with a net of $52.50. You netted a tidy $52.50 in profit from no investment of your own money. Your rate of return on the $52.50 is actually infinite because you had no money invested to get it!

Many books have been written extolling the virtues of using other people's money (OPM). This version is even finer. Your government's money (YGM) is available to you in the form of income tax deferral!

Income tax deferral can make a big difference in the amount of money over a period of years. To properly calculate the value of this deferral, you must consider the variables. The number of years that the money is left in the account will make a substantial difference. A five-year deferral will be less significant than a ten-year deferral. The earning's rate will also make a difference in the power of this deferral. Generally speaking, the greater the rate of return and the longer the deferral, the bigger the impact. Tax brackets are important as well. Obviously, the higher your income tax bracket, the greater advantage that tax deferral will have. If your tax bracket is zero, then deferral would be of absolutely no benefit.

POWER OF INCOME TAX DEFERRAL ILLUSTRATED

The following table illustrates the power of income tax deferral. Assume that you are in the 35 percent income tax bracket and could earn 10 percent on your investments annually. In twenty years, your spendable money, after all taxes are paid, is 34 percent more by using income tax deferral. So if you ended up with a net (spendable) $100,000 in your investment account using nondeferred investments, you could have a net (spendable) $134,000 by deferring the tax and then paying it after twenty years. If your investments only earned 5 percent during the same twenty-year period, you would have 20 percent more spendable money. Notice that time and tax bracket are most important to increasing the positive advantage of income tax deferral:

Advantage of Tax Deferral				
Year	Earnings of 10%		Earnings of 5%	
	25% Tax Rate	35% Tax Rate	25% Tax Rate	35% Tax Rate
5	2%	2%	0%	1%
10	7%	8%	2%	2%
15	14%	19%	4%	5%
20	25%	34%	7%	9%
25	37%	53%	11%	15%

The assumption in this table is that you would earn everything as ordinary income every year from the non-tax deferred account. This is the case if you invest in bonds, CDs, or high turnover investment funds.

You must be careful to compare like things to make the analysis accurate and meaningful. This causes us to compare retirement accounts with nonretirement accounts. We typically would use the same rates of return and other variables when comparing choices. Sometimes it is obvious that the choice would be wrong for a certain type of account. For example, tax-free municipal bonds generally pay less in interest than taxable bonds. This is a natural pricing reality due to the fact that the take-home amount (after-tax) of tax-free bonds would be higher than the take-home amount of taxable bonds if they pay the same rate. Therefore tax-free bonds are more suitable for people who could benefit from having more take-home money because of their tax bracket. Due to the fact that tax-free bonds and all other financial instruments are based on supply and demand for their pricing, tax-free bonds should always pay lower amounts of interest than taxable bonds with all other things being equal (credit rating, maturity, etc.). For obvious reasons, you would never use tax-free bonds in your IRA or retirement account.

Annuities are not directly comparable to non-annuities for the same reason. When I mention annuities here, I do not mean the CD-like fixed annuities or immediate income annuities, but the deferred variable type with underlying investment choices that are similar to mutual funds. Because annuities have built-in tax deferral, they are priced differently in the way they charge and calculate their expenses. Like the example of tax-free municipal bonds, annuities will tend to have a higher load or expense because of their tax-deferred feature. This does not mean that annuities are either good or bad, but they have to be weighed with their specific attributes and added loads to determine if they are appropriate. Annuities can also offer adverse income tax consequences because they are always subject to eventual income taxes at ordinary income tax rates, even if their underlying investments (held in other non-annuity vehicles) would have resulted in much lower long-term capital gain income tax treatment.

There are two favorable income tax advantages to long-term capital gains: lower income tax rates and income tax deferral. Remember, long-term capital gains are subject to a lower income tax rate of 15 percent maximum for 2009 and 2010 and 20 percent for 2011 and beyond. These long-term capital gain investments also enjoy income tax deferral. For example, if you invested $50,000 in a stock seven years ago and sold it today for $100,000, you would have a gain of $50,000. This gain would be taxed at a maximum of 15 percent and would only be taxed when you sold it. This "only taxed when you sell it" part is tax deferral.

ASSET ALLOCATION

Similar types of assets are often lumped together into *asset classes*. The theory is that different asset classes often perform very differently and asset classes of the same category will perform in a similar way. When you convert to multiple Roth IRAs to start the RCO period, the accounts are separated by asset class with each Roth IRA having no more than one type of asset class if possible. This anticipated disparate performance can help the Roth conversion strategy. The asset classes that go up the most during the RCO period might stay converted to Roth IRAs, while the lesser performers or losers can be unconverted to try again next year. If these different asset classes had been left together inside the same converted Roth IRA, then you have no choice of selecting specific investments within that IRA for recharacterizing or unconverting. If any amount of the Roth IRA is unconverted, it must be a proportional amount of all investments within it, called pro rata. You are not allowed to pick and choose within the Roth IRA. However, if you heeded my advice from Chapter 1 and converted into separate Roth IRAs by asset class, you can pick and choose to unconvert or not, any or all Roth IRAs, and have much greater selection and control over the process.

TURNOVER

Mutual funds and other money management vehicles buy and sell the investments within their funds. These investments are usually stocks or bonds. The longer they hold their specific investments, the lower the turnover. For regular non-tax deferred accounts, investments that have a lower turnover will cause less income tax than investments that have a higher turnover. This means that the lower-turnover investment choice will have a better after-tax return than the higher-turnover investment with exactly the same before-tax return. In general, stock mutual funds and other stock investment funds have much higher turnover than you might think. With Roth IRA conversions, it is important to estimate the turnover of non-IRA investment funds to determine the advantage of converting and paying the tax from these funds versus another source. Index mutual funds have almost no turnover and are therefore more income tax efficient.

CATEGORIES OF PEOPLE

I have found it useful to divide people into two general categories and situations. Here are my observations about these two groups.

SAVERS

Savers are a class of people who delay money gratification and typically have no debt. They often save for a large purchase like a car until they have saved all the cash that they need to buy it. Typically they have a large IRA rollover or retirement account that they do not intend to ever use, unless they encounter a financial emergency. They are disappointed that they have to start taking mandatory IRA distributions at age 70½ and wish they did not have to.

SPENDERS

Spenders are fun-loving people who like to spend money first and ask questions later. Spenders are loved by credit card companies and banks alike because they are unafraid of debt. They buy cars using financing or leasing. Spenders are attracted by zero percent financing offers and other "good deals" where they think they are saving money just by buying things on sale. No delay of gratification here. Spenders often drain their IRAs and retirement savings before they reach age 59½. Spenders are also unafraid of penalties and interest. Spenders believe that they could solve all of their financial problems by making more money. Spenders commonly are worried about Social Security not being enough and wonder if they can ever retire. Often it is hard to tell the exact magnitude of the debt hole a spender has dug because they do not easily disclose their debt obligations. They may look to the untrained eye like a saver who waited until they could afford to spend, but spenders are pretty often secretly stressed out about money as their spiraling debt and dearth of savings begins to catch up with them. Spenders find themselves robbing Peter to pay Paul in their personal lives, but they seem to have an unlimited capacity to justify and rationalize their next purchase.

The primary difference between the rich and the poor, besides the obvious fact of the rich having more money, is that the rich have learned the magic of delayed gratification. To the extent that you can spend less money than you have available, you will have more to spend in the future. When compound interest or the time value of money kicks in, the results will be astounding. Just a little delay of gratification can make a big difference in the future. This is a difficult lesson because everyone has so many things that they immediately desire. Often these are different things from moment to moment resulting in a myriad of individual purchases that are all independently affordable but in the sum total exceed the amount of available funds. This is facilitated by credit cards and other mechanisms to effectively provide immediate gratification.

In my estate planning practice, I have observed these two types of people and their attitudes about money and discipline. Growing up poor, I had always assumed the biggest factor in getting rich was the ability to earn a lot of money. Over the last few decades, I have learned that I was very wrong. The biggest ingredient in the wealth equation is the control you have over your relative spending. I have had very wealthy clients, many who never earned the level of income that I thought necessary to gain such a substantial net worth. Yet with the combination of time and savings or investments, I have been an eyewitness to the rule of 72 and how it can work for everyone. We have never had a client with a large estate who spent more money than he or she earned.

Roth IRA conversions may give you more incentive to save money and income taxes at the same time—a winning combination.

Earning huge amounts of money is not the key answer to wealth as you will see by reading the stories in your daily newspapers and magazines as they chronicle the financial woes of major award-winning movie actors and recently deceased pop stars. Even though they earned billions, they wound up broke.

NONDEDUCTIBLE IRAs REVISITED
—THE ROTH IRA SHUFFLE

I addressed the complexity of having nondeductible IRAs in Chapter 2. However, this complexity of nondeductible IRAs may indeed be worth it for more people after 2010. You can contribute up to the $5,000 or $6,000 (over age 50) every year to nondeductible IRAs no matter how much your income is and even if you have another retirement plan. So if you want to get more money into Roth IRAs but your income is too high, you can contribute to nondeductible IRAs every year and convert them immediately to Roth IRAs! Remember that you have to have earned income and not yet be age 70½ to do this, but this opens the Roth door for everyone else who would like to add to his or her income tax-free assets.

If you have contributed a substantial amount to nondeductible IRAs over the years, you will want to strongly consider converting to a Roth IRA as soon as you can. Remember the amount of your total nondeductible contributions or basis will not be taxed when you convert to a Roth IRA. You will only pay taxes on the total amount converted after subtracting the nondeductible contributions. After you convert to a Roth IRA, any subsequent growth will be tax-free! So if your nondeductible basis amount is $30,000 now, earning 7.2 percent, it will double in ten years to $60,000. If you convert it now to a Roth IRA, the future value will be $60,000—all tax-free. The cost to actually convert the specific $30,000 nondeductible part now is zero. If you wait until that part has grown to $60,000 to convert, then you will have to pay tax on the $30,000. You must convert all IRAs proportionally or pro rata with regard to what is nondeductible, but if the amount is substantial on the nondeductible side, it makes converting all of your IRAs (deductible and nondeductible) even more desirable sooner, instead of later.

BORROWING NOT PLEDGING

Borrowing money to pay the tax on Roth conversions may make sense to some people depending on their specific situation. Remember that you can never pledge IRA assets (Roth or regular) or use them as loan collateral without destroying the entire IRA. However, banks may actually make note of all of your resources including IRAs in extending you credit on a favorable basis.

LOAN MONEY TO PARENTS

Adult children of parents who have regular IRAs might be able to help their parents convert to Roth IRAs especially when the parents are in a lower income tax bracket than the children.

Nimrod's mother is 75, and Nimrod is an only child and sole heir to his mother's estate. His mother has $50,000 in an IRA but she feels that she has no money to pay the income tax on conversion to a Roth IRA. Nimrod may consider loaning his mother the money to pay the income tax on conversion or even give that money to her within the annual gift tax exemptions because Nimrod has the money and will be better off inheriting a larger Roth IRA in the future.

SPEND PRINCIPAL FROM OTHER PLACES
—IT IS ALL YOUR MONEY

One technique that the many IRA savers have learned over the years is that they can spend principal from other accounts and let the IRA grow to maximize the income tax deferral outcome.

Zacchaeus is age 65 and retired. He has an IRA that is worth $500,000 and other savings of $500,000, and he needs some additional income from his retirement over what his non-IRA assets are producing. He may start spending the principal from the non-IRA accounts to allow his IRA accounts to grow enjoying the maximum income tax deferral. He actually may see his net worth grow as a result of spending principal in one place and allowing other assets to grow.

After the Roth conversion, Zacchaeus has even more incentive to allow the Roth IRA to be untouched until he has depleted all his other resources. The Roth IRA becomes the ultimate rainy-day fund as he feels secure knowing that he may use all of the Roth IRA assets at any time but he will use those most valuable assets last—only after he has depleted all of his less favorable non-Roth IRA assets.

ROTH CONVERSION OPTION (REVISITED)

In Chapter 1, I compared the RCO to a golf mulligan or "do over." We recreational golfers or duffers may get mulligans, but there is no such thing in the official rules of golf. On the PGA tour, there are no mulligans or do overs; but there are provisionals.

The official penalty for hitting a golf ball out of bounds is severe. If you hit a golf ball out of bounds, you must hit another ball again from the place where you hit the original shot that went out of bounds. This penalty for going out of bounds is called "stroke and distance" in the rules of golf. The stroke part descriptively counts the stroke that went out of bounds and the one stroke penalty for actually going out of bounds as a total stroke cost of two. The distance part is that you do not get to hit again from where the golf ball went out of bounds but you must hit again from the same place where you hit the unfortunate shot. You get to start over with two strokes added, getting nothing for it except a lesson in anger management.

All golf balls that appear to have started out of bounds may not actually go out of bounds. If you were to find out that the first ball that you thought was out of bounds actually hit a tree or ended up in bounds, you would want to play that first ball without penalty. Here the rules of golf allow you to hit a second ball from the original place and preserve the option of playing the first ball if it is indeed in bounds by declaring it a *provisional.* You must make this declaration to your playing partners before you hit the second ball. This provisional rule is in the interest of time to keep the game moving. After you hit your provisional ball, you look for your first ball and hopefully you get lucky and find it in bounds. If your worst fears are realized and indeed the first ball is out of bounds, then your provisional is officially in play. If the first ball is in bounds, then it is as if the provisional shot never happened.

However, for you to have all of the options that come with the provisional ball in place, it must have been declared. If you did not declare the second shot a provisional before you hit it, the second ball becomes the only one in play (along with the two strokes added) and you are not allowed to play your first ball even if you discover it in bounds. So, if you want to have all the options, declare the second ball a provisional every time. It adds precious hopeful possibilities and costs you nothing except the utterance of the word.

This is analogous to the RCO. In early January, you must declare all of your IRA accounts to be Roth "provisionals" by converting them to Roth accounts. You can later recharacterize or unconvert each one of these accounts if you choose, but if you did not do the RCO you cannot have that option.

In finance, an option is a contract between a buyer and a seller that gives the buyer the right, but not the obligation, to buy a particular asset at a later day on an agreed price. In real estate, an option is a contract between a buyer and a seller that would give the buyer the same right to buy in the future, again without the obligation to buy. In both the finance world of stocks and the real estate world, these options cost real money. However, with the Roth IRA, you're able to take an option setting the date in advance when the assets in your regular IRA would be valued, with the option to complete the conversion of those assets in the future using the original date.

BE SURE TO REALLOCATE AFTER RCO

After the decision is made about which IRAs will stay converted and which are to be unconverted or recharacterizied (if any), be sure to reallocate back to a diversified portfolio with the investments in the now permanently converted Roth accounts. This reallocation and diversification at the end of the RCO period is an attempt to manage the Roth IRAs as a complete and unified portfolio, so that any one specific asset class's drop in value does not diminish the total Roth IRA (because it is well diversified again after the RCO period).

OUR INCOME TAX STRUCTURE

THE TAX SYSTEM IN THIS country is called a progressive tax system—the people who have higher incomes pay a higher percentage of tax. This is sort of like a frequent flyer program in reverse. This progressive tax system makes sense logistically because it is hard to tax the poor enough to make any difference to a country's total income tax needs. The old adage, "to whom much is given, much is expected," could refer to taxation as well.

CALCULATION OF INCOME TAX

The calculation of income tax can be a little confusing. They don't call it the tax code for nothing. The first step in figuring your income tax is choosing your filing status—actually you get little choice in the matter. The five possibilities for filing status are single, married filing jointly, married filing separately, head of household, and qualifying widow(er).

SINGLE

Your marital status is determined on the last day of the year. You file as single if you are unmarried, or legally separated under a divorce or separate maintenance decree, and you do not qualify for another filing status.

MARRIED FILING JOINTLY

You may file as married filing jointly if you are married as of the last day of the year and both spouses agree to file this way. If your spouse dies during the year, you may still file under this status, but only for this last year. Most married people file jointly because it almost always results in less tax than the married filing separately status. There is a Roth conversion advantage to making all conversions while you can claim this married filing jointly status because it is far more liberal at lower brackets than the single status. If you are married, converting to Roth IRAs may result in a substantial advantage while you and your spouse are both alive, instead of waiting until after the first spouse's death when the survivor is forced to use the single filing status.

MARRIED FILING SEPARATELY

You may choose to file as married filing separately if you are married as of the last day of the year. This will most often result in more total income taxes paid than filing jointly. Beginning in 2010 you may convert to a Roth IRA no matter what your filing status may be.

HEAD OF HOUSEHOLD

To file as head of household, you generally must have a dependent child or qualifying relative who lives with you the majority of the year. You also must pay for the majority of the costs associated with keeping up a home to use this status. Finally, you also must be unmarried or live apart from your spouse for the last six months of the year to use the head of household status.

QUALIFYING WIDOW(ER)

Remember you may file as married filing jointly for the year of a spouse's death. For each of the following two years after the death of a spouse, you may use qualifying widow(er) status if you do not remarry and if you have a dependent child who lives with you. You also must pay for the majority of the costs associated with keeping up a home to file this way. For all of the exciting details on the five filing status options, see IRS Publications 501 and 17. They can be found on the www.irs.gov website.

USE THE POWER OF DEDUCTION

After you "choose" your filing status and list all of your income, you then get to subtract all of your deductions before arriving at your taxable income. You may itemize or you may claim a standard deduction. You get to deduct for all of your dependents and even regular IRA or retirement plan contributions. All of these items are listed on the much-dreaded IRS Form 1040. After you subtract all of your deductions from your income, you come up with your taxable income. It is this taxable income that is used to calculate your actual income tax amount.

THE OLD BRACKET RACKET

Income tax brackets are utilized to compute income tax based on taxable income. These brackets are part of the progressive tax system that I mentioned earlier.

Take a look at the tax rate chart for 2009 on the next page.

2009 Tax Rate Chart

Single
(Schedule X)

- ☐ **10%** on income between $0 and $8,350
- ☐ **15%** on income between $8,351 and $33,950; *plus* $835
- ☐ **25%** on income between $33,951 and $82,250; *plus* $4,675
- ☐ **28%** on income between $82,251 and $171,550; *plus* $16,750
- ☐ **33%** on income between $171,551 and $372,950; *plus* $41,754
- ☐ **35%** on income over $372,950; *plus* $108,216

Married Filing Jointly or Qualifying Widow(er) Filing Status
(Schedule Y-1)

- ☐ **10%** on income between $0 and $16,700
- ☐ **15%** on income between $16,701 and $67,900; *plus* $1,670
- ☐ **25%** on income between $67,901 and $137,050; *plus* $9,350
- ☐ **28%** on income between $137,051 and $208,850; *plus* $26,637.50
- ☐ **33%** on income between $208,851 and $372,950; *plus* $46,741.50
- ☐ **35%** on income over $372,950; *plus* $100,894.50

Married Filing Separately Filing Status
(Schedule Y-2)

- ☐ **10%** on income between $0 and $8,350
- ☐ **15%** on income between $8,351 and $33,950; *plus* $835
- ☐ **25%** on income between $33,951 and $68,525; *plus* $4,675
- ☐ **28%** on income between $68,526 and $104,425; *plus* $13,318.75

- ☐ **33%** on income between $104,426 and $186,475; *plus* $23,370.75
- ☐ **35%** on income over $186,475; *plus* $50,447.25

Head of Household
(Schedule Z)

- ☐ **10%** on income between $0 and $11,950
- ☐ **15%** on income between $11,951 and $45,500; *plus* $1,195
- ☐ **25%** on income between $45,501 and $117,450; *plus* $6,227.50
- ☐ **28%** on income between $117,451 and $190,200; *plus* $24,215
- ☐ **33%** on income between $190,201 and $372,950; *plus* $44,585
- ☐ **35%** on income over $372,950; *plus* $104,892.50

Our income tax bracket rates reflect this progressive tax system, and it works like this: If you had taxable income of $208,850 in 2009 and filed jointly, you were in the 28 percent marginal income tax bracket. This is called a marginal bracket because all of your income was not taxed at 28 percent. Some of your income was taxed at 10 percent, 15 percent, and 25 percent as well. The fact that you are in the 28 percent bracket, with $208,850 of taxable income, means that your last dollars earned are taxed at this amount. From the tax rate chart, we see that the income tax on a married couple filing jointly with taxable income of $208,850 would be $46,671.50. This would actually be a tax percentage of 22.38 percent of the taxable income. However, because they are at the top of the 28 percent bracket, if they were to earn a dollar more than the $208,850, that next dollar would be taxed at the next bracket of 33 percent. This same 33 percent tax would also apply if they converted additional amounts to a Roth IRA during that same year. Roth IRA conversions are actually not possible during 2009 for this example due to the $100,000 limit on income for Roth IRA conversions. But you get the idea. Beginning in 2010 and beyond, there will no longer be any income limit for Roth IRA conversions.

If you were, as a joint or single filer, to have taxable income of more than $372,950, you would then be in the 35 percent marginal bracket. But only your dollars over this $372,950 threshold would actually be taxed at 35 percent. This top rate is what I call the pinnacle of patriotism.

You must examine the income tax impact that Roth IRA conversions would make in your situation. The best way to do that is to figure your income tax without the Roth IRA conversion and then figure the income tax with the Roth IRA conversion. The increase in actual taxes that would have to be paid as a result of the conversion will show you the actual tax cost and percentage for the conversion. Remember, you can convert as much or as little to the Roth as you choose. By calculating the taxes on several different amounts of Roth IRA conversions, you can get the exact tax and percentage of tax for each progressive conversion.

Your CPA or tax preparer can give you several scenarios for conversions and the resulting tax impact for comparison before you go firm on any actual Roth IRA conversion. You can also use one of several popular income tax software programs to run these numbers if you want to try it on your own.

Adam and Eve have taxable income of $150,000 in 2010 counting no Roth IRA conversions. They have a total of $700,000 in IRA rollovers. They have taken the Roth Conversion Option on January 4, 2010, by converting seven IRAs worth exactly $100,000 each. Assuming the same taxation rate from the 2009 chart, their findings would be as follows:

Scenario	Taxable Income	Total Tax	Tax Increase	Tax Rate Last Conversion
Convert 0	$150,000.00	$30,263.50		
Convert 1	$250,000.00	$60,321.00	$30,057.50	30.06%
Convert 2	$350,000.00	$93,321.00	$33,000.00	33.00%
Convert 3	$450,000.00	$127,862.00	$34,541.00	34.54%
Convert 4	$550,000.00	$162,862.00	$35,000.00	35.00%
Convert 5	$650,000.00	$197,862.00	$35,000.00	35.00%
Convert 6	$750,000.00	$232,862.00	$35,000.00	35.00%
Convert 7	$850,000.00	$267,862.00	$35,000.00	35.00%

This table illustrates the relatively cheaper income tax brackets for the first dollars converted. This is true for taxpayers who are not at the maximum tax brackets before they convert. Adam and Eve need to look at the rest of their situation to make an informed decision by their deadline on how much to leave converted to a Roth IRA, if any. This firm date or deadline is October 15 of the year following the year that they actually made the Roth IRA conversion or started the Roth conversion option. So Adam and Eve must make up their minds and recharacterize or unconvert any of these Roth accounts by October 17, 2011.

RIDE AND EXPLOIT LOWER INCOME TAX BRACKETS

Many people have converted smaller amounts every year using the methodology we just discussed to fill up their lower income tax brackets. So if they still had $100,000 of room until they have exhausted the 33 percent bracket, they would only convert $100,000 to a Roth that year, and do the same the next year until eventually all of their IRAs were converted at what they perceived were not excessive income tax brackets based on what they expected their income and brackets to be in the future. This is a great strategy if you have the luxury of time to get all of the IRAs and retirement accounts converted before you reach age 70½. However, if you are almost 70½ or over, you may want to make the conversion sooner rather than later, even if that conversion causes some of the money to be taxed in higher income tax brackets.

Adam and Eve need to go through the checklist in Appendix A for their situation. What are their ages and earned income forecast? How have the Roth accounts performed since they started the RCO process? What do they think the future holds regarding income tax rates?

TAXES WILL GO UP

You do not need to be a prophet to predict an increase in income tax rates in the near future. Considering the combined facts of a record high deficit in this country and historically low current income tax rates, future income tax increases are certain. In fact according to the nonpartisan think tank, The Tax Foundation, the current government overspending is so high that we will not be able to tax our way to a balanced budget. The Tax Foundation calculates that for taxes to actually keep up with spending already budgeted in the year 2010, income tax rates would need to rise from our current rates (10 percent to 35 percent) to a new tax range that starts at 27.2 percent and reaches up to 95.2 percent!

I do not predict tax rates in the near future of 95 percent, but clearly income taxes will need to increase. Tax rates for 2011 are scheduled to range from 15 percent to a top bracket of 39.6 percent. If that old rate of 39.6 percent sounds familiar, it is actually a return of the old rates from 2003. The current 35 percent top tax rate was a temporary income tax decrease that is set to expire at the end of 2010.

We could soon see, in addition to income tax bracket increases, an unfavorable adjustment to the income tax brackets that actually makes taxes higher as well. Also, we could see the politician's old friend return with the reintroduction of *bubble brackets.* Bubble brackets are income tax brackets that tax a certain portion of income at a higher rate, which effectively takes away any advantage of the lower brackets for high income earners. This is deceptive in that it appears that taxes have gone up by only a few percentage points, but in reality, for many it is much worse than it initially appears.

Roth IRA conversions can provide a wonderful hedge against increasing income tax rates no matter what name the politicians call these future tax hikes.

ASK YOURSELF SOME QUESTIONS

Just because income tax rates are going up does not mean that it will impact you. Consider your prospective earned income in the future. Are you making more and more money every year with no interest in slowing down? Do you have substantial assets in IRAs and retirement plans? Do you have a lot of unearned income from your savings and investments? Do you expect to be in a lower income tax bracket when you retire? When do you expect to retire? Do you believe that income tax rates are going up?

AVOID INCOME TAX PENALTIES

I hate paying penalties, or interest, for that matter. The IRS imposes a penalty for the underpayment of income tax even if you pay all the tax that you owe by the April 15 deadline under certain conditions. The IRS uses a pay-as-you-go system, which means that you are supposed to make tax payments on your income as you earn or receive it. Usually this is done through tax withholding for employees, and estimated quarterly tax payments for the self-employed and retired persons. The best things to know here are the exceptions, and how to make sure that you qualify for them, so you do not incur a penalty.

GIVE 110 PERCENT

One way to avoid any underpayment penalty is by paying in over the current year, through withholding or estimated tax payments, an amount of at least 110 percent of the income tax due in the year before. This is your get-out-of-penalty card. If you are going to owe substantially more tax in the current year than you did the previous year (maybe due to Roth IRA conversions), this allows you to wait to pay the balance of your income tax on April 15. If you follow this rule of 110 percent there will never be an underpayment tax penalty. It was probably a Texas football coach who was not satisfied with his high school players' efforts that first demanded 110 percent. Now even the IRS is doing it! You can actually get by with 100 percent if your prior year's adjusted gross income was $150,000 or less.

If you are employed, be sure that your withholding is set up to be at least 110 percent (or 100 percent) of last year's income tax total. You can increase the withholding later in the year and still qualify to avoid the underpayment penalty as long as the 110 percent (or 100 percent) total is reached from withholding by year's end. For quarterly estimated tax deposits, however, these need to be done in equal payments to be sure to avoid the underpayment penalty (see worksheet at the bottom of the page).

This great penalty avoidance methodology will help you to avoid this penalty even in unusual years. In the case of a substantial amount of income tax due as a result of a large Roth IRA conversion, you can now wait until April 15 to make the large payment of tax to the IRS. This way you may earn interest on your income tax payment up to the deadline and avoid penalties at the same time.

Estimated Tax Worksheet

1. What was the total income tax from the year before (IRS form 1040)?_____

2. Multiply (amount from 1) by 1.1 _____

3. Divide (amount from 2) by 4 _____

4. Make Estimated Tax Payments (amount from 3) on each of the dates below starting with April 15th of the tax year in question.

5. April 15 _____

   July 15 _____

   October 15_____

   January 15_____

   (Repeat next year)

STATE AND CITY INCOME TAX

Many states have a state income tax that will impose additional income tax on both IRA distributions and conversions. The higher the income tax bracket or rates, the better the advantage of the Roth conversion. Certainly in this case adding both federal and state income taxes can result in a very high income tax rate.

Let me suggest a possible effective planning option to eliminate state income tax. Move. Especially for folks considering Roth IRA conversions this may be a fantastic solution that will allow future flexibility to move again after the Roth IRA conversion.

There are currently seven states with no income tax at the state level—Alaska, Florida, Nevada, South Dakota, Texas, Washington, and Wyoming. Additionally New Hampshire and Tennessee apply their state tax only to interest and dividends—currently not taxing IRA distributions. Some other states with state income taxes exempt IRA distributions like Pennsylvania. Some municipalities like New York City have additional income taxes that apply to IRA distributions and conversions as well. Check the specifics of your state and city income tax as you contemplate your IRA planning.

Let's say you decide to move to Texas with no state income tax, and convert your sizeable regular IRA to a Roth IRA while a legal resident of the lone star state. You would have no state income tax on the Roth conversion. Then if you were homesick you could return, perhaps the following year to the state you originally came from with your newly converted tax-free Roth in tow.

Be careful to follow both states rules of residency to make sure that neither state attempts to make a claim of additional avoidable and unexpected income tax. Document your various proof or evidence of residency in case you ever come under scrutiny or examination in the future. California and a few other states have been very aggressive about claiming residency; so take great care to know the rules and document the facts as you go. That will save you a load of trouble down the road.

The very significant and unusual opportunity of state income tax planning with Roth IRA conversions can be found in the one-time income taxation event that then allows you to enjoy your converted Roth IRA income tax free for many years to come. You should always be aware of any applicable state income tax where you live or any place where you are contemplating moving to, until all your IRAs and retirement accounts have been converted to Roth IRAs.

The Roth IRA conversion provides an additional hedge for future state income tax in at least three ways:

1. If the state where you live imposes or creates a new state income tax in the future or increases the rates of the current income tax, you would be protected with a prior Roth IRA conversion.

2. If you move to a different state that has a state income tax, you would be protected with a prior Roth IRA conversion.

3. Should you not spend all of your Roth IRA conversion before you die, your heirs will be protected, no matter what state they reside in, from state income tax by inheriting a Roth IRA.

THE STRETCH IRA HOAX

NE OF THE MOST COMMON things that I have heard from many of my clients who were almost 70½ with large IRAs was that they wished they did not have to take money out of their IRAs. The wanted the ability to use their IRA if they ever needed it for the proverbial rainy day, but they had enjoyed their untouched IRA's tax deferral for so long, that they wanted to keep it intact as long as possible. For many years, mandatory IRAs involved many life expectancy tables and choices for mandatory distribution calculations as we looked among the complex maze for minimum distributions during their lifetime. This was called "stretch IRAs" based on the concept that we could prolong the inevitable unwinding and melting down of a person's IRA after age 70½. This was a feeble attempt, at best, because every year the mandatory withdrawal amount gets bigger and bigger. Even now, with the much-improved simplicity of recalculation of a person's life expectancy every year, plus having only one table to choose from for everyone (unless their spouse is more than 10 years younger and their sole beneficiary), the IRA decays pretty swiftly. Take a look at the life expectancy numbers for a minute using the main table on the following page starting at age 70:

Age	Distribution Period (Years)	Withdrawal (%)
70	27.4	3.65
71	26.5	3.77
72	25.6	3.91
73	24.7	4.05
74	23.8	4.20
75	22.9	4.37
76	22.0	4.55
77	21.2	4.72
78	20.3	4.93
79	19.5	5.13
80	18.7	5.35
81	17.9	5.59
82	17.1	5.85
83	16.3	6.13
84	15.5	6.45
85	14.8	6.76

This looks pretty innocuous until you realize the impact of these withdrawals on the total IRA versus converting to a Roth IRA and having no lifetime mandatory withdrawals. The first year you turn 70½, you have to divide your IRA balance from the end of the prior year by 27.4 and take that out. That is 3.65 percent of the IRA. This is applicable to folks born from January 1 though the end of June because you also happen to be 70 the same year. When you put the numbers on a spreadsheet they look worse.

Jude turns 70 in January 2010. He has a large IRA rollover worth $1,000,000 on December 31, 2009. He is married to a younger woman, age 67, so he has to use the regular life expectancy table. He must complete the minimum withdrawal for 2010 before his required beginning date of April 1, 2011, and beginning in 2011 take his minimum withdrawals before December 31 of that same year. Let's assume he earns 5 percent on his regular IRA and takes only the minimum distribution required at the end of each year for maximum deferral. The table that follows shows just how much money he has left in his

IRA compared to what he would have in a Roth IRA conversion starting with the same amount that has no withdrawals:

Age	Year	Reg IRA	Roth IRA	Reg IRA Deficit
70	2010	$1,013,504	$1,050,000	3.48%
71	2011	$1,025,933	$1,102,500	6.94%
72	2012	$1,037,155	$1,157,625	10.41%
73	2013	$1,047,022	$1,215,506	13.86%
74	2014	$1,055,381	$1,276,282	17.31%
75	2015	$1,062,063	$1,340,096	20.75%
76	2016	$1,066,891	$1,407,100	24.18%
77	2017	$1,069,910	$1,477,455	27.58%
78	2018	$1,070,701	$1,551,328	30.98%
79	2019	$1,069,328	$1,628,895	34.35%
80	2020	$1,065,611	$1,710,339	37.70%
81	2021	$1,059,361	$1,795,856	41.01%
82	2022	$1,050,378	$1,885,649	44.30%
83	2023	$1,038,456	$1,979,932	47.55%
84	2024	$1,023,382	$2,078,928	50.77%
85	2025	$1,005,404	$2,182,875	53.94%
86	2026	$984,369	$2,292,018	57.05%
87	2027	$960,127	$2,406,619	60.10%
88	2028	$932,532	$2,526,950	63.10%
89	2029	$901,448	$2,653,298	66.03%
90	2030	$867,446	$2,785,963	68.86%
91	2031	$830,499	$2,925,261	71.61%
92	2032	$790,603	$3,071,524	74.26%
93	2033	$747,778	$3,225,100	76.81%
94	2034	$702,994	$3,386,355	79.24%
95	2035	$656,400	$3,555,673	81.54%
96	2036	$608,183	$3,733,456	83.71%
97	2037	$558,568	$3,920,129	85.75%
98	2038	$507,825	$4,116,136	87.66%
99	2039	$457,421	$4,321,942	89.42%
100	2040	$407,686	$4,538,039	91.02%

Even though Jude is only taking the minimum from his IRA, it is decaying quite rapidly. By age 84, or in only 14 years of mandatory IRA distributions, more than half of his potential IRA has left this blessed tax-deferred state. Let's presume he earns 10 percent instead, maybe outrunning these mandatory IRA distributions by doubling his earnings. The following table shows that situation:

Age	Year	Reg IRA	Roth IRA	Reg IRA Deficit
70	2010	$1,063,504	$1,100,000	3.32%
71	2011	$1,129,722	$1,210,000	6.63%
72	2012	$1,198,564	$1,331,000	9.95%
73	2013	$1,269,896	$1,464,100	13.26%
74	2014	$1,343,528	$1,610,510	16.58%
75	2015	$1,419,212	$1,771,561	19.89%
76	2016	$1,496,623	$1,948,717	23.20%
77	2017	$1,575,690	$2,143,589	26.49%
78	2018	$1,655,639	$2,357,948	29.78%
79	2019	$1,736,298	$2,593,742	33.06%
80	2020	$1,817,078	$2,853,117	36.31%
81	2021	$1,897,273	$3,138,428	39.55%
82	2022	$1,976,049	$3,452,271	42.76%
83	2023	$2,052,424	$3,797,498	45.95%
84	2024	$2,125,252	$4,177,248	49.12%
85	2025	$2,194,179	$4,594,973	52.25%
86	2026	$2,257,981	$5,054,470	55.33%
87	2027	$2,315,273	$5,559,917	58.36%
88	2028	$2,364,496	$6,115,909	61.34%
89	2029	$2,403,904	$6,727,500	64.27%
90	2030	$2,433,425	$7,400,250	67.12%
91	2031	$2,451,451	$8,140,275	69.88%
92	2032	$2,456,258	$8,954,302	72.57%
93	2033	$2,446,023	$9,849,733	75.17%
94	2034	$2,421,832	$10,834,706	77.65%

Age	Year	Reg IRA	Roth IRA	Reg IRA Deficit
95	2035	$2,382,407	$11,918,177	80.01%
96	2036	$2,326,523	$13,109,994	82.25%
97	2037	$2,253,054	$14,420,994	84.38%
98	2038	$2,161,028	$15,863,093	86.38%
99	2039	$2,054,589	$17,449,402	88.23%
100	2040	$1,933,923	$19,194,342	89.92%

This did not make much of a difference in the percentage of IRA potential withdrawn, did it? He now would have more than half of his potential IRA gone during his 85th year or after only 15 years. What about earning 20 percent? Let's look at the next table:

Age	Year	Reg IRA	Roth IRA	Reg IRA Deficit
70	2010	$1,163,504	$1,200,000	3.04%
71	2011	$1,352,299	$1,440,000	6.09%
72	2012	$1,569,934	$1,728,000	9.15%
73	2013	$1,820,361	$2,073,600	12.21%
74	2014	$2,107,947	$2,488,320	15.29%
75	2015	$2,437,487	$2,985,984	18.37%
76	2016	$2,814,189	$3,583,181	21.46%
77	2017	$3,244,282	$4,299,817	24.55%
78	2018	$3,733,322	$5,159,780	27.65%
79	2019	$4,288,534	$6,191,736	30.74%
80	2020	$4,916,907	$7,430,084	33.82%
81	2021	$5,625,601	$8,916,100	36.91%
82	2022	$6,421,739	$10,699,321	39.98%
83	2023	$7,312,115	$12,839,185	43.05%
84	2024	$8,302,788	$15,407,022	46.11%
85	2025	$9,402,347	$18,488,426	49.14%
86	2026	$10,615,983	$22,186,111	52.15%
87	2027	$11,946,942	$26,623,333	55.13%
88	2028	$13,395,626	$31,948,000	58.07%
89	2029	$14,958,450	$38,337,600	60.98%

Age	Year	Reg IRA	Roth IRA	Reg IRA Deficit
90	2030	$16,637,995	$46,005,120	63.83%
91	2031	$18,425,039	$55,206,144	66.63%
92	2032	$20,303,670	$66,247,373	69.35%
93	2033	$22,249,438	$79,496,847	72.01%
94	2034	$24,254,333	$95,396,217	74.58%
95	2035	$26,284,928	$114,475,460	77.04%
96	2036	$28,296,861	$137,370,552	79.40%
97	2037	$30,232,962	$164,844,662	81.66%
98	2038	$32,021,391	$197,813,595	83.81%
99	2039	$33,646,357	$237,376,314	85.83%
100	2040	$35,034,937	$284,851,577	87.70%

Even at 20 percent, Jude has less than half of the money that he would have had by age 86 if there were no mandatory distributions from his IRA, or if he converted to a Roth IRA before age 70.

The results would be similar if Jude was age 70 in 2010 except that he had been born in the months of July through December. In this case, he is not 70½ until 2011, so he gets to wait a year until 2011 for his first year of mandatory distributions from his IRA. He has to use age 71 as the first year calculation because he was 71 that same year, perhaps as a penance for getting to wait a year to start his IRA withdrawals. His actual required beginning date is April 1, 2012. Let's assume his balance was $1,000,000 on December 31, 2010, and he earns 5 percent and distributes the mandatory IRA distribution amount on the last day of each year. Look at the following table:

Age	Year	Reg IRA	Roth IRA	Reg IRA Deficit
71	2011	$1,012,264	$1,050,000	3.59%
72	2012	$1,023,336	$1,102,500	7.18%
73	2013	$1,033,072	$1,157,625	10.76%
74	2014	$1,041,319	$1,215,506	14.33%
75	2015	$1,047,913	$1,276,282	17.89%
76	2016	$1,052,676	$1,340,096	21.45%
77	2017	$1,055,655	$1,407,100	24.98%

Age	Year	Reg IRA	Roth IRA	Reg IRA Deficit
78	2018	$1,056,435	$1,477,455	28.50%
79	2019	$1,055,081	$1,551,328	31.99%
80	2020	$1,051,413	$1,628,895	35.45%
81	2021	$1,045,246	$1,710,339	38.89%
82	2022	$1,036,383	$1,795,856	42.29%
83	2023	$1,024,620	$1,885,649	45.66%
84	2024	$1,009,747	$1,979,932	49.00%
85	2025	$992,008	$2,078,928	52.28%
86	2026	$971,253	$2,182,875	55.51%
87	2027	$947,334	$2,292,018	58.67%
88	2028	$920,108	$2,406,619	61.77%
89	2029	$889,437	$2,526,950	64.80%
90	2030	$855,888	$2,653,298	67.74%
91	2031	$819,434	$2,785,963	70.59%
92	2032	$780,069	$2,925,261	73.33%
93	2033	$737,815	$3,071,524	75.98%
94	2034	$693,627	$3,225,100	78.49%
95	2035	$647,654	$3,386,355	80.87%
96	2036	$600,080	$3,555,673	83.12%
97	2037	$551,126	$3,733,456	85.24%
98	2038	$501,059	$3,920,129	87.22%
99	2039	$451,327	$4,116,136	89.04%
100	2040	$402,254	$4,321,942	90.69%

Again, by the time Jude is age 85, he has had to remove more than half of his IRA from what could have remained if he had converted to a Roth IRA.

The individual life expectancy table that the IRS uses for beneficiaries states that at age 70 a person's life expectancy is 17 years or age 87. This is a statistical midpoint for a large number of 70-year-olds, meaning that one-half of the group will die before age 87 and the other half will live to age 87 or older. Even though the government's table does not specify gender, health, or lifestyle; the message here is that many people live for a long time after they turn 70. The current life expectancy at birth is now age 78 which is longer than it has ever been.

YEAR-OF-DEATH DISTRIBUTION

The longer you live after 70, however, the more damage you do to the concept of stretching your IRA by living. In the example, if Jude were to die after his required beginning date, mandatory IRA distributions must be taken for his last year of life just as if he were alive, and they must be taken before December 31 of the year that he died to avoid the 50 percent penalty. The entire year's required distribution must be taken the year of your death, even though you may not have been alive for the entire year.

THREE CHOICES FOR TAX DEFERRAL

If a person really wants to prolong the tax deferral of his or her regular IRA, that person only has three choices. They could marry a really young spouse and name him or her the sole beneficiary of their IRA. This seems expensive and impractical, but a few people have done this independent of tax advice. The second thing they could do is die before they reach their required beginning date. This requires an unusual commitment to one's IRA tax deferral, and I am not aware of anyone dying for that purpose.

There is a great third option, however: convert to a Roth IRA. If you convert all of your IRAs to Roth IRAs before your required beginning date, you will be able to stretch out and not make any mandatory lifetime distributions. You can pay the tax on conversion from outside funds, if available. If you have no outside funds whatsoever, you can pay the tax from your IRA. There is no 10 percent penalty or additional tax on the immediate withdrawal of funds from a Roth conversion as long as you are over age 59½. So, if Jude had converted his entire $1,000,000 to a Roth IRA, he would be able to use the whole amount—$1,000,000—from his Roth immediately without penalty or extra income tax. He would be judicious about spending such large amounts from this Roth account because of its obvious value. The Roth IRA has no lifetime required distributions and is unrestricted to grow tax-free! This Roth IRA would be considered the most valuable asset in his entire estate because of these benefits. But Jude is not restricted from using the money from his Roth IRA at anytime. If he spends the entire $1,000,000 from his Roth IRA and needs what leftover interest or earnings from his Roth IRA, he would need to wait on the five-year Roth clock to take out the final dregs from his Roth IRA, income tax free. If he has so quickly burned through the entire $1,000,000 of the most precious tax-free asset in the Roth IRA, he probably no longer needs to be concerned about income taxes at all. He is likely worried about being dead broke!

THE FIVE-YEAR RULE

As you can see from Jude in the last example, there really is no five-year rule for Roth IRA conversions as long as you are over age 59½. If you are under age 59½, then you had exactly the same problem with a regular IRA that you face with a Roth IRA. A penalty of 10 percent for withdrawals from a regular IRA or Roth IRA conversion may apply unless you qualify for an exception. The exceptions for this age 59½ early withdrawal penalty are exactly the same with the Roth IRA conversion as with the regular IRA. If you are looking for a way to take the money out of a Roth IRA before age 59½ without penalty, remember you can always take only up to the amount of your Roth contributions, then you must look to the exceptions.

ESTATE PLANNING AND THE IRA

I HAVE WORKED ON VARIOUS estate planning issues for my clients for over two decades. Many people overlook some important facts relating to estate planning, and there are many myths and misconceptions about this subject.

A common thing that people say and believe when their children are young and still dependent is," I don't want to give my kids so much money that it ruins them." What this sentiment means is that if the children inherited a lot of money early in life then their normal desire to work might never develop. A large inheritance might prove to be a stumbling block, or disincentive, if received at too young of an age.

Many people put their first estate plan together shortly after they begin their family. Most of these estate plans actually have great built-in protections to prevent children or other heirs from receiving a large inheritance until they are above a certain age. The usual choice is to allow the heir to use and control a portion of inherited funds (often a third), accessed when the heir reaches age 25. When the heir turns 30, the second third is released. The final third of the inheritance is released when the heir reaches age 35.

The chances of the children or other heirs inheriting at such a young age is usually very remote for pretty obvious reasons. Most people who are married give no inheritances to their children until both spouses have died. Life expectancy at birth is now age 78 in this country. If the average age of a parent at the birth of a child is around age 28, then you would expect the average person who inherits assets from his or her parents to be age 50. The age of the average person inheriting may actually be closer to age 60 or older.

If you are a child of a wealthy parent and you chose to wait for your inheritance instead of making productive financial and life choices…and you realize that you are going to have to wait until age 60 to inherit… you are a loser!

In fact, no matter how wealthy the parents are, most children become self-sustaining financially by the time they reach their mid- to late-twenties. This may be a result of nature, the children's maturity, or the parent's fatigue and subsequent decision to curtail support. Either way, whatever the reason, the system seems to be working.

Financial goals are most often only for the individual or couple involved. And as a matter of fact, the financial goal and objective for most people is that they be able to take care of themselves without becoming a financial burden on their children or others. People rarely list their financial goal as "to leave a lot of money for the children." It is by default that the children become heirs in the first place. The money saved is for the person who saved it, if they ever want it or need it, until they die.

Years ago, I heard a loud fellow proclaim that his plan was to spend all of his money with such good timing that he would "tip the undertaker his last dime"! The problem with this bold timing strategy is that most people run out of money first, and I am sure that this man did. I have always reflected on the unknown by saying that no one knows when he is going to die, except for my brother-in-law…and the warden told him! Most people are content to save extra money for a rainy day. Even if they don't ever need the extra money, they are more secure knowing that they have it available.

If I could offer a person an estate-planning menu option that would entail a good quality of life without ever having to die: this would be the most popular choice. So if the first estate-planning choice is not to die, the alternative choice is to have the assets at death go most often from one spouse to the survivor. Then at the death of the survivor spouse, the assets are usually directed equally among the children or other heirs. When folks die, they would rather their children or other heirs get the money instead of the IRS.

If a person is not married or does not have children, he or she must choose other heirs. This choice of heirs often includes relatives, friends, or charities. Whether you have children or not, you can direct your money to go the way you want, to the people that you want. It is your choice.

IRAs and retirement plans have a beneficiary designation that directs the assets in that account at your death. This beneficiary designation is incredibly important in that it supersedes anything your will or living trust may say about that asset. A common mistake that folks make when they change their estate plan is to forget to change the beneficiary designations at the same time. The beneficiary designation wins the inheritance war every time. So even if your other estate-planning documents say something entirely different and to the contrary, the beneficiary of your IRA is the recipient of that IRA at your death.

CONTINGENCIES

When you set up a beneficiary designation on an IRA, you are often asked for a contingent beneficiary designation as well. The contingent beneficiary is the person or persons who inherit the asset if the primary beneficiary dies before you do (fancy people call that predeceasing).

DISCLAIMER

A primary beneficiary might also refuse an inheritance by disclaiming it. If a beneficiary of an IRA disclaims, then the portion that the person disclaims goes to the next beneficiary just as if the person who made the disclaimer had died before the account holder. This disclaimer is often called a *qualified disclaimer.* People who disclaim have no say where the money goes if they disclaim it, but they are most often aware of whom the contingent beneficiary is and disclaim with that in mind. You usually have to disclaim in writing and irrevocably within nine months of receiving the property, and you should make the disclaimer without using the property. You can partially disclaim to pick and choose the assets and amounts that are disclaimed or accepted.

This disclaimer has always been an important, wonderful, and flexible tool. It is even better when used with IRAs, because of the continued income tax benefits that both Roth and traditional IRAs offer.

When Noah died he left his large Roth IRA to his three sons Ham, Shem, and Japheth. His contingent beneficiaries were his grandchildren *per stirpes.* This Latin word *per stirpes* means by branch of the family. So if Ham disclaims his part (or dies before his father Noah), then Ham's third goes to his children divided equally.

Noah left his IRA inheritance to his three sons. Each of the sons can now select whether to take his third share or let that pass to his children. One of the most critical things that affects inheritances from IRAs, both Roth and regular, is the age of the beneficiary. Inherited IRAs must distribute beginning with the year after the account holder's death. These inherited IRAs must distribute based on the age of the beneficiary: at least the minimum required to avoid the much-dreaded 50 percent penalty for not distributing enough.

We covered the mechanics of inherited IRAs and their mandatory distributions in Chapters 2 and 3. Both Roth IRAs and regular IRAs must be distributed in exactly the same amounts each year. The obvious difference is that an inherited regular IRA distribution is taxable to the beneficiary and the inherited Roth distribution is income tax free.

What if Noah had converted to a Roth IRA the last year of his life? What difference would it make mathematically to his beneficiaries if they took out only the minimum required distributions? Let's take Ham who is Noah's oldest son. Let's say Ham is age 60 the year that he inherits his dad's IRA. Assume a 7 percent return rate and an income tax rate of 25 percent. Let's say that Ham is a saver like his dad, and we want to measure the net assets in three different ways. So we will compare a straight non-IRA inheritance versus a regular IRA inheritance versus a Roth IRA inheritance. All three are worth exactly the same amount of spendable after-tax dollars the day Noah died. For these accounts to start with equal spendable assets of $250,000 the regular IRA also has an additional "side fund" of non-IRA money equal to $62,500. This is because the regular IRA has not yet paid taxes. The side fund is counted with the regular IRA for these comparisons. So let's see what the outcome would be in 10 and 20 years if Ham saves this money he inherited and his portion starts at $250,000. The outcome would be as follows:

After-Tax (Spendable) Inheritance			
Year	Non-IRA Inheritance	Regular IRA Inheritance	Roth IRA Inheritance
0	$250,000	$250,000	$250,000
10	$417,024	$463,058	$478,402
20	$695,636	$819,254	$860,460

Put another way, the Roth inheritance advantage (RIA) is the following percentages over the alternatives:

Roth Spendable Advantage		
Year	Non-IRA Inheritance	Regular IRA Inheritance
10	12.83%	3.21%
20	19.16%	4.79%

So Noah made a great choice in converting his IRA to a Roth IRA be-fore he died. If he had not done so, his children could not have converted any of his regular IRAs after his death. Executors are allowed to convert retirement plans to Roth IRAs after the participant's death, however. Even in a retirement plan situation, it is far more preferable not to leave such a decision to chance. And if you are still in the Roth Conversion Option period at death, the executor may unconvert (recharacterize) or leave converted before the October 15 deadline the year after the conver-sion. So you are in a far better condition to convert every IRA every year, as you learned in Chapter 1, for maximum benefit and flexibility.

Now as a result of Noah's Roth IRA conversion, his son Ham will receive more in total spendable dollars. The Roth IRA is worth more inherited than the equivalent amount of cash. In 20 years according to the last example, the spendable amount of the inherited Roth is worth 19 percent more than just plain cash. It is also worth almost 5 percent more than the regular IRA alternative. Ham's baby brother, Japheth is only 50 when daddy Noah died. The RIA is even better in Japheth's case:

Roth Spendable Advantage		
Year	Non-IRA Inheritance	Regular IRA Inheritance
10	13.48%	3.37%
20	21.81%	5.45%

If Noah had done a little more estate planning, he may have ended up with an IRA inheritance trust. These carefully drafted trusts are built to hold Roth or regular IRA assets and grant even more flexibility and advantages to inherited IRAs. As you can see from the last two examples, the best way to maximize the income tax advantages allowed to an inherited IRA is to withdraw only the minimum required per year. This special trust can do just that and add some extra features as well, including extra asset protection and management benefits. These management features of an IRA inheritance trust would allow Noah's sons to disclaim the inherited Roth IRA to their children.

Japeth has only one child—a son named Jehosaphat. He is age 10 the year of his grandfather Noah's death. If Japeth were to disclaim his portion to his son Jehosaphat via this IRA inheritance trust, the outcome would be amazing:

	Roth Spendable Advantage	
Year	Non-IRA Inheritance	Regular IRA Inheritance
10	14.42%	3.6%
20	25.33%	6.33%
30	33.67%	8.42%
40	10.0%	40.0%
50	44.64%	11.16%
60	47.75%	11.94%
70	49.23%	12.31%

These numbers would surely make Jehosaphat jump for joy. Japeth could be the trustee of this trust and reinvest the money and make distributions downstream as he saw fit according to the flexible provisions of this IRA inheritance trust.

If you have a sizeable Roth or regular IRA, then serious consideration of an IRA inheritance trust is in order. You would change the beneficiary of your IRAs to the trust after you had the trust executed, and one trust would accommodate many different beneficiary possibilities. The IRA inheritance trust accomplishes this by breaking off into individual smaller trusts at the appropriate times. Through the correct utilization of qualified disclaimers and an IRA inheritance trust, you can preserve the often-wasted income tax benefits of regular and Roth IRAs for many years to come. This strategy gives many more options after the death of the IRA holder.

The IRA inheritance trust combined with disclaimers also provides added flexibility because most folks want to keep their children (not the grandchildren) as their primary beneficiaries no matter what their children's financial situation may be. The children may choose to disclaim or not after the parent's death with the correct inheritance trust strategy in place.

ROTH IRAs ARE BETTER FOR ESTATE TAX

At the time of this writing, current estate tax law calls for no estate taxes to be due for deaths occurring in the year 2010 for all estates, no matter how large. This is a narrow window, however, because deaths occurring after 2010 will be subject to estate tax if the size of the estate exceeds $1,000,000, again based on current law. No matter what changes we have in store for the estate tax future by our lawmakers, the Roth IRA is more efficient than regular IRAs when there is a large estate that would be subject to this tax. For example, if a person dies with a $3,000,000 estate that consists of $2,000,000 of non-IRA assets and $1,000,000 in an IRA, the estate taxes are the same no matter whether the IRA is a regular or a Roth IRA with a $1,000,000 balance. This seems incorrect because the entire Roth IRA would be spendable money to the heirs and the regular IRA would still be subject to income tax as the heirs withdrew the money. If the heirs were in the 35 percent income tax bracket, as they withdrew the regular IRA it would only be worth $650,000 of spendable money. Yet both the regular IRA and Roth IRA would count exactly the same in figuring the estate tax. There may be some offsetting income tax deductions for the heirs of the regular IRA if there are estate taxes paid, but invariably the Roth IRA is superior for the heirs of a taxable estate.

TIMELINE FOR INHERITED ROTH AND REGULAR IRAs

December 31 of the same year as death	Deadline to make regular IRA required minimum distribution for that year if holder did not do so while alive.
September 30 of the year following death	Beneficiaries are identified for calculating the required distributions. Deadline to cash out a charity or other beneficiary who does not qualify as a designated beneficiary.
October 31 of the year following death	Deadline for trust documentation to be provided to IRA custodian; if using a trust beneficiary.
December 31 of the year following death	Deadline to take first regular or Roth IRA distribution for each beneficiary (unless beneficiary is spouse of deceased IRA holder). If more than one beneficiary, separate shares or accounts must be created for each to use different life expectancies by this date.
9 months after date of death	Deadline to make qualified disclaimer for estate tax purposes.

WHAT COULD GO
WRONG?

I HAVE SPENT A GREAT deal of time and effort extolling the hopefully now obvious virtues and advantages that Roth conversions will have for most people. However, nothing is perfect for everyone, and one size definitely does not fit all. So let's explore some of the areas where you need to be especially careful with Roth IRA conversions.

BEWARE OF FALLING INCOME TAX BRACKETS

A natural question seems to be one that you probably have already asked yourself: What if you convert to a Roth IRA and in the future income tax rates go down? You had to pay substantial income tax at the then current income tax rates way back when you made the Roth conversion—and now many years in the future you observe your own income tax rates drop below the percentage that you paid when you converted. This would look like a bad thing, right?

This future drop in your personal tax bracket could happen for two reasons: income tax rates go down in the future or your future taxable income decreases. Let's address these one at a time starting with income tax rates going down.

Maybe some future politician figures out Medicare, deficit spending, Social Security, health care, inflation, and the huge debt problem in this country, and all of us citizens are awarded lower tax brackets. Well dream on my friend, it doesn't cost much to be an optimist. However, most people believe that tax rates are going to go up instead of down. What about a flat tax, fair tax, or even a consumption tax being swapped out for income tax? Again, it sounds like a dream, and I believe that it is an unrealistic dream, at that.

There is a real possibility of your income tax bracket shrinking because you have less taxable income in the future, but we need to be realistic about this. What is your current level of saved assets in IRAs, other retirement plans, and other investments? What is your earned income stream likely to be in the future? How do those numbers relate to your expected spending and living expenses as a percentage? Do you plan on using your IRAs for income near term or just saving them in case of an emergency? In my experience, people who have successfully saved substantial assets will typically have higher rates of income after retirement than they ever suspected. You need to run your own probabilities based on your unique situation.

Lower income tax rates in the future will impact the Roth conversion advantage and could even make the Roth conversion a disadvantage if this rate drop is substantial. This occurrence is unlikely but should be addressed.

If your rates do go down, they would have to go down drastically for it to make a big negative difference to your IRA conversion.

Check out the last RCA tables in Appendix C to see the impact of falling income tax brackets on Roth IRA conversions.

WILL CONGRESS TAX ROTH IRAS IN THE FUTURE? (THE CONSPIRACY THEORY)

Conspiracy theories abound. I've heard delusional radio talk show hosts spin conspiracy theories about Nancy Pelosi and Barney Frank positioned with their tax rifles on a grassy knoll just waiting for everyone to convert to a Roth IRA so they could tax the heck out of it with a new law. The reality is that future taxation of Roth IRAs is not only unlikely, it is very logistically difficult. Roth contributions and conversions are made with after-tax dollars called *basis.* Roth IRA distributions are by law ordered as first in, first out (FIFO). What this means is that any money taken out of a Roth is literally your own money, which is not a tax event in any case. The gain in a Roth would be after all of your basis is exceeded and would be an accounting logistical nightmare.

There are much easier and more efficient ways for politicians to increase income tax revenue. Raising income tax rates and changing the brackets along with limiting deductions would be common first choices. Increasing capital gains taxes and the tax on dividends are strong considerations. Restoring lower exclusions on estate taxes is certainly a possibility.

Many years ago, there was a similar fear for people who set up retirement plans. Some people were so afraid of a conspiracy in that area that they took no advantage of retirement plans and lost a substantial financial windfall by opting out of that opportunity.

I strongly suggest that even if you are a believer in conspiracies that you use the Roth Conversion Option (RCO) and watch the results and tax horizon to give yourself every opportunity in the future.

FORGETTING TO UNCONVERT

If you use the RCO and do not recharacterize or unconvert by the October 15 (or the next business day) deadline, these Roth conversions are firm and cannot be undone. You should remember to examine the results of your RCO in process both at the end of the first year and again before the final deadline. Be sure to mark it on your calendar and *do not forget these important milestones.*

DON'T GET TOO CUTE

It seems that the attractive tax-free nature of the Roth IRA has drawn a fair number of aggressive schemes that seem too good to be true. Many of these clever plans are heavily marketed with the grace and subtleties of timeshares or Ginsu knives. Some of these contrivances involve an initial purchase of an annuity inside a regular IRA. This annuity has a high initial surrender charge. The regular IRA is immediately converted to a Roth IRA using the value of the annuity's much lower and temporary surrender value to create a "discount" of the converted IRA's value of around 20 percent. This way you only have to pay the income tax on around 80 percent of the Roth's true value, and in a few years, the surrender charge has expired leaving you with a much higher amount tax-free plus earnings. Well, the folks at the IRS say that the value of the annuity is not the surrender value in this case but the fair market value, so this trick will not work and may cost you substantial penalties and heartaches as well.

Some other failed plans had the holder putting the stock in a closely held business in a retirement plan and then converting the retirement plan to a Roth IRA using an artificially low value. Again, the IRS has placed such schemes on their "naughty list," and I suggest that you steer clear of anything that seems so esoteric and creative that it also appears to be illusory and abusive.

VALUATION IS IMPORTANT

If you have certain investments that are difficult to value, especially if they are worth a substantial amount, you may want to seek specific professional help to maximize any legal strategies to take best advantage of any valuation issues regarding Roth conversions.

TIPS AND TRICKS: THE REASON TO ROTH

THE GET-OUT-OF-TAX FREE CARD

I suggest that you make full use of the Roth Conversion Option (RCO) every year. Make several different Roth conversions in separate Roth accounts, divided by asset class, early in the year. This seems to be a no-brainer. Using the RCO is a must to preserve all of your future options. As my friend Ed Slot likes to say, "It's like betting on a horse race after it has been run." The IRS gives you a money-back guarantee if you decide to recharacterize or unconvert any and all Roth conversions before the deadline: January 4, 2010, until October 17, 2011—651 days—a long time.

No one can accurately predict what is going to happen to your account values during the RCO, not even Warren Buffett. Even if the RCO ends up being an academic exercise due to your accounts not going up, or you ultimately simply decide to unconvert everything for any reason, the

RCO exercise costs you nothing. If you have regular IRAs, then the safe and reasonable thing for you to do is the RCO, and see what happens.

Imagine the remorse of not having availed yourself of a completely free and non-obligatory option that may have made a significant amount of difference in your future after-tax retirement funds.

WHAT IF YOU MISSED IT? (JANUARY 4, 2010 AND BEYOND)

There is a saying, "It's not how you start, it's how you finish." The same can be said for Roth IRA conversion opportunities. Start the RCO when you can. If it is late in the year when you start, consider converting a smaller portion of your regular IRAs for the current year and the balance after the new year depending on the tax increase outlook.

TRY TO BECOME A TYPE 1

The best results and efficiency in Roth conversions are when you have some non-IRA assets to use to pay the tax on the conversion. The RCO period may allow you to become a Type 1 by giving you the time to scour your financial landscape and find the outside IRA money to pay the conversion tax. Don't go so far as to beg, borrow, or steal, but do everything in your power to pay the tax from non-IRA funds. You might want to consider borrowing, but begging and stealing are out of the question. Use your imagination. If you have great RCO results, you may boost your creativity and come up with a plan.

By paying the money with outside funds, you are enlarging the amount of net spendable money that will be available to be income tax free. The payment of tax due on a Roth conversion is not an expense. The income taxes paid at conversion are a debt that you have on your IRA, and if you wait, this debt will grow bigger and bigger proportionally. You are currently partnering with the IRS on your IRA, and the cheapest time to buy the IRS out of the IRA partnership may be now.

TAX DEFERRAL CAN BE ADDICTING

I am a big fan of tax deferral and even a bigger fan of tax-free money. Many people have had their IRAs so long that they have forgotten about the certain eventual income tax or at least blocked it from their minds. Folks do get lulled into thinking their IRA is forever. This problem might be called being "drunk on deferral." After age 70½, regular IRAs become unwound by the incessant annual increasing mandatory withdrawals. Tax free is superior to tax deferral. And Roth IRAs can stay tax free longer due to the joy of having no lifetime mandatory distributions.

PAY ATTENTION TO INCOME TAX BRACKETS

If your taxable income is not in the top bracket, and you do not have a huge amount in your IRAs, harvest and use the lower income tax brackets every year with some Roth conversions. For some situations, 15 percent is cheap and for others 30 percent is a bargain. If you have several years before reaching 70½, you may be able to slowly convert all your regular IRAs before your required distributions begin with the regular IRAs.

Set a goal for when you need to be fully converted to avoid required minimum distributions and convert every year based on your situation including the RCO results. Make sure that you are converting to Roth IRAs fast enough to meet your long-term goals and that your regular IRA is not growing faster than your total annual net Roth conversions.

LOOK AT YOUR SITUATION REALISTICALLY

Measure the time in years until you turn age 70½. Count the assets both inside and outside of IRAs and retirement plans. Give reasonable prospects and estimates to your earned and unearned income future. Realistically look at your resources. If you have a lifetime pension of $80,000 per year, are drawing social security, and also have $1,000,000 in your regular IRA, don't fantasize about being in the 15 percent bracket some day. Also, the married filing jointly income tax brackets are far more generous than the single brackets. If you are married, try to take full advantage of these married filing jointly brackets by converting larger amounts each year while both you and your spouse are alive.

RUN THE NUMBERS AND DO THE MATH

You cannot possibly make the best decision without knowing all the important facts like what happened to your Roth account's value during the RCO. You also will know more about the income tax rate outlook for the future. Most people will begin to calculate their options and potential results for keeping the Roth IRA conversions a few months before the RCO deadline. For 2010 conversions, that date is October 17, 2011. Say you begin to run the numbers in August. There are many tools to help you with this process. Almost every investment and insurance company has free Roth IRA conversion calculators. Many are even Internet based and on their company websites.

ROTH IRA CONVERSION CALCULATORS

Roth conversion calculators are powerful tools, but you must use them carefully. Many of the less powerful but simpler Roth calculators that I have tested produce some results that can be misleading and even incorrect. The more robust tools tend to be very complicated and hard for most people to operate correctly. One of the general problems with most of these Roth conversion calculator programs is that they want to calculate all or nothing as Roth conversion choices.

TRANCHE APPROACH

The most logical mathematical approach to calculating Roth IRA conversion scenarios is usually not just calculating the entire conversion but breaking up the regular IRA into several slices or tranches and running the numbers after you convert each added tranche. (Tranche is an old French word that means slice that is used frequently in finance.) By running the numbers both with the Roth conversion and without it and adding a larger portion each time to the amount to convert, you will get a more accurate depiction of the benefit of successive tranches.

If James had taxable income of $200,000 before he converted anything to a Roth and he was married filing jointly, he would begin in a current income tax bracket of 28 percent as you can see from the 2009 tax table that follows:

> 28% on the income between $137,051 and $208,850
>
> 33% on the income between $208,851 and $372,950
>
> 35% on the income over $372,950

At $200,000 in base taxable income, only the next $8,850 would still be in the 28 percent bracket. So the first tranche of $8,850 would be used. The next bracket is 33 percent, and it would apply to the next tranche of Roth conversion of $164,100. I got the number of $164,100 by looking at the tax chart and subtracting $208,850 from $372,950 to get the complete next income tax bracket of 33 percent. So tranche number 2 would be an additional Roth conversion of $164,100, and it would be subject to income tax of 33 percent. The third and final tranche of this Roth conversion would be the entire balance of the regular IRA minus the first two tranches of $8,850 and $164,100. Tranche number 3 will be subject to 35 percent tax.

Mathematically and intuitively you can see that the best results for Roth conversions as a percentage would be tranche number 1 because it will have the lowest income tax rate of 28 percent. The next-best Roth conversion results will be tranche number 2 taxed at 33 percent. The least-favorable Roth conversion results would be found in tranche 3 because it is taxed at a higher income tax rate of 35 percent.

We used the 2009 income tax rates on the last example because those are the latest ones that I have at this writing. If this person started the RCO on January 4, 2010, we would then run the numbers in early 2011 using the actual 2010 rates. Also, we would run the analysis with the 2010 special by using the estimated rates for 2011 and 2012. We would also take into account the actual RCO performance results, and we will have a pretty good idea on the Roth Conversion Advantage or RCA for each tranche or part of the conversion. At that time, we also may know more about the announced or proposed tax rates for future years that may influence these calculations.

You can see why you would want to make sure that you kept the option open to pay the income tax due on the 2010 conversion in 2010. If the income tax rates are going to be sharply higher in 2011 and in the future, paying a rate of 35 percent maximum in 2010 may be a real bargain. As long as you have correctly made the estimated tax deposits or withholding that was discussed in Chapter 3, you may pay the balance of 2010 taxes (including the Roth IRA conversion) in mid-April of 2011 and have no penalty for tax underpayment. You still have until the RCO deadline of October 17, 2011, to change your mind about the 2010 deferral special and to undo any and all 2010 conversions. You hold all the cards.

The RCO is a wonderful tool to help you take advantage of all the Roth IRA conversion rules. However, the Roth conversion alone may give a tremendous advantage to many people even without a gain in the RCO period. Even if tax rates are lower in the future than the rate that applies to you during the Roth conversion, you could still benefit greatly from a Roth conversion in many situations. Make sure to run your numbers and even seek professional analytical help before you unconvert or recharacterize.

Another thing to keep in mind is that Roth conversion calculators and many other financial projection tools are only tools. The factors that are entered may include, growth rate of investments, tax brackets, age, earned income, investment income, turnover of outside investments, state income tax rates, and others. We can even test downside potential by changing the future assumptions. These projections are forecast as a straight line into the future, however, actual results will not be a straight line.

Some of the Roth IRA conversion calculators seem to be designed to promote or sell a company's specific financial product. Beware of these.

WHY 9:57 AM?

When I was a little boy, I used to love to watch those late-night TV evangelists with their fine white suits and preacher hair. It always seemed that in between the healing and begging for donations, they would insert a special section that would scare the socks off me. This was the part where the wild-eyed zealot would talk about the coming of the end of the world. Some of them predicted this end of the world to a decade. Others had even honed it down to a certain year. But my favorite and by far the most convincing late-night preacher had the rest of the competition beat by a mile. He would smile at the camera with his craggy face and snow white goatee and look down his long nose through his reading glasses and reveal that the end of the world would be on such and such a date a few months from then at exactly 9:57AM Central Standard Time! Wow, I thought. This guy is good. And specific. He may have been joking but I was sure nervous for a few months.

Well, the date that he gave has long since come and gone. I have forgotten the date, but I never will forget the time. 9:57AM Central Standard Time. So when I wanted to communicate that January 4, 2010, was the best day to convert all of your regular IRAs and available retirement plans to Roth IRAs to start the RCO process, I thought it would sound more believable if I just added a time. I actually thought about normal times like 10:30 or 11:00, but as I mused about the time, I remembered that TV preacher and that wonderful time—9:57AM Central Standard Time.

So now you know the rest of the story. As long as you convert your regular IRAs and available retirement plans, as specified in Chapter 1, on January 4 of 2010 or as soon as you learn about this, any time will do.

May the good news continue!

QUESTIONS AND ANSWERS

Q: Why would a person consider converting from an ordinary IRA to a Roth IRA?

A: The reason so many people convert to a Roth is because they will have significantly more money in the future as a result of this conversion. As counterintuitive as it sounds, by paying taxes today to convert from a tax-deferred vehicle (regular IRA) to a tax-free vehicle (Roth IRA), the results may be overwhelmingly better. Also, since there are no mandatory lifetime distributions with the Roth, these advantages compound.

• •

Q: What are the disadvantages to a regular IRA?

A: Regular IRAs are tax-deferred instead of tax-free. Regular IRAs have strict and complicated mandatory distribution rules.

• •

Q: What type of person or situation would benefit the most from converting a regular IRA to a Roth IRA?

A: There are two categories of people who would most benefit from a Roth IRA conversion. First, people of any age who have money outside their regular IRA (which they can use to pay the conversion income tax) should benefit greatly in most cases. Let's call these Type 1 people. Second, folks who are over the age of 59½ (with or without these outside funds) would benefit from converting to a Roth in time to have all their regular IRA accounts converted before they reach age 70½. The period of time may be needed for Type 2 people (those without any outside funds to pay the conversion tax) from age 59½ and age 70½. This time between those ages can be used to maximize both their potential lower income tax brackets each year and the corresponding RCO opportunities. If you are a Type 1 or a Type 2, you can look up your Roth conversion advantage on the tables in this book found in Appendix C.

• •

Q: Who should not convert from a regular IRA to a Roth IRA?

A: There are a few types of people who should probably not convert to a Roth IRA. Folks who will need to use up their regular IRA to live before they turn 70½ or at least faster than the mandatory distributions often will not benefit from the Roth conversion. Also, people who are under age 59½ and have no money or income outside their IRA to pay the income tax on the conversion may not benefit from the conversion. Great results during the Roth Conversion Option (RCO) may change the math and make a Roth conversion attractive even to people in these situations.

• •

Q: Won't I be in a lower income tax bracket when I retire?

A: Most people who save adequate funds for their retirement will not be in a substantially lower income tax bracket at retirement. As a matter of fact you may be in a higher tax bracket, especially if you have a substantial regular IRA after age 70½.

• •

Q: What are the requirements to be able to convert my regular IRA to a Roth IRA? Can I convert after 2010?

A: Beginning in 2010 and beyond, anyone can convert to a Roth IRA regardless of income level or filing status, even married filing separately. After 2010 *anyone* can convert to a Roth IRA. Prior to 2010, you had to have modified adjusted gross income of $100,000 or less and not use married filing separately status to qualify for the Roth IRA conversion.

• •

Q: How do I actually make the conversion from a regular IRA to a Roth IRA?

A: There are three ways to make the Roth conversion:

1. *Rollover.* You can receive a distribution from your regular IRA and contribute or roll over that distribution amount to a Roth IRA within 60 days of the distribution.

2. *Trustee-to-trustee transfer.* You can have the trustee of your regular IRA transfer an amount from the regular IRA to the trustee of your Roth IRA.

3. *Same trustee transfer.* If you are using the same trustee for both accounts, simply direct the trustee to transfer a certain amount from the regular to the Roth IRA. This often is done by the trustee renaming or redesignating the regular IRA as a Roth IRA instead of opening a new account.

If you can avoid it, stay away from the rollover method because that is where most mistakes are made. Make sure the recipient account has the designation "Roth IRA" in the name of the account.

• •

Q: If I decide to convert from my regular IRA to a Roth IRA, do I have to convert the entire amount?

A: No. You may convert any amount that you like to a Roth IRA. And you do not have to decide exactly how much to keep converted until the deadline if you use the RCO.

• •

Q: Can I convert my nondeductible IRA to a Roth IRA?

A: Yes. If you have both nondeductible and deductible regular IRAs, you cannot pick and choose, but your conversions are calculated as a percentage or ratio of each type. If you convert all your IRAs in the same year, you simply deduct your basis (or nondeductible total contributions) from the total amount converted to find the net amount of taxable income that the Roth conversion will add to your taxable income.

• •

Q: At what age do I have to distribute my Roth IRA?

A: There are never any mandatory distributions from a Roth IRA while you are alive.

• •

Q: Can a beneficiary roll over an inherited Roth IRA to his or her own name?

A: Only a spouse can roll over an inherited Roth IRA to his or her name.

• •

Q: When must the money from a Roth IRA be distributed?

A: After the Roth IRA holder dies, the nonspouse beneficiary must begin distributions. These distributions are made over the beneficiary's life expectancy.

••

Q: How quickly after death must the Roth IRA be distributed?

A: The Roth IRA is distributed over the life expectancy of the beneficiary after it is inherited. It can be distributed more quickly if desired.

••

Q: Do I have to pay income taxes on the amount that I convert from a regular to a Roth IRA?

A: Yes. Taxes have to be paid on the amount converted to a Roth IRA.

••

Q: How soon do these taxes have to be paid?

A: These taxes have to be paid in the normal fashion in the year of conversion, just as regular income taxes are paid. However, if the Roth conversion is done in 2010 you can choose to defer the taxes until 2011 and 2012. There is no interest charged for this deferral, but income tax rates might be higher in those years.

••

Q: How can the income taxes on my 2010 Roth conversion be higher if I defer the tax until 2011 and 2012?

A: You are actually deferring the income, and tax rates can change. If you defer the payment on a 2010 conversion of $200,000, you will have to add half of the conversion or $100,000 to your 2011 tax return and the same for 2012. Your actual income tax rates will depend on your income tax situation and tax rates during those two years.

• •

Q: If I convert my regular IRA to a Roth in 2010, do I have to defer the income tax on the conversion until 2011 and 2012?

A: No. You may elect to pay the income tax on the conversion in 2010 if you like. You will have to opt out of the two-year special by October 17, 2011, and indicate that you are doing so on your 2010 income tax return.

• •

Q: I know there is a special deal for 2010 Roth IRA conversions so I do not have to pay the taxes until 2011 and 2012. Is that the best thing to do?

A: Maybe not. What you should do is use the RCO and convert to Roth IRAs in 2010 and wait and see what the outlook is by the first part of 2010 in regard to income tax rates. If income tax rates are going to be higher in 2011 and beyond, you may want to opt out of the two-year special and pay the income taxes on 2010 Roth conversions with your 2010 taxes. Be careful to avoid underpayment penalties with the easy foolproof method described in that section of this book found on page 111.

• •

Q: Can I pick and choose which Roth conversions I made in 2010 to defer and which ones to pay the taxes on for 2010?

A: No. You must either count all of your 2010 Roth conversions in 2010 or defer all of your 2010 Roth conversions until 2011 and 2012. You may not pick and choose. However, if you are married and both spouses convert to Roth IRAs in 2010, one spouse can use the deferral and the other spouse can opt out.

• •

Q: How do I undo a Roth IRA conversion?

A: Before the October 15 deadline of the year after you make the conversion, you simply notify the Roth IRA trustee or custodian where your IRA is held (bank, brokerage, or insurance company) that you want to unconvert or recharacterize a particular Roth IRA. The trustee will have a specific form exactly for this purpose. In this notification form, you instruct the IRA trustee to recharacterize the entire account, or if you only want to unconvert part, the exact percentage or amount that you want undone. Assuming that this is the same custodian or trustee that you used when you made the Roth conversion, they just rename the account back to the old designation of regular IRA. If you have moved your account (changed trustees) during the RCO period, you will need to give them the specifics on the original Roth conversion, as well. If you unconvert any amount from a Roth IRA back to a regular IRA you report the recharacterization specifics on IRS Form 8606 of your tax return for the year of the Roth IRA conversion. By no coincidence, this October tax return deadline is the same one as the recharacterization deadline.

• •

Q: My income is substantially over $100,000 per year. Is 2010 my only year that I am allowed to convert to a Roth IRA?

A: No. The income restriction for Roth IRAs is lifted for conversions beginning in 2010, and anyone with any level of income may convert to a Roth IRA starting in 2010 or any following year.

• •

Q: I missed the conversion date of January 4, 2010. Am I too late to convert?

A: No. You should convert some of your IRAs as soon as you can in the current year to start the RCO described in Chapter 1. If it is already late in the year this year, you may want to leave at least half or more of your regular IRAs to be converted in early January depending on your situation and the outlook on increasing tax rates.

• •

Q: You talked about the deadline for recharacterizing or unconverting my 2010 converted Roth IRAs all the way until October 17, 2011. Do I have to file an extension to be able to do this?

A: No. You do not have to extend your return to use the mid-October un-conversion deadline. The deadline for recharacterizing or unconverting a Roth is October 15 of the year following the Roth conversion. That is also the final due date of the income tax return, including extensions. You may still file your income taxes before then and simply amend the return if you convert more or less than you indicated on your previously filed 1040.

• •

Q: If I die during my Roth Conversion Option (RCO) period, are my heirs stuck with the conversion?

A: No. The executor of your estate can recharacterize or unconvert up until the October 15 deadline, with exactly the same options as you had when you were alive. If you had not converted your regular IRAs before death however, there would be no choice or ability to convert them to a Roth afterward. The RCO preserves more options in every situation.

• •

Q: What are the reasons that I would want to recharacterize or unconvert my Roth conversion?

A: You may want to recharacterize some or all of your Roth conversions for several reasons. If a Roth account has gone down substantially in value since converting it, you will probably want to unconvert that account. If you are maximizing only your lower income tax brackets, then you may want to reconvert the lesser performing Roth accounts for later conversions in later years. If you will indeed not have funds to pay the tax from a non-IRA source, and especially if you are under the age of 59½, you will probably want to unconvert. The key with the RCO is that you have the choice of unconverting; without the RCO you do not have the choice to backdate a Roth conversion.

Q: Are there any extra restrictions for 2010 conversions using the two-year deferral?

A: Yes. If you convert to a Roth IRA in 2010 and defer the income tax until 2011 and 2012, you will need to leave that conversion intact until the beginning of 2012 to have all of the income deferred as planned. Any amount distributed from the 2010 Roth conversion before 2012 will accelerate the income tax on that distribution to the actual year of the distribution, instead of half in 2011 and half in 2012.

Q: I am age 65 and interested in converting my large IRA to a Roth. I do not think I will need any income from my Roth IRA conversion right away, but I read somewhere that I would be restricted by some five-year rule to get money out.

A: This is not true. For people over age 59½, you can take all of the money that you converted out of a Roth IRA at any time with no penalty or tax. The five-year rule only applies to any money removed after you have taken out the amount you converted or basis. So if you converted $200,000 on Tuesday to a Roth IRA, you could take out the entire $200,000 on Wednesday and spend it without any penalties as long as you are over age 59½. You have the peace of mind knowing the access is available if necessary.

Q: This Roth IRA conversion thing sounds too good to be true. Why would the government let me do such a thing?

A: It is true that the Roth is a great deal for many people, but it is a good deal for the government as well. Even though the U.S. treasury would reap more in the future by not allowing you to convert to a Roth now, these current Roth IRA conversions trigger taxes right away. Money in taxes now versus more money in taxes way in the future is not a hard choice for politicians. They would like the money now.

• •

Q: I want to leave my Roth IRAs to my children, but I sure like the idea of my heirs postponing the tax-free Roth withdrawals even more by using younger beneficiaries like my grandchildren. What do you recommend?

A: You should look into an IRA Inheritance Trust. This carefully drafted trust can preserve many options for both regular and Roth IRAs. This trust can actually allow your children the flexibility to disclaim some or all of their inherited Roth or regular IRAs for the benefit of their children (your grandchildren). The IRA assets and distributions can stay in the trust and be distributed and controlled by each of your children independently (their respective portions) and provides maximum protection and flexibility to IRA inheritances.

• •

Q: Do you think that income tax rates will go up in the future?

A: Yes. Tax rates are actually set in the current law to go up to a maximum bracket of 39.6 in 2011. With the deficit and national debt at very high levels, I believe tax increases are a certainty.

• •

Q: What about a future law change down the road that taxes Roth IRAs? Could that happen?

A: Not likely. Roth IRAs are set up by their design to be tax free. The accounting method of first in, first out (FIFO) would make it logistically very difficult to tax Roth IRAs, because the money that comes out of a Roth first is a return of your investment or basis. Anything could happen, but I expect that politicians will use one or more of the easier methods to increase taxes, like raising rates and lowering deductions. Also, the public outcry would likely be deafening if there ever was a threat of taxing the Roth IRA.

• •

Q: How do I avoid penalty for underpayment?

A: Pay in at least 110 percent of your prior year's total income tax liability during the current year. Be sure to read the part about the specifics under that section in this book on pages 111–112.

• •

Q: I am approaching age 70½ with a substantial IRA that I want to keep intact as long as I can. Should I marry a young person to stretch out my distributions?

A: Converting to a Roth would be a far more effective way to keep your IRA intact. Creative question, though.

• •

Q: Is a Roth IRA a good investment?

A: Roth IRAs and regular IRAs are not specific investments. They are just the containers in which you put money to be invested. Within Roth and regular IRAs, you may direct the funds to be invested virtually any way that you like and make changes in these investments as you elect.

• •

Q: What are the ordering rules of Roth IRA distributions?

A: Money coming out of a Roth IRA is considered to have been taken from the Roth in the following order, regardless of which actual Roth account it came from. First removed are Roth IRA contributions up to the total. Second, conversions are considered to be removed year-by-year starting with the oldest year's conversions. Each year's conversions are considered to be taxable first and nontaxable (nondeductible IRA portion) second. Finally, earnings are considered to be withdrawn last, after all contributions and conversions are exhausted.

• •

Q: How does the five-year clock work on qualified distributions from the Roth IRA?

A: There is a five-year clock for qualified distributions. The clock started by Roth contributions begins January 1 in the year for which the first Roth contribution is made. The clock started by Roth conversions begins on January 1 of the year of that year's conversion. You use the Roth clock that is earliest for all Roth distributions.

• •

Q: Can I convert my qualified retirement plan to a Roth IRA?

A: Yes. Subject to the rules of your specific retirement plan, you can convert retirement plans directly to Roth IRAs. These plans can be qualified pension, profit-sharing, stock bonus, 401(k), qualified annuity, tax-sheltered annuity, 403(b), Keogh, government deferred compensation, or section 457 plans. SEP IRA and SIMPLE IRA plans also can be directly converted to Roth IRAs.

• •

Q: Can I roll over my Roth IRA into another Roth IRA?

A: Yes, you can roll over a Roth IRA into another Roth IRA.

●●

Q: What are the income limits to Roth IRA contributions?

A: For 2009, if you are single or married filing jointly you can have modified adjusted gross income (MAGI) of up to $105,000 and $166,000, respectively, to contribute up to the maximum to a Roth IRA. No contributions are allowed to a Roth if your MAGI is $120,000 or more if you are single. If you are married filing jointly with a MAGI of $176,000 or above, no Roth contributions are allowed.

●●

Q: How much can I contribute to a Roth IRA?

A: If your income is under the limit, you may contribute up to $5,000 to a Roth IRA if you are age 49 or under. If you are age 50 or older, you may contribute up to $6,000 if your income qualifies. You may never contribute more than your taxable earned income to a Roth IRA.

●●

Q: May a contribution to a Roth IRA be made if a person has a retirement plan at work?

A: Yes, as long as a person otherwise qualifies for a Roth IRA contribution; it makes no difference whether a person or that person's spouse is covered by other retirement plans at work.

●●

Q: Can I contribute to a Roth IRA after age 70½?

A: Yes. If you qualify income wise, you may contribute to a Roth IRA at any age.

• •

Q: Can my nonworking spouse contribute to a Roth IRA?

A: Yes. As long as one spouse has earned income, you may contribute up to the maximum for both spouses, if you qualify.

• •

Q: Can I contribute to both a regular IRA and a Roth IRA in the same year?

A: Yes. However, the annual maximum total for both regular and Roth contributions may not exceed $5,000 or $6,000 for those age 50 or older.

• •

Q: Can a trust be the beneficiary of a Roth IRA?

A: Yes. A trust can be a great beneficiary choice for Roth IRAs. Make sure that the trust is specifically drafted for IRAs to qualify it for all of the available potential benefits of an IRA inheritance trust.

• •

Q: Are Roth IRA distributions subject to state income taxes?

A: Not usually. Most states tie their state income tax system to the federal income tax resulting in qualified Roth distributions being completely free from state income tax. Many states are so desperate for revenue that they might consider some form of taxation that would affect Roth IRAs, including a so-called "wealth tax."

• •

Q: Are Roth IRAs protected from the claims of creditors?

A: In many states, Roth IRAs are specifically protected (at least to a certain maximum limit) from the claims of creditors. In other states, there may be less certainty. If asset protection is a concern, be sure to check the exact rules of your state regarding Roth IRAs. Caution is advised: Just because a protection exists for regular IRAs does not mean that Roth IRAs receive equal protection.

• •

Q: What are the disadvantages to a Roth IRA?

A: Roth IRAs are not tax deductible, and income taxes must be paid when converting from a regular to a Roth IRA. The psychology of paying taxes now is very difficult for many, especially large amounts of tax. There is also the fear of Congress later changing the rules, negatively affecting Roth IRAs. State income tax issues and creditor protection are also cautions for some considering the Roth IRA.

• •

Q: Can I give my children Roth IRAs?

A: Yes, as long as the child has met both the earned income and income maximum requirements, a gift of a Roth IRA may be made. Each person can only contribute up to the total annual maximum regardless of the source of funds.

• •

Q: Should I keep all of my Roth IRAs separate?

A: After the deadline has passed for recharacterizing or unconverting, you may consolidate all of your Roth IRAs into one account if you like. It makes no difference if you made both contributions and conversions to Roth IRAs because any distributions are considered to be withdrawn in a certain order no matter what actual Roth account was the source. Be sure to keep all Roth IRA accounts separate until the RCO is over and the October deadline has passed.

. . . .

Q: I have a large regular IRA and my income tax on the Roth conversion will cost me almost $300,000. How long will I have to live before I break even on this $300,000 expense?

A: You actually are starting out with an advantage with the Roth IRA conversion in most cases. The $300,000 "cost" is actually a debt that you owe against your IRA in taxes. You cannot spend the money in your regular IRA without paying the corresponding income taxes. I do hope that you live a long time after you convert to a Roth to enjoy the extra tax-free money that you will have available.

. . . .

Q: I have a large retirement plan at work and cannot take a distribution or convert it to a Roth because I am still working. Is there anything I can do to convert this account to a Roth IRA?

A: Yes. Convince your company's retirement plan administrator to allow "in service" distributions or Roth conversions. If that were done, you would be able to convert to a Roth IRA. Many companies' retirement plans will already allow this at a certain age. The reluctance to have this feature in a retirement plan is often based on fear that the employees will take distributions early and squander their valuable retirement funds.

. . . .

Q: When do I pay taxes on my Roth IRA?

A: Never! Roth IRAs accumulate income tax free. Qualified distributions are also income tax free.

• •

Q: My father has a regular IRA and I think he would benefit by converting it to a Roth because he does not need the income. The trouble is he does not have the money to pay the taxes on the conversion. What should I tell him?

A: If he is near or over age 70½, he should probably convert his IRA to a Roth, even if he has to pay the taxes from the Roth conversion. Alternatively, if you have the resources and depending on other facts in his situation, consider a gift or loan to him for the income tax on the conversion and perhaps you could be repaid as the beneficiary of his Roth IRA.

• •

Q: My son wants to start saving as soon as he can. He has a good job but has no retirement plan at work. Should he start a Roth IRA?

A: He certainly should consider a Roth IRA if he qualifies to contribute to one. Contributions to a Roth can be withdrawn without penalties or tax at any time, so he should max out the Roth every year and know he is also building emergency reserves, as well as saving for his future. Have him check the chapter on Roth IRAs to make sure he qualifies.

• •

Q: What is the downside to converting to a Roth IRA?

A: If you convert to a Roth IRA now and your income tax rate is substantially lower in the future, you could lose spendable dollars by making the conversion. For most people, this will not be the case, but you still need to do the RCO and run the numbers in your situation.

•••

Q: I will need the income from my regular IRA, should I convert to a Roth?

A: For many people, converting to a Roth IRA will provide more income depending on the specifics of their situation. Run the numbers for your specific case and do the RCO before you decide.

•••

Q: I have IRA rollovers from retirement plans and contributory IRAs. Should I bring them all together in one account?

A: No. IRAs that originated in retirement plans should always be kept separate from contributory IRAs. See the section in this book that relates to that to learn more. There is no harm, however, in consolidating all of your contributory IRAs and also consolidating all of your IRAs that came from retirement plans. Just do not mix the two. Once converted to Roth IRAs and after the RCO deadline to unconvert has passed, all Roth IRAs can be consolidated.

•••

Q: I have only a small IRA in one investment account. Do I need to break it up into five different Roth IRAs to do the RCO?

A: No. Most people who have larger IRAs and retirement plans with different investments need to break up their Roth IRA conversions into at least five accounts to start their RCO. The advantage of this is the ability to convert the winners and unconvert the losers at the end of the RCO period. If all you have is one investment and do not wish to diversify, or just CD type assets, it is okay to convert it into one Roth account.

•••

Q: Is my Roth IRA conversion going to impact the taxation on my Social Security benefits?

A: Yes. When you convert to a Roth IRA the additional income for that year (or two years, if you use the 2010 special) will typically count in higher income taxes against your Social Security benefits. This can also increase your Medicare Part B premiums. However, in subsequent years after conversion, having a Roth IRA can be a real plus because the regular IRA required distributions would no longer be a factor. Roth IRA earnings or distributions are not counted in the taxation of Social Security benefits. Converting to a Roth will be a real advantage regarding Social Security benefits and Medicare Part B premiums for many folks.

• •

Q: I am over 70½ and want to convert my regular IRA to a Roth IRA. If I convert in 2010 can I stop taking my required minimum distributions?

A: No. And yes. If you convert to a Roth in 2010, you still have to take your 2010 required minimum distribution because you are past your RBD or required beginning date. The good news is that you will have no more required distributions for your lifetime starting in 2011, if you convert all of your regular IRAs in 2010.

• •

Q: You suggest converting several different Roth IRAs separated by asset class to maximize the potential of the RCO. Will these multiple accounts cost me more in expenses from my investment firm than if I had only one Roth account?

A: Typically not. Many investment firms and insurance companies charge the same administrative fee for a single Roth IRA as they do for multiple Roth accounts for the same account holder.

• •

Q: I am 69 and still working with no plans to quit. I have participated in a Roth 401(k) at work and am concerned that I will have to make mandatory distributions soon. Is this true?

A: Yes. For some reason, Roth 401(k) plans have mandatory distributions after age 70½ just like IRAs. The way to avoid these mandatory distributions is to do a rollover of your Roth 401(k) to a Roth IRA before you turn 70½. This rollover is tax-free because it is from one Roth to another Roth. In future years, you can still make contributions to your Roth 401(k). Just be sure to roll over the entire balance from the Roth 401(k) every December to your Roth IRA, and you will never have to have any mandatory distributions.

• •

Q: Do inherited IRAs have to be distributed immediately after the beneficiaries' death?

A: No. Regular and Roth inherited IRAs may continue the same distribution schedule after the beneficiaries' death if so desired.

• •

APPENDIX A:
QUESTIONS TO ANSWER

WHEN FINANCIAL PROFESSIONALS ASK ME about how to advise their clients on Roth IRA conversions, I like to stress the importance of asking all the right questions. If you and I were sitting down at my conference table discussing your own Roth IRA conversion, my questions would be similar to the ones that follow.

This conversation would be ideal to have with your advisor after you have started the Roth Conversion Option but before the deadline to unconvert. So if you converted all of your regular IRAs and available retirement plans on January 4, 2010, we might have this conversation in March 2011. I would ask you:

What day did you convert all your regular IRAs and available retirement plans to start the RCO? _____

What is the value of each of the Roth conversion accounts on both the day you converted and today? _____

How many days are left before the recharacterization deadline? __

_____

What is your date of birth and marital status? (If married, I would get answers for the spouse as well) _____

What is the state of your health? _____

_____

_____

What is your net worth summary? (Assets and liabilities) _____

_____

_____

What is your income history from working? _____

_____

_____

Are you working now and what are your plans for working in the future? _____

_____

_____

_____

How would you forecast your future income?_____

_____

_____

Do you expect to receive an inheritance or have a parent become a dependent in the future?_____

_____

_____

What is your investment performance and selection history (both outside and retirement funds)? What is the investment turnover and tax treatment of your non-IRA investments? _____

_____

_____

_____

What is your outlook for investment performance in the future?

_____

_____

_____

What are your living expenses now and what is expected in the future? _____

_____

_____

_____

What was your income tax situation the last three years and do you expect it to change in the future?_____

_____

_____

What are your plans for using the money in your IRAs and retirement plans? _____

_____

_____

Do you plan to move to another state in the future? _____

_____

_____

Who are your beneficiaries and contingent beneficiaries of your IRAs and estate plan? _____

_____

_____

What are the ages and basic information about your children, grandchildren, and other heirs? _____

_____

_____

What type of estate plan do you have and what are the specifics?

_____

_____

_____

_____

_____

_____

_____

What do you think the outlook is for future income tax increases or reductions? _____

_____

_____

What are your specific concerns about your situation now and in the future? _____

_____

_____

Date: _____

Name: _____

Address: _____

City, State, Zip: _____

Phone: _____

E-mail: _____

Results of RCO/When Converted/ Amount Converted /Current Value:_____

_____

_____

Date of Birth (DOB): _____

Marital Status: _____

Health Concerns: _____

_____

_____

Spouse:

Name: _____

DOB: _____

Health Concerns: _____

_____

_____

CHILDREN

CHILD 1

Name _____

DOB _____Approximate Income _____

Marital Status _____

State of Residence _____

Number of Children _____

Names _____

_____

DOBs _____

CHILD 2

Name _____

DOB _____Approximate Income _____

Marital Status _____

State of Residence _____

Number of Children _____

Names _____

_____

DOBs _____

CHILD 3

Name _____

DOB _____Approximate Income _____

Marital Status _____

State of Residence _____

Number of Children _____

Names _____

_____

DOBs _____

CHILD 4

Name _____

DOB _____Approximate Income _____

Marital Status _____

State of Residence _____

Number of Children _____

Names _____

_____

DOBs _____

CHILD 5

Name _____

DOB _____Approximate Income _____

Marital Status _____

State of Residence _____

Number of Children _____

Names _____

_____

DOBs _____

INCOME TAX INFORMATION
FOR THE LAST 3 YEARS

Year _____

Taxable Income _____

Earned_____

Unearned _____

Year _____

Taxable Income _____

Earned_____

Unearned _____

Year _____

Taxable Income _____

Earned_____

Unearned _____

INCOME TAX PROJECTIONS

Year _____

Taxable Income _____

Earned_____

Unearned _____

Year _____

Taxable Income _____

Earned_____

Unearned _____

Changes / Plans to Retire? / Spouse _____

_____

_____

IRA Totals, How Invested, Projected Rate of Return _____

_____

_____

Retirement Plan Totals, How Invested, Projected Rate of Return, Eligible to Roll Over _____

_____

_____

Non IRA Investable Assets, Details, Projected Rate of Return, Turnover _____

_____

_____

Real Estate Owned _____

_____

_____

Do you have a second home? Where? _____

_____

_____

Business Interests _____

_____

_____

Primary Beneficiary(s) _____

_____

_____

Contingent Beneficiary(s) _____

_____

_____

Details if not children _____

_____

_____

Alternate heirs if any _____

_____

_____

Parents Alive / IRAs / Ages / Expected Inheritances _____

_____

_____

Spouse's Parents Alive / IRAs / Ages / Expected Inheritances ____

_____

_____

Special Concerns _____

_____

_____

_____

_____

_____

_____

APPENDIX B:
NINE ROTH IRA
CONVERSION MISTAKES

MISTAKE 1. NOT TAKING THE ROTH CONVERSION OPTION.

To properly judge whether to commit to a Roth IRA conversion, you must make the Roth conversion(s) first and wait until near the end of the recharacterization deadline to decide. For 2010, the first day to convert is January 4, and the unconversion deadline is 651 days later on October 17, 2011. Any decision not to convert before participation in the RCO is potentially a huge mistake. You can always undo any and all Roth conversions before the deadline, but you cannot backdate the conversion. Account performance and announced future tax rates during the RCO period may make your decision easier.

MISTAKE 2. CONVERTING TO A ROTH IRA TOO QUICKLY.

If you have the benefit of time (as in several years before you are age 70½) and your income tax brackets are not near the top brackets, you may benefit by converting only partial amounts of your regular IRA to a Roth each year. By converting to Roth IRAs over several years, you may better utilize the lower tax brackets and increase the Roth conversion advantage. You still will want to convert the entire regular IRA at first by using the RCO so you can pick and choose the accounts that remain Roth IRAs and preserve all of your future options.

MISTAKE 3. CONVERTING TO A ROTH IRA TOO SLOWLY.

If you are near age 70½, you may want to complete your Roth conversions more quickly based on your specific situation. Also, top tax bracket earners (Type 1s) who have outside non-IRA funds to pay the income tax may want to convert sooner as well. The threat of higher income tax rates in the future and avoiding mandatory regular IRA distributions should be considered. The complete RCO should be utilized as always to preserve future options.

MISTAKE 4. NOT CONVERTING INTO SEVERAL NEW SEPARATE ROTH ACCOUNTS.

Roth IRA conversions may be undone or recharacterized on an account-by-account basis without affecting the status of other conversion accounts. If one of your Roth conversion investments goes way up and another goes down before the deadline to unconvert, you may undo the loser and keep the winner only if you converted the two investments into separate accounts. I suggest you convert into several new separate accounts based on asset class. Be sure to convert into new Roth IRA accounts for the RCO period. After the deadline for recharacterizations, you may consolidate all of your Roth accounts.

MISTAKE 5. NOT USING AN IRA INHERITANCE TRUST.

There are many benefits in using a trust as the beneficiary of your Roth and regular IRAs. Beneficiaries of IRAs often make mistakes with inherited IRAs by removing the money more quickly than the IRS required distributions instead of extending the tax benefits as allowed. By using a specifically designed IRA Inheritance Trust, you can provide maximum protection and flexibility as well. You can financially protect the heirs from divorces, creditor claims, and sometimes even the heirs themselves.

MISTAKE 6. NOT REALLOCATING INVESTMENT ASSETS AFTER RCO.

After the deadline to unconvert or recharacterize has passed, you should reallocate and rebalance the Roth IRA assets. This is especially true if some accounts were unconverted back to regular IRAs; you definitely want to protect the Roth IRAs from sharp declines if possible by using asset allocation. If you enjoyed a large gain during the RCO period with an investment that has great volatility, care should be taken to not give back the gain in the Roth, if you can shift the more volatile investments to the regular IRAs for the next RCO period. You also will want to allocate all of your assets (IRA and non-IRA), for maximum income tax efficiency because some assets are better suited for non-IRA accounts.

MISTAKE 7. IGNORING STATE INCOME TAX.

State income tax is a factor that must be considered with the Roth IRA conversion. Generally, the consideration of state income tax makes the appeal of Roth IRA conversions even greater. Even if you live in a state with no income tax, consider where you may live in the future as well the state(s) were your heirs reside. Also, many states may sharply increase their income tax rates in the future.

MISTAKE 8. NOT BECOMING A TYPE 1.

Before you have completed the RCO period, make sure that you are not at least a partial Type 1. Type 1s are folks who have the money to pay the income tax when converting to a Roth from non-IRA funds. Consider every other possibility and resource before you unconvert or pay the tax from the IRA. Remember, if you are over age 59½, you may remove immediately any amount from the converted Roth with no penalty or additional income tax, up to the total converted. So the Roth IRA conversion funds could be considered your emergency account if you are over age 59½.

MISTAKE 9. TAKING ADVICE FROM THE WRONG PEOPLE.

Many newspapers and magazines have had articles about Roth IRA conversions. Many have led people to the wrong conclusions or at least been confusing. Most insurance and investment companies have Roth IRA conversion calculators and literature. Most financial advisors have opinions as well. Warren Buffett said, "Wall Street is the only place that people ride to in a Rolls Royce to get advice from those who take the subway. Make sure that you do the Roth Conversion Option and analyze your situation before the deadline to unconvert very carefully. Expert advice on this process may be very helpful, but be sure your advice is coming from a true expert in this subject.

APPENDIX C:
ROTH CONVERSION
ADVANTAGE TABLES

YOU MAY GET A GOOD idea of the potential outcome of a Roth IRA conversion by looking at the following Roth Conversion Advantage (RCA) tables. These tables compare converting to a Roth IRA versus leaving funds in a regular IRA. The comparison on these tables counts the net spendable or after-tax money in both cases at certain points in the future without using the money before then. The critical inputs and factors to these calculations include income tax rates, time periods, earnings rates, and age of the IRA owner. A change to any one of these inputs will change the calculation. We also must consider the important and different results depending on whether you have available outside or non-IRA (money market) funds to pay the income taxes on conversion to a Roth IRA.

First, determine if you are a Type 1 or a Type 2 person. A Type 1 person has outside (non-IRA) funds to pay the income taxes for the Roth IRA conversion. A Type 2 person has no other resource to pay the income tax on a Roth IRA conversion except from the IRA. Due to the 10 percent penalty for IRA withdrawals before age 59½, these charts start for Type 2s at age 60. We start the charts for Type 1s at age 40.

Second, determine your tax rate possibilities by looking at the income tax rate chart found on pages 106–107 or in the instructions to IRS Form 1040. You may want to consider your results by breaking your IRA conversion into separate slices of tranches and using different tax rate calculations on each increasing tranche.

We have calculated the advantage percentage at several different earnings rates 10, 20, and 30 years. The percentage reflects how much more spending money you would have with a Roth than with a regular IRA by using these parameters. For example, if the results were that you would have had $100,000 in spendable money with a regular IRA, and $120,000 with a Roth conversion, the RCA percentage would be 20 percent.

Look up the age nearest your own in the tables that follow to find the RCA percentage. If you are younger than age 40 and a Type 1, just use the age 40 percentages because they will be the same for you.

For example, let's assume you are age 60, Type 1 and in the 35 percent income tax bracket. At an 8 percent earnings rate, your advantage in 20 years is 20.15 percent. On the basis of these assumptions, by converting to a Roth IRA, you will have 20 percent more spendable money in 20 years. If you are having trouble with this concept, reread Chapter 4 and pay close attention to the examples and tables.

ASSUMPTIONS FOR THE
RCA PERCENTAGE TABLES

The assumptions in these tables do not take into account any advantage of the account rising within the RCO period above the selected earnings rate. These tables assume that the non-IRA investment portion is in CDs, taxable bonds, or high turnover mutual fund investments where all gains are taxed each year. I have not included the additional Roth IRA conversion advantage of the delay of the payment of income taxes if income taxes on the conversion are deferred using the 2010 special. The earnings rates are assumed to be the same for the IRA as for the non-IRA funds for Type 1s. The mandatory regular IRA distributions are calculated to be taken out on the last day of the year and added (after-tax) to the non-IRA assets. I have assumed the IRA owner is using the standard life expectancy table.

CHANGING TAX RATES

The first RCA percentage tables presume the income tax rates are the same for the Roth IRA conversion as the future income tax rates. On pages 194 and 195, the RCA tables reflect a conversion income tax rate of 35 percent with an immediate income tax rate reduction to a 25 percent tax rate. As you can see from these tables, this situation would produce a negative RCA percentage. In other words, if you converted to a Roth IRA and paid taxes at 35 percent and your income tax rate in the future was 25 percent, you may have had more spendable money by not making the conversion. If you are age 65 and a Type 1 with this income tax rate scenario, in 10 years at an earnings rate of 12 percent, your RCA percentage would be −1.01 percent. However, in 20 years, your RCA percentage would be a positive number of 12.34, even under such a drastic and immediate drop in tax rates.

As you can see by these RCA percentage tables, the negative results are rather finite and temporary even with a sharp fall in your income tax rate after the Roth conversion. However, if your income tax rate goes up in the future, the results of a Roth conversion can be much more positively dramatic. The final RCA percentage table shows a Roth conversion income tax rate of 35 percent rising after the conversion to 40 percent. This 5 percent increase in tax rates produces a major increase in the future spendable money with a Roth conversion. Under this tax scenario, the same Type 1, 65-year-old, with an earnings rate of 12 percent has an RCA percentage of 22.32 in 10 years. The RCA percentage is 49.26 at 20 years.

In general, the upside of a Roth conversion with future tax rate increases is much greater than the downside of the same conversion with future tax rate decreases.

CAUTION

These RCA percentage tables and Roth IRA conversion calculators are a guide but not a predictor of exact outcome. If thoughtful and rational parameters are entered into these calculators using your specific situation, you can find the output very helpful. However, many of these calculators can produce misleading results. You may want to consult with a Roth IRA conversion specialist to help you with this important process. The best time to bring this conversion math into play is toward the end of the RCO period when more of the important facts are known for this decision.

TYPE 1: 15% TAX RATE

Age	Year	Earnings Rate			
		5%	8%	12%	15%
40	10	1.05%	1.61%	2.30%	2.76%
	20	2.04%	3.10%	4.33%	5.15%
	30	2.99%	4.46%	6.13%	7.19%
45	10	1.05%	1.61%	2.30%	2.76%
	20	2.04%	3.10%	4.33%	5.15%
	30	3.32%	4.98%	6.87%	8.09%
50	10	1.05%	1.61%	2.30%	2.76%
	20	2.04%	3.10%	4.33%	5.15%
	30	4.20%	6.34%	8.82%	10.44%
55	10	1.05%	1.61%	2.30%	2.76%
	20	2.37%	3.60%	5.05%	6.01%
	30	5.62%	8.55%	12.01%	14.30%
60	10	1.05%	1.61%	2.30%	2.76%
	20	3.23%	4.93%	6.94%	8.28%
	30	7.56%	11.62%	16.49%	19.77%
65	10	1.37%	2.10%	2.98%	3.59%
	20	4.62%	7.08%	10.01%	11.98%
	30	10.02%	15.55%	22.34%	27.00%
70	10	2.04%	3.12%	4.42%	5.29%
	20	6.24%	9.60%	13.67%	16.42%
	30	12.57%	19.72%	28.70%	35.00%
75	10	2.23%	3.41%	4.83%	5.80%
	20	3.30%	10.78%	15.43%	18.60%
80	10	2.48%	3.80%	5.40%	6.47%
	20	7.86%	12.21%	17.61%	21.34%

TYPE 1: 25% TAX RATE

Age	Year	Earnings Rate			
		5%	**8%**	**12%**	**15%**
40	10	2.90%	4.45%	6.32%	7.59%
	20	5.62%	8.46%	11.70%	13.79%
	30	8.16%	12.02%	16.18%	18.70%
45	10	2.90%	4.45%	6.32%	7.59%
	20	5.62%	8.46%	11.70%	13.79%
	30	8.53%	12.62%	17.08%	19.80%
50	10	2.90%	4.45%	6.32%	7.59%
	20	5.62%	8.46%	11.70%	13.79%
	30	9.81%	14.68%	20.14%	23.57%
55	10	2.90%	4.45%	6.32%	7.59%
	20	5.98%	9.02%	12.53%	14.80%
	30	11.98%	18.19%	25.39%	30.05%
60	10	2.90%	4.45%	6.32%	7.59%
	20	7.20%	10.95%	15.36%	18.26%
	30	15.04%	23.21%	33.01%	39.54%
65	10	3.24%	4.97%	7.07%	8.50%
	20	9.27%	14.23%	20.19%	24.18%
	30	18.97%	29.79%	43.26%	52.53%
70	10	4.40%	6.76%	9.63%	11.58%
	20	12.18%	18.91%	27.17%	32.80%
	30	23.72%	37.94%	56.40%	69.59%
75	10	4.69%	7.22%	10.29%	12.39%
	20	13.35%	20.87%	30.22%	36.70%
80	10	5.07%	7.83%	11.18%	13.47%
	20	14.77%	23.28%	34.07%	41.68%

TYPE 1: 28% TAX RATE

Age	Year	Earnings Rate			
		5%	8%	12%	15%
40	10	3.65%	5.59%	7.94%	9.53%
	20	7.06%	10.60%	14.64%	17.23%
	30	10.23%	15.03%	20.15%	23.20%
45	10	3.65%	5.59%	7.94%	9.53%
	20	7.06%	10.60%	14.64%	17.23%
	30	10.65%	15.71%	21.18%	24.47%
50	10	3.65%	5.59%	7.94%	9.53%
	20	7.06%	10.60%	14.64%	17.23%
	30	12.07%	18.04%	24.69%	28.81%
55	10	3.65%	5.59%	7.94%	9.53%
	20	7.45%	11.23%	15.58%	18.38%
	30	14.49%	22.00%	30.69%	36.26%
60	10	3.65%	5.59%	7.94%	9.53%
	20	8.79%	13.38%	18.76%	22.30%
	30	17.89%	27.67%	39.41%	47.21%
65	10	4.01%	6.16%	8.76%	10.54%
	20	11.07%	17.03%	24.20%	28.99%
	30	22.28%	35.13%	51.22%	62.31%
70	10	5.27%	8.12%	11.58%	13.94%
	20	15.27%	22.24%	32.05%	38.76%
	30	27.58%	44.41%	66.46%	82.32%
75	10	5.59%	8.62%	12.31%	14.84%
	20	15.56%	24.43%	35.53%	43.25%
80	10	6.01%	9.28%	13.30%	16.05%
	20	17.14%	27.15%	39.94%	49.01%

TYPE 1: 33% TAX RATE

Age	Year	Earnings Rate			
		5%	8%	12%	15%
40	10	5.08%	7.80%	11.08%	13.31%
	20	9.84%	14.79%	20.39%	23.93%
	30	14.26%	20.91%	27.86%	31.90%
45	10	5.08%	7.80%	11.08%	13.31%
	20	9.84%	14.79%	20.39%	23.93%
	30	14.75%	21.73%	29.14%	33.50%
50	10	5.08%	7.80%	11.08%	13.31%
	20	9.84%	14.79%	20.39%	23.93%
	30	16.42%	24.53%	33.45%	38.89%
55	10	5.08%	7.80%	11.08%	13.31%
	20	10.29%	15.53%	21.52%	25.34%
	30	19.25%	29.29%	40.83%	48.14%
60	10	5.08%	7.80%	11.08%	13.31%
	20	11.83%	18.05%	25.33%	30.08%
	30	23.24%	36.12%	51.59%	61.81%
65	10	5.49%	8.45%	12.04%	14.49%
	20	14.44%	22.32%	31.81%	38.16%
	30	28.39%	45.14%	66.28%	80.86%
70	10	6.90%	10.67%	15.27%	18.43%
	20	18.11%	28.41%	41.20%	49.98%
	30	34.63%	56.42%	85.45%	106.50%
75	10	7.26%	11.24%	16.12%	19.47%
	20	19.61%	31.01%	45.44%	55.54%
80	10	7.73%	12.00%	17.26%	20.89%
	20	21.44%	32.24%	50.84%	62.74%

TYPE 1: 35% TAX RATE

Age	Year	Earnings Rate			
		5%	8%	12%	15%
40	10	5.72%	8.80%	12.51%	15.03%
	20	11.10%	16.69%	23.01%	26.99%
	30	16.09%	23.59%	31.37%	35.84%
45	10	5.72%	8.80%	12.51%	15.03%
	20	11.10%	16.69%	23.01%	26.99%
	30	16.61%	24.47%	32.75%	37.58%
50	10	5.72%	8.80%	12.51%	15.03%
	20	11.10%	16.69%	23.01%	26.99%
	30	18.38%	27.47%	37.42%	43.44%
55	10	5.72%	8.80%	12.51%	15.03%
	20	11.57%	17.48%	24.22%	28.51%
	30	21.38%	32.57%	45.40%	53.48%
60	10	5.72%	8.80%	12.51%	15.03%
	20	13.20%	20.15%	28.29%	33.60%
	30	25.60%	39.88%	57.05%	68.36%
65	10	6.15%	9.48%	13.52%	16.27%
	20	15.93%	24.67%	35.22%	42.28%
	30	31.06%	49.56%	73.01%	89.18%
70	10	7.62%	11.80%	16.91%	20.43%
	20	19.78%	31.11%	45.25%	54.97%
	30	37.68%	61.71%	93.92%	117.37%
75	10	7.99%	12.39%	17.80%	21.53%
	20	21.36%	33.88%	49.82%	61.00%
80	10	8.48%	13.19%	19.00%	23.03%
	20	23.28%	17.48%	55.64%	68.82%

TYPE 2: 15% TAX RATE

Age	Year	Earnings Rate			
		5%	8%	12%	15%
60	10	0.00%	0.00%	0.00%	0.00%
	20	1.35%	2.03%	2.82%	3.34%
	30	5.10%	7.78%	10.94%	13.03%
65	10	0.37%	0.56%	0.78%	0.92%
	20	2.92%	4.43%	6.18%	7.33%
	30	7.87%	12.11%	17.22%	20.65%
70	10	1.14%	1.72%	2.39%	2.83%
	20	4.77%	7.26%	10.21%	12.15%
	30	10.77%	16.75%	24.14%	29.22%
75	10	1.36%	2.06%	2.87%	3.39%
	20	5.61%	8.59%	12.16%	14.54%
80	10	1.65%	2.51%	3.50%	4.16%
	20	6.62%	10.22%	14.59%	17.55%

TYPE 2: 25% TAX RATE

Age	Year	Earnings Rate			
		5%	8%	12%	15%
60	10	0.00%	0.00%	0.00%	0.00%
	20	2.23%	3.35%	4.64%	5.47%
	30	8.53%	12.99%	18.22%	21.63%
65	10	0.61%	0.92%	1.28%	1.51%
	20	4.86%	7.33%	10.19%	12.03%
	30	13.27%	20.49%	29.18%	34.98%
70	10	1.89%	2.84%	3.93%	4.64%
	20	7.96%	12.12%	16.98%	20.16%
	30	18.35%	28.81%	41.86%	50.85%
75	10	2.26%	3.40%	4.73%	5.58%
	20	9.41%	14.44%	20.45%	24.44%
80	10	2.75%	4.16%	5.80%	6.87%
	20	11.18%	17.34%	24.87%	29.99%

TYPE 2: 28% TAX RATE

Age	Year	Earnings Rate			
		5%	8%	12%	15%
60	10	0.00%	0.00%	0.00%	0.00%
	20	2.49%	3.75%	5.18%	6.09%
	30	9.56%	14.55%	20.39%	24.18%
65	10	0.69%	1.03%	1.43%	1.69%
	20	5.43%	8.20%	11.37%	13.40%
	30	14.91%	23.04%	32.82%	39.32%
70	10	2.11%	3.17%	4.39%	5.17%
	20	8.92%	13.57%	19.00%	22.53%
	30	20.68%	32.56%	47.40%	57.62%
75	10	2.53%	3.81%	5.28%	6.23%
	20	10.56%	16.22%	22.96%	27.43%
80	10	3.08%	4.65%	6.48%	7.67%
	20	12.57%	19.53%	28.03%	33.82%

TYPE 2: 33% TAX RATE

Age	Year	Earnings Rate			
		5%	8%	12%	15%
60	10	0.00%	0.00%	0.00%	0.00%
	20	2.93%	4.39%	6.06%	7.12%
	30	11.27%	17.16%	23.99%	28.39%
65	10	0.81%	1.21%	1.68%	1.98%
	20	6.39%	9.63%	13.32%	15.67%
	30	17.66%	27.34%	38.93%	46.59%
70	10	2.48%	3.72%	5.14%	6.04%
	20	10.52%	16.00%	22.35%	26.45%
	30	24.63%	38.94%	56.86%	69.15%
75	10	2.97%	4.47%	6.19%	7.29%
	20	12.48%	19.19%	27.15%	32.41%
80	10	3.62%	5.47%	7.61%	9.00%
	20	14.91%	23.21%	33.38%	40.28%

TYPE 2: 35% TAX RATE

Age	Year	Earnings Rate			
		5%	8%	12%	15%
60	10	0.00%	0.00%	0.00%	0.00%
	20	3.10%	4.65%	6.41%	7.52%
	30	11.96%	18.20%	25.42%	30.05%
65	10	0.85%	1.28%	1.78%	2.09%
	20	6.77%	10.20%	14.09%	16.56%
	30	18.77%	29.06%	41.38%	49.49%
70	10	2.63%	3.94%	5.43%	6.38%
	20	11.16%	16.96%	23.68%	28.00%
	30	26.23%	41.53%	60.71%	73.84%
75	10	3.15%	4.73%	6.55%	7.71%
	20	13.26%	20.38%	28.83%	34.40%
80	10	3.84%	5.80%	8.06%	9.53%
	20	15.85%	24.70%	35.55%	42.90%

TYPE 1: 35% at Conversion Future Rate of 25%

Age	Year	Earnings Rate	
		9%	12%
45	10	-3.30%	-1.69%
	20	1.98%	4.89%
	30	7.30%	11.31%
65	10	-2.81%	-1.01%
	20	7.59%	12.34%
	30	24.40%	34.71%

TYPE 2: 35% at Conversion Future Rate of 25%

Age	Year	Earnings Rate	
		9%	12%
	10	-10.62%	-9.92%
70	20	-1.72%	1.39%
	30	14.55%	22.94%

TYPE 1: 35% Conversion Future Rate of 40%

Age	Year	Earnings Rate	
		9%	12%
	10	17.63%	21.09%
45	20	28.40%	34.09%
	30	38.67%	45.83%
	10	18.55%	22.32%
65	20	39.54%	49.26%
	30	74.97%	96.97%

TYPE 2: 35% Conversion Future Rate of 40%

Age	Year	Earnings Rate	
		9%	12%
	10	13.68%	15.01%
70	20	31.53%	37.58%
	30	66.73%	84.70%

APPENDIX D:
MUST-HAVE IRS FORMS

I HAVE INCLUDED SOME OF the common and more useful IRS forms, worksheets and instructions in the pages ahead. Understanding more about tax brackets and the way that taxes are calculated will be helpful in planning for the future. Be sure and get the latest tax form or worksheet from the IRS website at www.irs.gov.

2009 Tax Rate Schedules

 CAUTION

The Tax Rate Schedules are shown so you can see the tax rate that applies to all levels of taxable income. Do not use them to figure your tax. Instead, see the instructions for line 44 that begin on page 37.

Schedule X—If your filing status is Single

If your taxable income is: Over—	But not over—	The tax is:	of the amount over—
$0	$8,350	.... 10%	$0
8,350	33,950	$835.00 + 15%	8,350
33,950	82,250	4,675.00 + 25%	33,950
82,250	171,550	16,750.00 + 28%	82,250
171,550	372,950	41,754.00 + 33%	171,550
372,950	....	108,216.00 + 35%	372,950

Schedule Y-1—If your filing status is Married filing jointly or Qualifying widow(er)

If your taxable income is: Over—	But not over—	The tax is:	of the amount over—
$0	$16,700	.... 10%	$0
16,700	67,900	$1,670.00 + 15%	16,700
67,900	137,050	9,350.00 + 25%	67,900
137,050	208,850	26,637.50 + 28%	137,050
208,850	372,950	46,741.50 + 33%	208,850
372,950	....	100,894.50 + 35%	372,950

Schedule Y-2—If your filing status is Married filing separately

If your taxable income is: Over—	But not over—	The tax is:	of the amount over—
$0	$8,350	.... 10%	$0
8,350	33,950	$835.00 + 15%	8,350
33,950	68,525	4,675.00 + 25%	33,950
68,525	104,425	13,318.75 + 28%	68,525
104,425	186,475	23,370.75 + 33%	104,425
186,475	....	50,447.25 + 35%	186,475

Schedule Z—If your filing status is Head of household

If your taxable income is: Over—	But not over—	The tax is:	of the amount over—
$0	$11,950	.... 10%	$0
11,950	45,500	$1,195.00 + 15%	11,950
45,500	117,450	6,227.50 + 25%	45,500
117,450	190,200	24,215.00 + 28%	117,450
190,200	372,950	44,585.00 + 33%	190,200
372,950	....	104,892.50 + 35%	372,950

- 101 -

2009 Tax Rate Schedule

| Form **1040** | Department of the Treasury—Internal Revenue Service
U.S. Individual Income Tax Return | 20**09** | (99) | IRS Use Only—Do not write or staple in this space. | OMB No. 1545-0074 |

For the year Jan. 1–Dec. 31, 2009, or other tax year beginning , 2009, ending , 20

Label
(See instructions on page 14.)
Use the IRS label.
Otherwise, please print or type.

L A B E L   H E R E

Your first name and initial | Last name | Your social security number

If a joint return, spouse's first name and initial | Last name | Spouse's social security number

Home address (number and street). If you have a P.O. box, see page 14. | Apt. no.

▲ You **must** enter your SSN(s) above. ▲

City, town or post office, state, and ZIP code. If you have a foreign address, see page 14.

Checking a box below will not change your tax or refund.

Presidential Election Campaign ▶ Check here if you, or your spouse if filing jointly, want $3 to go to this fund (see page 14) ▶ ☐ You ☐ Spouse

Filing Status
Check only one box.

1 ☐ Single
2 ☐ Married filing jointly (even if only one had income)
3 ☐ Married filing separately. Enter spouse's SSN above and full name here. ▶
4 ☐ Head of household (with qualifying person). (See page 15.) If the qualifying person is a child but not your dependent, enter this child's name here. ▶
5 ☐ Qualifying widow(er) with dependent child (see page 16)

Exemptions

6a ☐ **Yourself.** If someone can claim you as a dependent, **do not** check box 6a .
b ☐ Spouse
c Dependents:

| (1) First name   Last name | (2) Dependent's social security number | (3) Dependent's relationship to you | (4) ✔ If qualifying child for child tax credit (see page 17) |

If more than four dependents, see page 17 and check here ▶ ☐

Boxes checked on 6a and 6b ___
No. of children on 6c who:
• lived with you ___
• did not live with you due to divorce or separation (see page 18) ___
Dependents on 6c not entered above ___
Add numbers on lines above ▶ ___

d Total number of exemptions claimed . . . .

Income

Attach Form(s) W-2 here. Also attach Forms W-2G and 1099-R if tax was withheld.

If you did not get a W-2, see page 22.

Enclose, but do not attach, any payment. Also, please use Form 1040-V.

7	Wages, salaries, tips, etc. Attach Form(s) W-2	7	
8a	**Taxable** interest. Attach Schedule B if required	8a	
b	**Tax-exempt** interest. Do not include on line 8a . . .	8b		
9a	Ordinary dividends. Attach Schedule B if required	9a	
b	Qualified dividends (see page 22)	9b		
10	Taxable refunds, credits, or offsets of state and local income taxes (see page 23) . .	10	
11	Alimony received	11	
12	Business income or (loss). Attach Schedule C or C-EZ	12	
13	Capital gain or (loss). Attach Schedule D if required. If not required, check here ▶ ☐	13	
14	Other gains or (losses). Attach Form 4797	14	
15a	IRA distributions .	15a		b Taxable amount (see page 24)	15b	
16a	Pensions and annuities	16a		b Taxable amount (see page 25)	16b	
17	Rental real estate, royalties, partnerships, S corporations, trusts, etc. Attach Schedule E	17	
18	Farm income or (loss). Attach Schedule F	18	
19	Unemployment compensation in excess of $2,400 per recipient (see page 27) . . .	19	
20a	Social security benefits	20a		b Taxable amount (see page 27)	20b	
21	Other income. List type and amount (see page 29) ___	21	
22	Add the amounts in the far right column for lines 7 through 21. This is your **total income** ▶	22	

Adjusted Gross Income

23	Educator expenses (see page 29)	23		
24	Certain business expenses of reservists, performing artists, and fee-basis government officials. Attach Form 2106 or 2106-EZ	24		
25	Health savings account deduction. Attach Form 8889 .	25		
26	Moving expenses. Attach Form 3903	26		
27	One-half of self-employment tax. Attach Schedule SE .	27		
28	Self-employed SEP, SIMPLE, and qualified plans . .	28		
29	Self-employed health insurance deduction (see page 30)	29		
30	Penalty on early withdrawal of savings	30		
31a	Alimony paid b Recipient's SSN ▶	31a		
32	IRA deduction (see page 31)	32		
33	Student loan interest deduction (see page 34) . . .	33		
34	Tuition and fees deduction. Attach Form 8917 . . .	34		
35	Domestic production activities deduction. Attach Form 8903	35		
36	Add lines 23 through 31a and 32 through 35	36	
37	Subtract line 36 from line 22. This is your **adjusted gross income** . . . . ▶	37	

For Disclosure, Privacy Act, and Paperwork Reduction Act Notice, see page 97. | Cat. No. 11320B | Form **1040** (2009)

2009 IRS Form 1040 (page 1).

Form 1040 (2009)   Page **2**

Tax and Credits	38	Amount from line 37 (adjusted gross income)		38	
	39a	Check { ☐ **You** were born before January 2, 1945, ☐ Blind. } Total boxes if: { ☐ **Spouse** was born before January 2, 1945, ☐ Blind. } checked ▶ 39a ☐			
Standard Deduction for—	b	If your spouse itemizes on a separate return or you were a dual-status alien, see page 35 and check here▶ 39b ☐			
	40a	**Itemized deductions** (from Schedule A) **or** your **standard deduction** (see left margin) . .		40a	
• People who check any box on line 39a, 39b, or 40b or who can be claimed as a dependent, see page 35.	b	If you are increasing your standard deduction by certain real estate taxes, new motor vehicle taxes, or a net disaster loss, attach Schedule L and check here (see page 35) . ▶ 40b ☐			
	41	Subtract line 40a from line 38		41	
	42	**Exemptions.** If line 38 is \$125,100 or less and you did not provide housing to a Midwestern displaced individual, multiply \$3,650 by the number on line 6d. Otherwise, see page 37 . .		42	
• All others:	43	**Taxable income.** Subtract line 42 from line 41. If line 42 is more than line 41, enter -0- . .		43	
Single or Married filing separately, \$5,700	44	**Tax** (see page 37). Check if any tax is from: a ☐ Form(s) 8814 b ☐ Form 4972 .		44	
	45	**Alternative minimum tax** (see page 40). Attach Form 6251		45	
Married filing jointly or Qualifying widow(er), \$11,400	46	Add lines 44 and 45 . . . . ▶		46	
	47	Foreign tax credit. Attach Form 1116 if required . . .	47		
	48	Credit for child and dependent care expenses. Attach Form 2441	48		
Head of household, \$8,350	49	Education credits from Form 8863, line 29	49		
	50	Retirement savings contributions credit. Attach Form 8880	50		
	51	Child tax credit (see page 42)	51		
	52	Credits from Form: a ☐ 8396 b ☐ 8839 c ☐ 5695	52		
	53	Other credits from Form: a ☐ 3800 b ☐ 8801 c ☐	53		
	54	Add lines 47 through 53. These are your **total credits**		54	
	55	Subtract line 54 from line 46. If line 54 is more than line 46, enter -0- . . . . . ▶		55	
Other Taxes	56	Self-employment tax. Attach Schedule SE		56	
	57	Unreported social security and Medicare tax from Form: a ☐ 4137 b ☐ 8919 .		57	
	58	Additional tax on IRAs, other qualified retirement plans, etc. Attach Form 5329 if required . .		58	
	59	Additional taxes: a ☐ AEIC payments b ☐ Household employment taxes. Attach Schedule H		59	
	60	Add lines 55 through 59. This is your **total tax** . . . . ▶		60	
Payments	61	Federal income tax withheld from Forms W-2 and 1099 . .	61		
	62	2009 estimated tax payments and amount applied from 2008 return	62		
If you have a qualifying child, attach Schedule EIC.	63	Making work pay and government retiree credits. Attach Schedule M	63		
	64a	**Earned income credit (EIC)**	64a		
	b	Nontaxable combat pay election 64b			
	65	Additional child tax credit. Attach Form 8812	65		
	66	Refundable education credit from Form 8863, line 16 . .	66		
	67	First-time homebuyer credit. Attach Form 5405	67		
	68	Amount paid with request for extension to file (see page 72) .	68		
	69	Excess social security and tier 1 RRTA tax withheld (see page 72)	69		
	70	Credits from Form: a ☐ 2439 b ☐ 4136 c ☐ 8801 d ☐ 8885	70		
	71	Add lines 61, 62, 63, 64a, and 65 through 70. These are your **total payments** . . . . . ▶		71	
Refund	72	If line 71 is more than line 60, subtract line 60 from line 71. This is the amount you **overpaid**		72	
Direct deposit? See page 73 and fill in 73b, 73c, and 73d, or Form 8888.	73a	Amount of line 72 you want **refunded to you.** If Form 8888 is attached, check here . ▶ ☐		73a	
	▶ b	Routing number |__|__|__|__|__|__|__|__|__| ▶c Type: ☐ Checking ☐ Savings			
	▶ d	Account number |__|__|__|__|__|__|__|__|__|			
	74	Amount of line 72 you want **applied to your 2010 estimated tax ▶** 74			
Amount You Owe	75	**Amount you owe.** Subtract line 71 from line 60. For details on how to pay, see page 74 . ▶		75	
	76	Estimated tax penalty (see page 74)	76		

Third Party Designee   Do you want to allow another person to discuss this return with the IRS (see page 75)? ☐ **Yes.** Complete the following. ☐ **No**

Designee's name ▶	Phone no. ▶	Personal identification number (PIN) ▶

Sign Here

Under penalties of perjury, I declare that I have examined this return and accompanying schedules and statements, and to the best of my knowledge and belief, they are true, correct, and complete. Declaration of preparer (other than taxpayer) is based on all information of which preparer has any knowledge.

Joint return? See page 15. Keep a copy for your records.

Your signature	Date	Your occupation	Daytime phone number
Spouse's signature. If a joint return, **both** must sign.	Date	Spouse's occupation	

Paid Preparer's Use Only

Preparer's signature ▶	Date	Check if self-employed ☐	Preparer's SSN or PTIN
Firm's name (or yours if self-employed), address, and ZIP code ▶		EIN	
		Phone no.	

Form **1040** (2009)

2009 IRS Form 1040 (page 2).

Appendix C. Life Expectancy Tables

	Table I (Single Life Expectancy) (For Use by Beneficiaries)		
Age	**Life Expectancy**	**Age**	**Life Expectancy**
0	82.4	28	55.3
1	81.6	29	54.3
2	80.6	30	53.3
3	79.7	31	52.4
4	78.7	32	51.4
5	77.7	33	50.4
6	76.7	34	49.4
7	75.8	35	48.5
8	74.8	36	47.5
9	73.8	37	46.5
10	72.8	38	45.6
11	71.8	39	44.6
12	70.8	40	43.6
13	69.9	41	42.7
14	68.9	42	41.7
15	67.9	43	40.7
16	66.9	44	39.8
17	66.0	45	38.8
18	65.0	46	37.9
19	64.0	47	37.0
20	63.0	48	36.0
21	62.1	49	35.1
22	61.1	50	34.2
23	60.1	51	33.3
24	59.1	52	32.3
25	58.2	53	31.4
26	57.2	54	30.5
27	56.2	55	29.6

Publication 590 (2008)

Life Expectancy Table I for Beneficiaries Used for inherited Roth and Regular IRAs (page 1).

Appendix C. (Continued)

Table I (Single Life Expectancy) (For Use by Beneficiaries)				
Age	**Life Expectancy**		**Age**	**Life Expectancy**
56	28.7		84	8.1
57	27.9		85	7.6
58	27.0		86	7.1
59	26.1		87	6.7
60	25.2		88	6.3
61	24.4		89	5.9
62	23.5		90	5.5
63	22.7		91	5.2
64	21.8		92	4.9
65	21.0		93	4.6
66	20.2		94	4.3
67	19.4		95	4.1
68	18.6		96	3.8
69	17.8		97	3.6
70	17.0		98	3.4
71	16.3		99	3.1
72	15.5		100	2.9
73	14.8		101	2.7
74	14.1		102	2.5
75	13.4		103	2.3
76	12.7		104	2.1
77	12.1		105	1.9
78	11.4		106	1.7
79	10.8		107	1.5
80	10.2		108	1.4
81	9.7		109	1.2
82	9.1		110	1.1
83	8.6		111 and over	1.0

Life Expectancy Table I for Beneficiaries Used for inherited Roth and Regular IRAs (page 2).

Appendix C. Life Expectancy Tables (Continued)

Ages	20	21	22	23	24	25	26	27	28	29
				Table II (Joint Life and Last Survivor Expectancy) (For Use by Owners Whose Spouses Are More Than 10 Years Younger and Are the Sole Beneficiaries of Their IRAs)						
20	70.1	69.6	69.1	68.7	68.3	67.9	67.5	67.2	66.9	66.6
21	69.6	69.1	68.6	68.2	67.7	67.3	66.9	66.6	66.2	65.9
22	69.1	68.6	68.1	67.6	67.2	66.7	66.3	65.9	65.6	65.2
23	68.7	68.2	67.6	67.1	66.6	66.2	65.7	65.3	64.9	64.6
24	68.3	67.7	67.2	66.6	66.1	65.6	65.2	64.7	64.3	63.9
25	67.9	67.3	66.7	66.2	65.6	65.1	64.6	64.2	63.7	63.3
26	67.5	66.9	66.3	65.7	65.2	64.6	64.1	63.6	63.2	62.8
27	67.2	66.6	65.9	65.3	64.7	64.2	63.6	63.1	62.7	62.2
28	66.9	66.2	65.6	64.9	64.3	63.7	63.2	62.7	62.1	61.7
29	66.6	65.9	65.2	64.6	63.9	63.3	62.8	62.2	61.7	61.2
30	66.3	65.6	64.9	64.2	63.6	62.9	62.3	61.8	61.2	60.7
31	66.1	65.3	64.6	63.9	63.2	62.6	62.0	61.4	60.8	60.2
32	65.8	65.1	64.3	63.6	62.9	62.2	61.6	61.0	60.4	59.8
33	65.6	64.8	64.1	63.3	62.6	61.9	61.3	60.6	60.0	59.4
34	65.4	64.6	63.8	63.1	62.3	61.6	60.9	60.3	59.6	59.0
35	65.2	64.4	63.6	62.8	62.1	61.4	60.6	59.9	59.3	58.6
36	65.0	64.2	63.4	62.6	61.9	61.1	60.4	59.6	59.0	58.3
37	64.9	64.0	63.2	62.4	61.6	60.9	60.1	59.4	58.7	58.0
38	64.7	63.9	63.0	62.2	61.4	60.6	59.9	59.1	58.4	57.7
39	64.6	63.7	62.9	62.1	61.2	60.4	59.6	58.9	58.1	57.4
40	64.4	63.6	62.7	61.9	61.1	60.2	59.4	58.7	57.9	57.1
41	64.3	63.5	62.6	61.7	60.9	60.1	59.3	58.5	57.7	56.9
42	64.2	63.3	62.5	61.6	60.8	59.9	59.1	58.3	57.5	56.7
43	64.1	63.2	62.4	61.5	60.6	59.8	58.9	58.1	57.3	56.5
44	64.0	63.1	62.2	61.4	60.5	59.6	58.8	57.9	57.1	56.3
45	64.0	63.0	62.2	61.3	60.4	59.5	58.6	57.8	56.9	56.1
46	63.9	63.0	62.1	61.2	60.3	59.4	58.5	57.7	56.8	56.0
47	63.8	62.9	62.0	61.1	60.2	59.3	58.4	57.5	56.7	55.8
48	63.7	62.8	61.9	61.0	60.1	59.2	58.3	57.4	56.5	55.7
49	63.7	62.8	61.8	60.9	60.0	59.1	58.2	57.3	56.4	55.6
50	63.6	62.7	61.8	60.8	59.9	59.0	58.1	57.2	56.3	55.4
51	63.6	62.6	61.7	60.8	59.9	58.9	58.0	57.1	56.2	55.3
52	63.5	62.6	61.7	60.7	59.8	58.9	58.0	57.1	56.1	55.2
53	63.5	62.5	61.6	60.7	59.7	58.8	57.9	57.0	56.1	55.2
54	63.5	62.5	61.6	60.6	59.7	58.8	57.8	56.9	56.0	55.1
55	63.4	62.5	61.5	60.6	59.6	58.7	57.8	56.8	55.9	55.0
56	63.4	62.4	61.5	60.5	59.6	58.7	57.7	56.8	55.9	54.9
57	63.4	62.4	61.5	60.5	59.6	58.6	57.7	56.7	55.8	54.9
58	63.3	62.4	61.4	60.5	59.5	58.6	57.6	56.7	55.8	54.8
59	63.3	62.3	61.4	60.4	59.5	58.5	57.6	56.7	55.7	54.8

Publication 590 (2008)

Life Expectancy Table II for IRA Holders Used for IRA holders who have a spouse/beneficiary that is more than 10 years younger than the holder. See IRS Publication 590 for the rest of this lengthy table at www.irs.gov.

Appendix C. Uniform Lifetime Table

<table>
<tr><td colspan="4" align="center">Table III
(Uniform Lifetime)</td></tr>
<tr><td colspan="4">(For Use by:
• Unmarried Owners,
• Married Owners Whose Spouses Are Not More Than 10 Years Younger, and
• Married Owners Whose Spouses Are Not the Sole Beneficiaries of Their IRAs)</td></tr>
<tr><th>Age</th><th>Distribution Period</th><th>Age</th><th>Distribution Period</th></tr>
<tr><td>70</td><td>27.4</td><td>93</td><td>9.6</td></tr>
<tr><td>71</td><td>26.5</td><td>94</td><td>9.1</td></tr>
<tr><td>72</td><td>25.6</td><td>95</td><td>8.6</td></tr>
<tr><td>73</td><td>24.7</td><td>96</td><td>8.1</td></tr>
<tr><td>74</td><td>23.8</td><td>97</td><td>7.6</td></tr>
<tr><td>75</td><td>22.9</td><td>98</td><td>7.1</td></tr>
<tr><td>76</td><td>22.0</td><td>99</td><td>6.7</td></tr>
<tr><td>77</td><td>21.2</td><td>100</td><td>6.3</td></tr>
<tr><td>78</td><td>20.3</td><td>101</td><td>5.9</td></tr>
<tr><td>79</td><td>19.5</td><td>102</td><td>5.5</td></tr>
<tr><td>80</td><td>18.7</td><td>103</td><td>5.2</td></tr>
<tr><td>81</td><td>17.9</td><td>104</td><td>4.9</td></tr>
<tr><td>82</td><td>17.1</td><td>105</td><td>4.5</td></tr>
<tr><td>83</td><td>16.3</td><td>106</td><td>4.2</td></tr>
<tr><td>84</td><td>15.5</td><td>107</td><td>3.9</td></tr>
<tr><td>85</td><td>14.8</td><td>108</td><td>3.7</td></tr>
<tr><td>86</td><td>14.1</td><td>109</td><td>3.4</td></tr>
<tr><td>87</td><td>13.4</td><td>110</td><td>3.1</td></tr>
<tr><td>88</td><td>12.7</td><td>111</td><td>2.9</td></tr>
<tr><td>89</td><td>12.0</td><td>112</td><td>2.6</td></tr>
<tr><td>90</td><td>11.4</td><td>113</td><td>2.4</td></tr>
<tr><td>91</td><td>10.8</td><td>114</td><td>2.1</td></tr>
<tr><td>92</td><td>10.2</td><td>115 and over</td><td>1.9</td></tr>
</table>

Life Expectancy Table III for Mandatory IRA Distributions Used for everyone *except* those with spouse/beneficiary who is more than 10 years younger.

☐ CORRECTED (if checked)

TRUSTEE'S or ISSUER'S name, street address, city, state, and ZIP code	**1** IRA contributions (other than amounts in boxes 2–4, 8–10, 13a, 14a, and 15a) $	OMB No. 1545-0747	**IRA Contribution Information**
	2 Rollover contributions $	**20**09 Form **5498**	
	3 Roth IRA conversion amount $	**4** Recharacterized contributions $	**Copy B**
TRUSTEE'S or ISSUER'S federal identification no. PARTICIPANT'S social security number	**5** Fair market value of account $	**6** Life insurance cost included in box 1 $	**For Participant**
PARTICIPANT'S name	**7** IRA ☐ SEP ☐ SIMPLE ☐ Roth IRA ☐		This information
	8 SEP contributions $	**9** SIMPLE contributions $	is being
Street address (including apt. no.)	**10** Roth IRA contributions $	**11** Check if RMD for 2010 ☐	provided to the Internal
	12a RMD date	**12b** RMD amount $	Revenue Service.
City, state, and ZIP code	**13a** Postponed contribution $	**13b** Year	**13c** Code
	14a Repayments $	**14b** Code	
Account number (see instructions)	**15a** Other contributions $	**15b** Code	

Form **5498**   (keep for your records)   Department of the Treasury - Internal Revenue Service

Instructions for Participant

The information on Form 5498 is submitted to the Internal Revenue Service by the trustee or issuer of your individual retirement arrangement (IRA) to report contributions, including any catch-up contributions, required minimum distributions (RMDs), and the fair market value (FMV) of the account. For information about IRAs, see Pubs. 590 and 560.

What's new. The size of Form 5498 has been increased to allow for separate entry boxes for information that was previously reported in the blank box to the left of box 10. See the instructions for boxes 12a–15b below.

Account number. May show an account or other unique number the trustee assigned to distinguish your account.

Box 1. Shows traditional IRA contributions for 2009 you made in 2009 and through April 15, 2010. These contributions may be deductible on your Form 1040 or 1040A. However, if you or your spouse was an active participant in an employer's pension plan, these contributions may not be deductible. This box does not include amounts in boxes 2–4, 8–10, 13a, 14a, and 15a.

Box 2. Shows any amount, including a direct rollover to a traditional IRA or Roth IRA, or a qualified rollover contribution (including a military death gratuity, SGLI payment, qualified settlement income, or airline payments) to a Roth IRA, you made in 2009. It does not show any amounts you converted from your traditional IRA, SEP IRA, or SIMPLE IRA to a Roth IRA. They are shown in box 3. See the Form 1040 or 1040A instructions for information on how to report rollovers. If you have ever made any nondeductible contributions to your traditional IRA or SEP IRA and you did not roll over the total distribution, use Form 8606 to figure the taxable amount. If property was rolled over, see Pub. 590. For a qualified rollover to a Roth IRA, also see Pub. 590.

Box 3. Shows the amount converted from a traditional IRA, SEP IRA, or SIMPLE IRA to a Roth IRA in 2009. Use Form 8606 to figure the taxable amount.

Box 4. Shows amounts recharacterized from transferring any part of the contribution (plus earnings) from one type of IRA to another. See Pub. 590.

Box 5. Shows the FMV of all investments in your account at year end. However, if a decedent's name is shown, the amount reported may be the FMV on the date of death. If the FMV is zero for a decedent, the executor or administrator of the estate may request a date-of-death value from the financial institution.

Box 6. For endowment contracts only, shows the amount allocable to the cost of life insurance. Subtract this amount from your allowable IRA contribution included in box 1 to compute your IRA deduction.

Box 7. May show the kind of IRA reported on this Form 5498.

Box 8. Shows SEP contributions made in 2009, including contributions made in 2009 for 2008, but not including contributions made in 2010 for 2009. If made by your employer, do not deduct on your income tax return. If you made the

contributions as a self-employed person (or partner), they may be deductible. See Pub. 560.

Box 9. Shows SIMPLE contributions made in 2009. If made by your employer, do not deduct on your income tax return. If you made the contributions as a self-employed person (or partner), they may be deductible. See Pub. 560.

Box 10. Shows Roth IRA contributions you made in 2009 and through April 15, 2010. Do not deduct on your income tax return.

Box 11. If the box is checked, you must take an RMD for 2010. An RMD may be required even if the box is not checked. If you do not take the RMD for 2010, you are subject to a 50% excise tax on the amount not distributed. See Pub. 590 for details.

Box 12a. Shows the date by which the RMD amount in box 12b must be distributed to avoid the 50% excise tax on the undistributed amount for 2010.

Box 12b. Shows the amount of the RMD for 2010. If box 11 is checked and there is no amount in this box, the trustee or issuer must provide you the amount or offer to calculate the amount in a separate statement by February 1, 2010.

Box 13a. Shows the amount of any postponed contribution made in 2009 for a prior year.

Box 13b. Shows the year to which the postponed contribution in box 13a was credited.

Box 13c. For participants who made a postponed contribution due to an extension of the contribution due date because of a federally designated disaster, shows the code FD.

For participants who served in designated combat zones and made postponed contributions, shows the code for the combat zone or hazardous duty area in which the participant served. The codes are: AF—Allied Force; JE—Joint Endeavor; EF—Enduring Freedom; and IF—Iraqi Freedom. For additional information, including a list of locations within the designated combat zones and qualified hazardous duty areas, see Pub. 3, Armed Forces' Tax Guide.

Box 14a. Shows the amount of any repayment of a qualified reservist distribution or federally designated disaster withdrawal repayment. See Pub. 590 for reporting repayments.

Box 14b. Shows the code QR for the repayment of a qualified reservist distribution or code DD for repayment of a federally designated disaster distribution.

Box 15a. Shows the amount of any catch-up contributions you made in the case of certain employer bankruptcies in lieu of the higher contribution limit for individuals who are age 50 or older. See Pub. 590.

Box 15b. Shows the code BK for special catch-up contributions elected by the participant in certain employer bankruptcies. See Pub. 590.

IRS Form 5498 Completed by IRA trustee or custodian.

Instructions for Trustees and Issuers

We provide general and specific form instructions as separate products. The products you should use for 2009 are the General Instructions for Forms 1099, 1098, 3921, 3922, 5498, and W-2G and the 2009 Instructions for Forms 1099-R and 5498. To order these instructions and additional forms, visit the IRS website at *www.irs.gov* or call 1-800-TAX-FORM (1-800-829-3676).

Caution: *Because paper forms are scanned during processing, you cannot file with the IRS Forms 1096, 1098, 1099, 3921, 3922, or 5498 that you print from the IRS website.*

Due dates. Furnish Copy B of this form to the participant by June 1, 2010, but furnish fair market value information and RMD if applicable by February 1, 2010.

File Copy A of this form with the IRS by June 1, 2010. If you file electronically, you must have software that generates a file according to the specifications in Pub. 1220, Specifications for Filing Forms 1098, 1099, 3921, 3922, 5498, and W-2G Electronically. IRS does not provide a fill-in form option.

Need help? If you have questions about reporting on Form 5498, call the information reporting customer service site toll free at 1-866-455-7438 or 304-263-8700 (not toll free). For TTY/TDD equipment, call 304-267-3367 (not toll free).

 Printed on recycled paper

IRS Form 5498 Instructions for IRA trustee or custodian.

Form **8606**	**Nondeductible IRAs**	OMB No. 1545-0074
	▶ See separate instructions.	2009
Department of the Treasury Internal Revenue Service (99)	▶ Attach to Form 1040, Form 1040A, or Form 1040NR.	Attachment Sequence No. **48**

Name. If married, file a separate form for each spouse required to file Form 8606. See page 5 of the instructions.	Your social security number

Fill in Your Address Only If You Are Filing This Form by Itself and Not With Your Tax Return ▶

Home address (number and street, or P.O. box if mail is not delivered to your home)	Apt. no.
City, town or post office, state, and ZIP code	

Part I   **Nondeductible Contributions to Traditional IRAs and Distributions From Traditional, SEP, and SIMPLE IRAs**

Complete this part only if one or more of the following apply.
- You made nondeductible contributions to a traditional IRA for 2009.
- You took distributions from a traditional, SEP, or SIMPLE IRA in 2009 **and** you made nondeductible contributions to a traditional IRA in 2009 or an earlier year. For this purpose, a distribution does not include a rollover (other than a repayment of a qualified disaster recovery assistance distribution), qualified charitable distribution, one-time distribution to fund an HSA, conversion, recharacterization, or return of certain contributions.
- You converted part, but not all, of your traditional, SEP, and SIMPLE IRAs to Roth IRAs in 2009 (excluding any portion you recharacterized) **and** you made nondeductible contributions to a traditional IRA in 2009 or an earlier year.

1	Enter your nondeductible contributions to traditional IRAs for 2009, including those made for 2009 from January 1, 2010, through April 15, 2010 (see page 5 of the instructions)	**1**	
2	Enter your total basis in traditional IRAs (see page 5 of the instructions)	**2**	
3	Add lines 1 and 2	**3**	

> **In 2009, did you take a distribution from traditional, SEP, or SIMPLE IRAs, or make a Roth IRA conversion?** ── **No** ──▶ Enter the amount from line 3 on line 14. Do not complete the rest of Part I.
> ── **Yes** ──▶ Go to line 4.

4	Enter those contributions included on line 1 that were made from January 1, 2010, through April 15, 2010	**4**	
5	Subtract line 4 from line 3	**5**	
6	Enter the value of **all** your traditional, SEP, and SIMPLE IRAs as of December 31, 2009, plus any outstanding rollovers. Subtract any repayments of qualified disaster recovery assistance distributions. If the result is zero or less, enter -0- (see page 6 of the instructions) . .	**6**	
7	Enter your distributions from traditional, SEP, and SIMPLE IRAs in 2009. **Do not** include rollovers (other than repayments of qualified disaster recovery assistance distributions), qualified charitable distributions, a one-time distribution to fund an HSA, conversions to a Roth IRA, certain returned contributions, or recharacterizations of traditional IRA contributions (see page 6 of the instructions)	**7**	
8	Enter the net amount you converted from traditional, SEP, and SIMPLE IRAs to Roth IRAs in 2009. **Do not** include amounts converted that you later recharacterized (see page 6 of the instructions). Also enter this amount on line 16	**8**	
9	Add lines 6, 7, and 8	**9**	
10	Divide line 5 by line 9. Enter the result as a decimal rounded to at least 3 places. If the result is 1.000 or more, enter "1.000"	**10** × .
11	Multiply line 8 by line 10. This is the nontaxable portion of the amount you converted to Roth IRAs. Also enter this amount on line 17 . . .	**11**	
12	Multiply line 7 by line 10. This is the nontaxable portion of your distributions that you did not convert to a Roth IRA	**12**	
13	Add lines 11 and 12. This is the nontaxable portion of all your distributions	**13**	
14	Subtract line 13 from line 3. This is **your total basis in traditional IRAs for 2009 and earlier years**	**14**	
15a	Subtract line 12 from line 7	**15a**	
b	Amount on line 15a attributable to qualified disaster recovery assistance distributions (see page 6 of the instructions). Also enter this amount on Form 8930, line 22	**15b**	
c	**Taxable amount.** Subtract line 15b from line 15a. If more than zero, also include this amount on Form 1040, line 15b; Form 1040A, line 11b; or Form 1040NR, line 16b	**15c**	

Note: *You may be subject to an additional 10% tax on the amount on line 15c if you were under age 59¹/₂ at the time of the distribution (see page 7 of the instructions).*

For Privacy Act and Paperwork Reduction Act Notice, see page 8 of the instructions.	Cat. No. 63966F	Form **8606** (2009)

IRS Form 8606 For non-deductible IRAs (page 1).

Form 8606 (2009)

Page **2**

Part II | **2009 Conversions From Traditional, SEP, or SIMPLE IRAs to Roth IRAs**

Complete this part if you converted part or all of your traditional, SEP, and SIMPLE IRAs to a Roth IRA in 2009 (excluding any portion you recharacterized).

Caution: *If your modified adjusted gross income is over $100,000* **or** *you are married filing separately and you lived with your spouse at any time in 2009, you* **cannot** *convert any amount from traditional, SEP, or SIMPLE IRAs to Roth IRAs for 2009. If you erroneously made a conversion, you must recharacterize (correct) it (see page 7 of the instructions).*

16	If you completed Part I, enter the amount from line 8. Otherwise, enter the net amount you converted from traditional, SEP, and SIMPLE IRAs to Roth IRAs in 2009. **Do not** include amounts you later recharacterized back to traditional, SEP, or SIMPLE IRAs in 2009 or 2010 (see page 7 of the instructions)	16
17	If you completed Part I, enter the amount from line 11. Otherwise, enter your basis in the amount on line 16 (see page 7 of the instructions)	17
18	**Taxable amount.** Subtract line 17 from line 16. Also include this amount on Form 1040, line 15b; Form 1040A, line 11b; or Form 1040NR, line 16b	18

Part III | **Distributions From Roth IRAs**

Complete this part only if you took a distribution from a Roth IRA in 2009. For this purpose, a distribution does not include a rollover (other than a repayment of a qualified disaster recovery assistance distribution), qualified charitable distribution, one-time distribution to fund an HSA, recharacterization, or return of certain contributions (see page 7 of the instructions).

19	Enter your total nonqualified distributions from Roth IRAs in 2009 including any qualified first-time homebuyer distributions (see page 7 of the instructions)	19
20	Qualified first-time homebuyer expenses (see page 7 of the instructions). **Do not** enter more than $10,000	20
21	Subtract line 20 from line 19. If zero or less, enter -0- and skip lines 22 through 25	21
22	Enter your basis in Roth IRA contributions (see page 7 of the instructions)	22
23	Subtract line 22 from line 21. If zero or less, enter -0- and skip lines 24 and 25. If more than zero, you may be subject to an additional tax (see page 7 of the instructions)	23
24	Enter your basis in conversions from traditional, SEP, and SIMPLE IRAs and rollovers from qualified retirement plans to a Roth IRA (see page 7 of the instructions)	24
25a	Subtract line 24 from line 23. If zero or less, enter -0- and skip lines 25b and 25c	25a
b	Amount on line 25a attributable to qualified disaster recovery assistance distributions (see page 7 of the instructions). Also enter this amount on Form 8930, line 23	25b
c	**Taxable amount.** Subtract line 25b from line 25a. If more than zero, also include this amount on Form 1040, line 15b; Form 1040A, line 11b; or Form 1040NR, line 16b	25c

Sign Here Only If You Are Filing This Form by Itself and Not With Your Tax Return

Under penalties of perjury, I declare that I have examined this form, including accompanying attachments, and to the best of my knowledge and belief, it is true, correct, and complete. Declaration of preparer (other than taxpayer) is based on all information of which preparer has any knowledge.

Your signature ▶   Date

Paid Preparer's Use Only	Preparer's signature ▶	Date	Check if self-employed ☐	Preparer's SSN or PTIN
	Firm's name (or yours if self-employed), address, and ZIP code ▶		EIN	
			Phone no.	

Form **8606** (2009)

IRS Form 8606 For non-deductible IRAs (page 2).

Form **5329**	**Additional Taxes on Qualified Plans (Including IRAs) and Other Tax-Favored Accounts**	OMB No. 1545-0074
	▶ Attach to Form 1040 or Form 1040NR.	**20**09
Department of the Treasury Internal Revenue Service (99)	▶ See separate instructions.	Attachment Sequence No. **29**

Name of individual subject to additional tax. If married filing jointly, see instructions. **Your social security number**

Fill in Your Address Only If You Are Filing This Form by Itself and Not With Your Tax Return ▶

Home address (number and street), or P.O. box if mail is not delivered to your home   Apt. no.

City, town or post office, state, and ZIP code

If this is an amended return, check here ▶ ☐

If you **only** owe the additional 10% tax on early distributions, you may be able to report this tax directly on Form 1040, line 58, or Form 1040NR, line 54, without filing Form 5329. See the instructions for Form 1040, line 58, or for Form 1040NR, line 54.

Part I Additional Tax on Early Distributions

Complete this part if you took a taxable distribution (other than a qualified disaster recovery assistance distribution), before you reached age 59½, from a qualified retirement plan (including an IRA) or modified endowment contract (unless you are reporting this tax directly on Form 1040 or Form 1040NR—see above). You may also have to complete this part to indicate that you qualify for an exception to the additional tax on early distributions or for certain Roth IRA distributions (see instructions).

1	Early distributions included in income. For Roth IRA distributions, see instructions	**1**	
2	Early distributions included on line 1 that are not subject to the additional tax (see instructions). Enter the appropriate exception number from the instructions: _____	**2**	
3	Amount subject to additional tax. Subtract line 2 from line 1	**3**	
4	**Additional tax.** Enter 10% (.10) of line 3. Include this amount on Form 1040, line 58, or Form 1040NR, line 54 . . . . **Caution:** *If any part of the amount on line 3 was a distribution from a SIMPLE IRA, you may have to include 25% of that amount on line 4 instead of 10% (see instructions).*	**4**	

Part II Additional Tax on Certain Distributions From Education Accounts

Complete this part if you included an amount in income, on Form 1040 or Form 1040NR, line 21, from a Coverdell education savings account (ESA) or a qualified tuition program (QTP).

5	Distributions included in income from Coverdell ESAs and QTPs	**5**	
6	Distributions included on line 5 that are not subject to the additional tax (see instructions) . . .	**6**	
7	Amount subject to additional tax. Subtract line 6 from line 5	**7**	
8	**Additional tax.** Enter 10% (.10) of line 7. Include this amount on Form 1040, line 58, or Form 1040NR, line 54	**8**	

Part III Additional Tax on Excess Contributions to Traditional IRAs

Complete this part if you contributed more to your traditional IRAs for 2009 than is allowable or you had an amount on line 17 of your 2008 Form 5329.

9	Enter your excess contributions from line 16 of your 2008 Form 5329 (see instructions). If zero, go to line 15		**9**	
10	If your traditional IRA contributions for 2009 are less than your maximum allowable contribution, see instructions. Otherwise, enter -0-	**10**		
11	2009 traditional IRA distributions included in income (see instructions) .	**11**		
12	2009 distributions of prior year excess contributions (see instructions) .	**12**		
13	Add lines 10, 11, and 12		**13**	
14	Prior year excess contributions. Subtract line 13 from line 9. If zero or less, enter -0-		**14**	
15	Excess contributions for 2009 (see instructions)		**15**	
16	Total excess contributions. Add lines 14 and 15		**16**	
17	**Additional tax.** Enter 6% (.06) of the **smaller** of line 16 **or** the value of your traditional IRAs on December 31, 2009 (including 2009 contributions made in 2010). Include this amount on Form 1040, line 58, or Form 1040NR, line 54 .		**17**	

Part IV Additional Tax on Excess Contributions to Roth IRAs

Complete this part if you contributed more to your Roth IRAs for 2009 than is allowable or you had an amount on line 25 of your 2008 Form 5329.

18	Enter your excess contributions from line 24 of your 2008 Form 5329 (see instructions). If zero, go to line 23		**18**	
19	If your Roth IRA contributions for 2009 are less than your maximum allowable contribution, see instructions. Otherwise, enter -0-	**19**		
20	2009 distributions from your Roth IRAs (see instructions)	**20**		
21	Add lines 19 and 20		**21**	
22	Prior year excess contributions. Subtract line 21 from line 18. If zero or less, enter -0-.		**22**	
23	Excess contributions for 2009 (see instructions)		**23**	
24	Total excess contributions. Add lines 22 and 23		**24**	
25	**Additional tax.** Enter 6% (.06) of the **smaller** of line 24 **or** the value of your Roth IRAs on December 31, 2009 (including 2009 contributions made in 2010). Include this amount on Form 1040, line 58, or Form 1040NR, line 54 .		**25**	

For Privacy Act and Paperwork Reduction Act Notice, see page 6 of the instructions.   Cat. No. 13329Q   Form **5329** (2009)

IRS Form 5329 For penalty and additional tax from Regular and Roth IRAs (page 1).

Form 5329 (2009)   Page **2**

Part V — Additional Tax on Excess Contributions to Coverdell ESAs

Complete this part if the contributions to your Coverdell ESAs for 2009 were more than is allowable or you had an amount on line 33 of your 2008 Form 5329.

26	Enter the excess contributions from line 32 of your 2008 Form 5329 (see instructions). If zero, go to line 31	**26**	
27	If the contributions to your Coverdell ESAs for 2009 were less than the maximum allowable contribution, see instructions. Otherwise, enter -0-	**27**	
28	2009 distributions from your Coverdell ESAs (see instructions)	**28**	
29	Add lines 27 and 28	**29**	
30	Prior year excess contributions. Subtract line 29 from line 26. If zero or less, enter -0-.	**30**	
31	Excess contributions for 2009 (see instructions)	**31**	
32	Total excess contributions. Add lines 30 and 31	**32**	
33	**Additional tax.** Enter 6% (.06) of the **smaller** of line 32 **or** the value of your Coverdell ESAs on December 31, 2009 (including 2009 contributions made in 2010). Include this amount on Form 1040, line 58, or Form 1040NR, line 54	**33**	

Part VI — Additional Tax on Excess Contributions to Archer MSAs

Complete this part if you or your employer contributed more to your Archer MSAs for 2009 than is allowable or you had an amount on line 41 of your 2008 Form 5329.

34	Enter the excess contributions from line 40 of your 2008 Form 5329 (see instructions). If zero, go to line 39	**34**	
35	If the contributions to your Archer MSAs for 2009 are less than the maximum allowable contribution, see instructions. Otherwise, enter -0-	**35**	
36	2009 distributions from your Archer MSAs from Form 8853, line 8	**36**	
37	Add lines 35 and 36	**37**	
38	Prior year excess contributions. Subtract line 37 from line 34. If zero or less, enter -0-.	**38**	
39	Excess contributions for 2009 (see instructions)	**39**	
40	Total excess contributions. Add lines 38 and 39	**40**	
41	**Additional tax.** Enter 6% (.06) of the **smaller** of line 40 **or** the value of your Archer MSAs on December 31, 2009 (including 2009 contributions made in 2010). Include this amount on Form 1040, line 58, or Form 1040NR, line 54	**41**	

Part VII — Additional Tax on Excess Contributions to Health Savings Accounts (HSAs)

Complete this part if you, someone on your behalf, or your employer contributed more to your HSAs for 2009 than is allowable or you had an amount on line 49 of your 2008 Form 5329.

42	Enter the excess contributions from line 48 of your 2008 Form 5329. If zero, go to line 47	**42**	
43	If the contributions to your HSAs for 2009 are less than the maximum allowable contribution, see instructions. Otherwise, enter -0-	**43**	
44	2009 distributions from your HSAs from Form 8889, line 16	**44**	
45	Add lines 43 and 44	**45**	
46	Prior year excess contributions. Subtract line 45 from line 42. If zero or less, enter -0-.	**46**	
47	Excess contributions for 2009 (see instructions)	**47**	
48	Total excess contributions. Add lines 46 and 47	**48**	
49	**Additional tax.** Enter 6% (.06) of the **smaller** of line 48 **or** the value of your HSAs on December 31, 2009 (including 2009 contributions made in 2010). Include this amount on Form 1040, line 58, or Form 1040NR, line 54	**49**	

Part VIII — Additional Tax on Excess Accumulation in Qualified Retirement Plans (Including IRAs)

Complete this part if you did not receive the minimum required distribution from your qualified retirement plan.

50	Minimum required distribution, if any, for 2009 (including the minimum required distribution for 2008 that is permitted to be made in 2009 for an individual with a required beginning date of April 1, 2009) (see instructions)	**50**	
51	Amount actually distributed to you in 2009 (plus any distributions actually made in 2008 that were permitted to be made in 2009 for an individual with a required beginning date of April 1, 2009) .	**51**	
52	Subtract line 51 from line 50. If zero or less, enter -0-	**52**	
53	**Additional tax.** Enter 50% (.50) of line 52. Include this amount on Form 1040, line 58, or Form 1040NR, line 54	**53**	

Sign Here Only If You Are Filing This Form by Itself and Not With Your Tax Return

Under penalties of perjury, I declare that I have examined this form, including accompanying attachments, and to the best of my knowledge and belief, it is true, correct, and complete. Declaration of preparer (other than taxpayer) is based on all information of which preparer has any knowledge.

▶ Your signature _____   ▶ Date _____

Paid Preparer's Use Only	Preparer's signature ▶		Date	Check if self-employed ☐	Preparer's SSN or PTIN
	Firm's name (or yours if self-employed), address, and ZIP code ▶			EIN	
				Phone no.	

Form **5329** (2009)

IRS Form 5329 For penalty and additional tax from Regular and Roth IRAs (page 2).

Form 1040—Line 32

Were You Covered by a Retirement Plan?

If you were covered by a retirement plan (qualified pension, profit-sharing (including 401(k)), annuity, SEP, SIMPLE, etc.) at work or through self-employment, your IRA deduction may be reduced or eliminated. But you can still make contributions to an IRA even if you cannot deduct them.

In any case, the income earned on your IRA contributions is not taxed until it is paid to you.

The "Retirement plan" box in box 13 of your Form W-2 should be checked if you were covered by a plan at work even if you were not vested in the plan. You are also covered by a plan if you were self-em-

ployed and had a SEP, SIMPLE, or qualified retirement plan.

If you were covered by a retirement plan and you file Form 2555, 2555-EZ, or 8815, or you exclude employer-provided adoption benefits, see Pub. 590 to figure the amount, if any, of your IRA deduction.

Married persons filing separately. If you were not covered by a retirement plan but

IRA Deduction Worksheet—Line 32

Keep for Your Records

⚠ **CAUTION**
If you were age 70½ or older at the end of 2009, you cannot deduct any contributions made to your traditional IRA or treat them as nondeductible contributions. Do not complete this worksheet for anyone age 70½ or older at the end of 2009. If you are married filing jointly and only one spouse was under age 70½ at the end of 2009, complete this worksheet only for that spouse.

Before you begin:
✓ Be sure you have read the list on page 31. You may not be eligible to use this worksheet.
✓ Figure any write-in adjustments to be entered on the dotted line next to line 36 (see the instructions for line 36 on page 35).
✓ If you are married filing separately and you lived apart from your spouse for all of 2009, enter "D" on the dotted line next to Form 1040, line 32. If you do not, you may get a math error notice from the IRS.

		Your IRA	Spouse's IRA
1a.	Were you covered by a retirement plan (see page 31)? .... **1a.** ☐ Yes ☐ No		
b.	If married filing jointly, was your spouse covered by a retirement plan? .... **1b.** ☐ Yes ☐ No		

Next. If you checked "No" on line 1a (and "No" on line 1b if married filing jointly), skip lines 2 through 6, enter the applicable amount below on line 7a (and line 7b if applicable), and go to line 8.
- $5,000, if under age 50 at the end of 2009.
- $6,000, if age 50 or older but under age 70½ at the end of 2009.
Otherwise, go to line 2.

2. Enter the amount shown below that applies to you.
- Single, head of household, or married filing separately and you **lived apart** from your spouse for all of 2009, enter $65,000
- Qualifying widow(er), enter $109,000
- Married filing jointly, enter $109,000 in both columns. But if you checked "No" on either line 1a or 1b, enter $176,000 for the person who was not covered by a plan
- Married filing separately and you lived with your spouse at any time in 2009, enter $10,000

2a. _____ **2b.** _____

3. Enter the amount from Form 1040, line 22 .... **3.** _____

4. Enter the total of the amounts from Form 1040, lines 23 through 31a, plus any write-in adjustments you entered on the dotted line next to line 36 .... **4.** _____

5. Subtract line 4 from line 3. If married filing jointly, enter the result in both columns   **5a.** _____ **5b.** _____

6. Is the amount on line 5 less than the amount on line 2?
☐ **No.** 🛑 None of your IRA contributions are deductible. For details on nondeductible IRA contributions, see Form 8606.
☐ **Yes.** Subtract line 5 from line 2 in each column. Follow the instruction below that applies to you.
- If single, head of household, or married filing separately, and the result is $10,000 or more, enter the applicable amount below on line 7 for that column and go to line 8.
  i. $5,000, if under age 50 at the end of 2009.
  ii. $6,000, if age 50 or older but under age 70½ at the end of 2009.
  Otherwise, go to line 7.
- If married filing jointly or qualifying widow(er), and the result is $20,000 or more ($10,000 or more in the column for the IRA of a person who was not covered by a retirement plan), enter the applicable amount below on line 7 for that column and go to line 8.
  i. $5,000, if under age 50 at the end of 2009.
  ii. $6,000, if age 50 or older but under age 70½ at the end of 2009.
  Otherwise, go to line 7.

6a. _____ **6b.** _____

Need more information or forms? See page 96.   - 32 -

Regular IRA Deduction Worksheet (page 1).

Form 1040—Line 32

IRA Deduction Worksheet—*Continued from page 32*

	Your IRA	Spouse's IRA
7. Multiply lines 6a and 6b by the percentage below that applies to you. If the result is not a multiple of $10, increase it to the next multiple of $10 (for example, increase $490.30 to $500). If the result is $200 or more, enter the result. But if it is less than $200, enter $200. • Single, head of household, or married filing separately, multiply by 50% (.50)(or by 60% (.60) in the column for the IRA of a person who is age 50 or older at the end of 2009) • Married filing jointly or qualifying widow(er), multiply by 25% (.25) (or by 30% (.30) in the column for the IRA of a person who is age 50 or older at the end of 2009). But if you checked "No" on either line 1a or 1b, then in the column for the IRA of the person who was not covered by a retirement plan, multiply by 50% (.50) (or by 60% (.60) if age 50 or older at the end of 2009) **7a.**		**7b.**

8. Enter the total of your (and your spouse's if filing jointly):
   • Wages, salaries, tips, etc. Generally, this is the amount reported in box 1 of Form W-2. See page 31 for exceptions
   • Alimony and separate maintenance payments reported on Form 1040, line 11
   • Nontaxable combat pay. This amount should be reported in box 12 of Form W-2 with code Q   **8.**

9. Enter the earned income you (and your spouse if filing jointly) received as a self-employed individual or a partner. Generally, this is your (and your spouse's if filing jointly) net earnings from self-employment if your personal services were a material income-producing factor, minus any deductions on Form 1040, lines 27 and 28. If zero or less, enter -0-. For more details, see Pub. 590 . . . .   **9.**

10. Add lines 8 and 9. . . . .   **10.**

> ⚠ **CAUTION**
> *If married filing jointly and line 10 is less than $10,000 ($11,000 if one spouse is age 50 or older at the end of 2009; $12,000 if both spouses are age 50 or older at the end of 2009), **stop here** and see Pub. 590 to figure your IRA deduction.*

11. Enter traditional IRA contributions made, or that will be made by April 15, 2010, for 2009 to your IRA on line 11a and to your spouse's IRA on line 11b . . . . **11a.** | | **11b.**

12. On line 12a, enter the **smallest** of line 7a, 10, or 11a. On line 12b, enter the **smallest** of line 7b, 10, or 11b. This is the most you can deduct. Add the amounts on lines 12a and 12b and enter the total on Form 1040, line 32. Or, if you want, you can deduct a smaller amount and treat the rest as a nondeductible contribution (see Form 8606) . . . . **12a.** | | **12b.**

your spouse was, you are considered covered by a plan unless you lived apart from your spouse for all of 2009.

TIP *You may be able to take the retirement savings contributions credit. See the instructions for line 50 that begin on page 40.*

Need more information or forms? See page 96.

Regular IRA Deduction Worksheet (page 2).

2009 Tax Computation Worksheet—Line 44

 See the instructions for line 44 that begin on page 37 to see if you must use the worksheet below to figure your tax.

Note. If you are required to use this worksheet to figure the tax on an amount from another form or worksheet, such as the Qualified Dividends and Capital Gain Tax Worksheet, the Schedule D Tax Worksheet, Schedule J, Form 8615, or the Foreign Earned Income Tax Worksheet, enter the amount from that form or worksheet in column (a) of the row that applies to the amount you are looking up. Enter the result on the appropriate line of the form or worksheet that you are completing.

Section A—Use if your filing status is **Single.** Complete the row below that applies to you.

Taxable income. If line 43 is—	(a) Enter the amount from line 43	(b) Multiplication amount	(c) Multiply (a) by (b)	(d) Subtraction amount	Tax. Subtract (d) from (c). Enter the result here and on Form 1040, line 44
At least $100,000 but not over $171,550	$	× 28% (.28)	$	$ 6,280.00	$
Over $171,550 but not over $372,950	$	× 33% (.33)	$	$ 14,857.50	$
Over $372,950	$	× 35% (.35)	$	$22,316.50	$

Section B—Use if your filing status is **Married filing jointly** or **Qualifying widow(er).** Complete the row below that applies to you.

Taxable income. If line 43 is—	(a) Enter the amount from line 43	(b) Multiplication amount	(c) Multiply (a) by (b)	(d) Subtraction amount	Tax. Subtract (d) from (c). Enter the result here and on Form 1040, line 44
At least $100,000 but not over $137,050	$	× 25% (.25)	$	$ 7,625.00	$
Over $137,050 but not over $208,850	$	× 28% (.28)	$	$ 11,736.50	$
Over $208,850 but not over $372,950	$	× 33% (.33)	$	$ 22,179.00	$
Over $372,950	$	× 35% (.35)	$	$ 29,638.00	$

Section C—Use if your filing status is **Married filing separately.** Complete the row below that applies to you.

Taxable income. If line 43 is—	(a) Enter the amount from line 43	(b) Multiplication amount	(c) Multiply (a) by (b)	(d) Subtraction amount	Tax. Subtract (d) from (c). Enter the result here and on Form 1040, line 44
At least $100,000 but not over $104,425	$	× 28% (.28)	$	$ 5,868.25	$
Over $104,425 but not over $186,475	$	× 33% (.33)	$	$ 11,089.50	$
Over $186,475	$	× 35% (.35)	$	$ 14,819.00	$

Section D—Use if your filing status is **Head of household.** Complete the row below that applies to you.

Taxable income. If line 43 is—	(a) Enter the amount from line 43	(b) Multiplication amount	(c) Multiply (a) by (b)	(d) Subtraction amount	Tax. Subtract (d) from (c). Enter the result here and on Form 1040, line 44
At least $100,000 but not over $117,450	$	× 25% (.25)	$	$ 5,147.50	$
Over $117,450 but not over $190,200	$	× 28% (.28)	$	$ 8,671.00	$
Over $190,200 but not over $372,950	$	× 33% (.33)	$	$ 18,181.00	$
Over $372,950	$	× 35% (.35)	$	$ 25,640.00	$

Need more information or forms? See page 96.

2009 Tax Computation Worksheet

Table I-2. **How Are a Traditional IRA and a Roth IRA Different?**
This table shows the differences between traditional and Roth IRAs. Answers in the middle column apply to traditional IRAs. Answers in the right column apply to Roth IRAs.

Question	Answer	
	Traditional IRA?	**Roth IRA?**
Is there an age limit on when I can set up and contribute to a	Yes. You must not have reached age 70½ by the end of the year. See *Who Can Set Up a Traditional IRA?* in chapter 1.	No. You can be any age. See *Can You Contribute to a Roth IRA?* in chapter 2.
If I earned more than $5,000 in 2008 ($6,000 if I was 50 or older by the end of 2008), is there a limit on how much I can contribute to a	Yes. For 2008, you can contribute to a traditional IRA up to: • $5,000, or • $6,000 if you were age 50 or older by the end of 2008. There is no upper limit on how much you can earn and still contribute. See *How Much Can Be Contributed?* in chapter 1.	Yes. For 2008, you may be able to contribute to a Roth IRA up to: • $5,000, or • $6,000 if you were age 50 or older by the end of 2008, but the amount you can contribute may be less than that depending on your income, filing status, and if you contribute to another IRA. See *How Much Can Be Contributed?* and Table 2-1 in chapter 2.
Can I deduct contributions to a	Yes. You may be able to deduct your contributions to a traditional IRA depending on your income, filing status, whether you are covered by a retirement plan at work, and whether you receive social security benefits. See *How Much Can You Deduct?* in chapter 1.	No. You can never deduct contributions to a Roth IRA. See *What Is a Roth IRA?* in chapter 2.
Do I have to file a form just because I contribute to a	Not unless you make nondeductible contributions to your traditional IRA. In that case, you must file Form 8606. See *Nondeductible Contributions* in chapter 1.	No. You do not have to file a form if you contribute to a Roth IRA. See *Contributions not reported* in chapter 2.
Do I have to start taking distributions when I reach a certain age from a	Yes. You must begin receiving required minimum distributions by April 1 of the year following the year you reach age 70½. See *When Must You Withdraw Assets? (Required Minimum Distributions)* in chapter 1.	No. If you are the original owner of a Roth IRA, you do not have to take distributions regardless of your age. See *Are Distributions Taxable?* in chapter 2. However, if you are the beneficiary of a Roth IRA, you may have to take distributions. See *Distributions After Owner's Death* in chapter 2.
How are distributions taxed from a	Distributions from a traditional IRA are taxed as ordinary income, but if you made nondeductible contributions, not all of the distribution is taxable. See *Are Distributions Taxable?* in chapter 1.	Distributions from a Roth IRA are not taxed as long as you meet certain criteria. See *Are Distributions Taxable?* in chapter 2.
Do I have to file a form just because I receive distributions from a	Not unless you have ever made a nondeductible contribution to a traditional IRA. If you have, file Form 8606.	Yes. File Form 8606 if you received distributions from a Roth IRA (other than a rollover, qualified charitable distribution, one-time distribution to fund an HSA, recharacterization, certain qualified distributions, or a return of certain contributions).

Note. You may be able to contribute up to $8,000 if you participated in a 401(k) plan and the employer who maintained the plan went into bankruptcy in an earlier year. For more information, see *Catch-up contributions in certain employer bankruptcies* in chapter 1 for traditional IRAs and in chapter 2 for Roth IRAs.

Difference in Regular and Roth IRAs

1. The plan you participate in is established for its employees by:

   a. The United States,

   b. A state or political subdivision of a state, or

   c. An instrumentality of either (a) or (b) above.

2. You did not serve more than 90 days on active duty during the year (not counting duty for training).

Volunteer firefighters. If the only reason you participate in a plan is because you are a volunteer firefighter, you may not be covered by the plan. You are not covered by the plan if both of the following conditions are met.

1. The plan you participate in is established for its employees by:

   a. The United States,

   b. A state or political subdivision of a state, or

   c. An instrumentality of either (a) or (b) above.

2. Your accrued retirement benefits at the beginning of the year will not provide more than $1,800 per year at retirement.

Limit if Covered by Employer Plan

As discussed earlier, the deduction you can take for contributions made to your traditional IRA depends on whether you or your spouse was covered for any part of the year by an employer retirement plan. Your deduction is also affected by how much income you had and by your filing status. Your deduction may also be affected by social security benefits you received.

Reduced or no deduction. If either you or your spouse was covered by an employer retirement plan, you may be entitled to only a partial (reduced) deduction or no deduction at all, depending on your income and your filing status.

Your deduction begins to decrease (phase out) when your income rises above a certain amount and is eliminated altogether when it reaches a higher amount. These amounts vary depending on your filing status.

To determine if your deduction is subject to the phaseout, you must determine your modified adjusted gross income (AGI) and your filing status, as explained later under *Deduction Phaseout*. Once you have determined your modified AGI and your filing status, you can use Table 1-2 or Table 1-3 to determine if the phaseout applies.

Social Security Recipients

Instead of using Table 1-2 or Table 1-3 and Worksheet 1-2, Figuring Your Reduced IRA Deduction for 2008, later, complete the worksheets in Appendix B of this publication if, for the year, all of the following apply.

- You received social security benefits.

- You received taxable compensation.

- Contributions were made to your traditional IRA.

- You or your spouse was covered by an employer retirement plan.

Use the worksheets in Appendix B to figure your IRA deduction, your nondeductible contribution, and the taxable portion, if any, of your social security benefits. Appendix B includes an example with filled-in worksheets to assist you.

Table 1-2. **Effect of Modified AGI[1] on Deduction if You Are Covered by a Retirement Plan at Work**

If you are covered by a retirement plan at work, use this table to determine if your modified AGI affects the amount of your deduction.

IF your filing status is ...	AND your modified adjusted gross income (modified AGI) is ...	THEN you can take ...
single or **head of household**	$53,000 or less	a full deduction.
	more than $53,000 but less than $63,000	a partial deduction.
	$63,000 or more	no deduction.
married filing jointly or **qualifying widow(er)**	$85,000 or less	a full deduction.
	more than $85,000 but less than $105,000	a partial deduction.
	$105,000 or more	no deduction.
married filing separately[2]	less than $10,000	a partial deduction.
	$10,000 or more	no deduction.

[1] Modified AGI (adjusted gross income). See *Modified adjusted gross income (AGI),* later.
[2] If you did not live with your spouse at any time during the year, your filing status is considered Single for this purpose (therefore, your IRA deduction is determined under the "Single" filing status).

Regular IRA Deductibility

Table 1-3. Effect of Modified AGI[1] on Deduction if You Are NOT Covered by a Retirement Plan at Work

If you are not covered by a retirement plan at work, use this table to determine if your modified AGI affects the amount of your deduction.

IF your filing status is ...	AND your modified adjusted gross income (modified AGI) is ...	THEN you can take ...
single, head of household, or qualifying widow(er)	any amount	a full deduction.
married filing jointly or separately with a spouse who *is not* covered by a plan at work	any amount	a full deduction.
married filing jointly with a spouse who *is* covered by a plan at work	$159,000 or less	a full deduction.
	more than $159,000 but less than $169,000	a partial deduction.
	$169,000 or more	no deduction.
married filing separately with a spouse who *is* covered by a plan at work[2]	less than $10,000	a partial deduction.
	$10,000 or more	no . deduction.

[1] Modified AGI (adjusted gross income). See *Modified adjusted gross income (AGI)*, later.
[2] You are entitled to the full deduction if you did not live with your spouse at any time during the year.

For 2009, if you are not covered by a retirement plan at work and you are married filing jointly with a spouse who is covered by a plan at work, your deduction is phased out if your modified AGI is more than $166,000 but less than $176,000. If your AGI is $176,000 or more, you cannot take a deduction for a contribution to a traditional IRA.

Deduction Phaseout

The amount of any reduction in the limit on your IRA deduction (phaseout) depends on whether you or your spouse was covered by an employer retirement plan.

Covered by a retirement plan. If you are covered by an employer retirement plan and you did not receive any social security retirement benefits, your IRA deduction

may be reduced or eliminated depending on your filing status and modified AGI, as shown in Table 1-2.

For 2009, if you are covered by a retirement plan at work, your IRA deduction will not be reduced (phased out) unless your modified AGI is:

- *More than $55,000 but less than $65,000 for a single individual (or head of household),*
- *More than $89,000 but less than $109,000 for a married couple filing a joint return (or a qualifying widow(er)), or*
- *Less than $10,000 for a married individual filing a separate return.*

If your spouse is covered. If you are not covered by an employer retirement plan, but your spouse is, and you did not receive any social security benefits, your IRA deduction may be reduced or eliminated entirely depending on your filing status and modified AGI as shown in Table 1-3.

Filing status. Your filing status depends primarily on your marital status. For this purpose, you need to know if your filing status is single or head of household, married filing jointly or qualifying widow(er), or married filing separately. If you need more information on filing status, see Publication 501, Exemptions, Standard Deduction, and Filing Information.

Lived apart from spouse. If you did not live with your spouse at any time during the year and you file a separate return, your filing status, for this purpose, is single.

Modified adjusted gross income (AGI). You can use Worksheet 1-1 to figure your modified AGI. If you made contributions to your IRA for 2008 and received a distribution from your IRA in 2008, see *Both contributions for 2008 and distributions in 2008*, later.

Do not assume that your modified AGI is the same as your compensation. Your modified AGI may include income in addition to your compensation such as interest, dividends, and income from IRA distributions.

Form 1040. If you file Form 1040, refigure the amount on the page 1 "adjusted gross income" line without taking into account any of the following amounts.

- IRA deduction.
- Student loan interest deduction.
- Tuition and fees deduction.
- Domestic production activities deduction.
- Foreign earned income exclusion.
- Foreign housing exclusion or deduction.
- Exclusion of qualified savings bond interest shown on Form 8815.
- Exclusion of employer-provided adoption benefits shown on Form 8839.

Regular IRA Deductibility

Worksheet 1-1. **Figuring Your Modified AGI**
Use this worksheet to figure your modified AGI for traditional IRA purposes.

1.	Enter your adjusted gross income (AGI) from Form 1040, line 38; Form 1040A, line 22; or Form 1040NR, line 36, figured without taking into account the amount from Form 1040, line 32; Form 1040A, line 17; or Form 1040NR, line 31	1. _____
2.	Enter any student loan interest deduction from Form 1040, line 33; Form 1040A, line 18; or Form 1040NR, line 32	2. _____
3.	Enter any tuition and fees deduction from Form 1040, line 34 or Form 1040A, line 19	3. _____
4.	Enter any domestic production activities deduction from Form 1040, line 35, or Form 1040NR, line 33	4. _____
5.	Enter any foreign earned income exclusion and/or housing exclusion from Form 2555, line 45, or Form 2555-EZ, line 18	5. _____
6.	Enter any foreign housing deduction from Form 2555, line 50	6. _____
7.	Enter any excludable savings bond interest from Form 8815, line 14	7. _____
8.	Enter any excluded employer-provided adoption benefits from Form 8839, line 30 . . .	8. _____
9.	Add lines 1 through 8. This is your **Modified AGI** for traditional IRA purposes	9. _____

This is your modified AGI.

Form 1040A. If you file Form 1040A, refigure the amount on the page 1 "adjusted gross income" line without taking into account any of the following amounts.

- IRA deduction.
- Student loan interest deduction.
- Tuition and fees deduction.
- Exclusion of qualified savings bond interest shown on Form 8815.

This is your modified AGI.

Form 1040NR. If you file Form 1040NR, refigure the amount on the page 1 "adjusted gross income" line without taking into account any of the following amounts.

- IRA deduction.
- Student loan interest deduction.
- Domestic production activities deduction.
- Exclusion of qualified savings bond interest shown on Form 8815.
- Exclusion of employer-provided adoption benefits shown on Form 8839.

This is your modified AGI.

Income from IRA distributions. If you received distributions in 2008 from one or more traditional IRAs and your traditional IRAs include only deductible contributions, the distributions are fully taxable and are included in your modified AGI.

Both contributions for 2008 and distributions in 2008. If all three of the following apply, any IRA distributions you received in 2008 may be partly tax free and partly taxable.

- You received distributions in 2008 from one or more traditional IRAs,
- You made contributions to a traditional IRA for 2008, and
- Some of those contributions may be nondeductible contributions. (See *Nondeductible Contributions* and Worksheet 1-2, later.)

If this is your situation, you must figure the taxable part of the traditional IRA distribution before you can figure your modified AGI. To do this, you can use Worksheet 1-5, Figuring the Taxable Part of Your IRA Distribution.

If at least one of the above does not apply, figure your modified AGI using Worksheet 1-1.

How To Figure Your Reduced IRA Deduction

If you or your spouse is covered by an employer retirement plan and you did not receive any social security benefits, you can figure your reduced IRA deduction by using Worksheet 1-2, Figuring Your Reduced IRA Deduction for 2008. The instructions for both Form 1040 and Form 1040A include similar worksheets that you can use instead of the worksheet in this publication. If you file Form 1040NR, use the worksheet in this publication.

If you or your spouse is covered by an employer retirement plan, and you received any social security benefits, see *Social Security Recipients*, earlier.

Regular IRA MAGI Worksheet

Worksheet 1-2. Figuring Your Reduced IRA Deduction for 2008

(Use only if you or your spouse is covered by an employer plan and your modified AGI falls between the two amounts shown below for your coverage situation and filing status.)

Note. If you were married and both you and your spouse contributed to IRAs, figure your deduction and your spouse's deduction separately.

Certain employer bankruptcies. See *Catch-up contributions in certain employer bankruptcies* earlier, for instructions to complete lines 4 and 6 of this worksheet.

IF you ...	AND your filing status is ...	AND your modified AGI is over ...	THEN enter on line 1 below ...
are **covered** by an employer plan	single or head of household	$53,000	$63,000
	married filing jointly or qualifying widow(er)	$85,000	$105,000
	married filing separately	$0	$10,000
are **not covered** by an employer plan, but your spouse is **covered**	married filing jointly	$159,000	$169,000
	married filing separately	$0	$10,000

1. Enter applicable amount from table above .... 1. _____

2. Enter your ***modified AGI*** (that of both spouses, if married filing jointly) .... 2. _____

   Note. If line 2 is equal to or more than the amount on line 1, **stop here.**
   Your IRA contributions are not deductible. See *Nondeductible Contributions.*

3. Subtract line 2 from line 1. **If line 3 is $10,000 or more ($20,000 or more if married filing jointly or qualifying widow(er) and you are covered by an employer plan), stop here.** You can take a full IRA deduction for contributions of up to $5,000 ($6,000 if you are age 50 or older) or 100% of your (and if married filing jointly, your spouse's) compensation, whichever is less ... 3. _____

4. Multiply line 3 by the percentage below that applies to you. If the result is not a multiple of $10, round it to the next highest multiple of $10. (For example, $611.40 is rounded to $620.) However, if the result is less than $200, enter $200.

   - Married filing jointly or qualifying widow(er) **and** you are covered by an employer plan, multiply line 3 by 25% (.25). (by 30% (.30) if you are age 50 or older).
   - All others, multiply line 3 by 50% (.50) (by 60% (.60) if you are age 50 or older).   } .... 4. _____

5. Enter your compensation minus any deductions on Form 1040, line 27 (one-half of self-employment tax) and line 28 (self-employed SEP, SIMPLE, and qualified plans); or on Form 1040NR, line 27 (self-employed SEP, SIMPLE, and qualified plans). If you are filing a joint return and your compensation is less than your spouse's, include your spouse's compensation reduced by his or her traditional IRA and Roth IRA contributions for this year. If you file Form 1040 or Form 1040NR, do not reduce your compensation by any losses from self-employment .... 5. _____

6. Enter contributions made, or to be made, to your IRA for 2008 but **do not** enter more than $5,000 ($6,000 if you are age 50 or older). If contributions are more than $5,000 ($6,000 if you are age 50 or older), see *Excess Contributions,* later.................................. 6. _____

7. **IRA deduction.** Compare lines 4, 5, and 6. Enter the smallest amount (or a smaller amount if you choose) here and on the Form 1040, 1040A, or 1040NR line for your IRA, whichever applies. If line 6 is more than line 7 and you want to make a nondeductible contribution, go to line 8 ..... 7. _____

8. **Nondeductible contribution.** Subtract line 7 from line 5 or 6, whichever is smaller. Enter the result here and on line 1 of your Form 8606 .... 8. _____

Reduced Regular IRA Deductibility

Worksheet 1-5. **Figuring the Taxable Part of Your IRA Distribution**
Use only if you made contributions to a traditional IRA for 2008 and have to figure the taxable part of your 2008 distributions to determine your modified AGI. See *Limit if Covered by Employer Plan.* Form 8606 and the related instructions will be needed when using this worksheet.
Note. When used in this worksheet, the term **outstanding rollover** refers to an amount distributed from a traditional IRA as part of a rollover that, as of December 31, 2008, had not yet been reinvested in another traditional IRA, but was still eligible to be rolled over tax free.

1. Enter the basis in your traditional IRAs as of December 31, 2007 .... **1.** _____

2. Enter the total of all contributions made to your traditional IRAs during 2008 and all contributions made during 2009 that were for 2008, **whether or not deductible**. Do not include rollover contributions properly rolled over into IRAs. Also, do not include certain returned contributions described in the instructions for line 7, Part I, of Form 8606. .... **2.** _____

3. Add lines 1 and 2 .... **3.** _____

4. Enter the value of all your traditional IRAs as of December 31, 2008 (include any outstanding rollovers from traditional IRAs to other traditional IRAs). Subtract any repayments of qualified disaster recovery assistance or recovery assistance distributions .... **4.** _____

5. Enter the total distributions from traditional IRAs (including amounts converted to Roth IRAs that will be shown on line 16 of Form 8606) received in 2008. (Do not include outstanding rollovers included on line 4 or any rollovers between traditional IRAs completed by December 31, 2008. Also, do not include certain returned contributions described in the instructions for line 7, Part I, of Form 8606.) Include any repayments of qualified disaster recovery assistance or recovery assistance distributions .... **5.** _____

6. Add lines 4 and 5 .... **6.** _____

7. Divide line 3 by line 6. Enter the result as a decimal (rounded to at least three places). If the result is 1.000 or more, enter 1.000 .... **7.** _____

8. **Nontaxable portion of the distribution.**
   Multiply line 5 by line 7. Enter the result here and on lines 13 and 17 of Form 8606 ... **8.** _____

9. **Taxable portion of the distribution (before adjustment for conversions).**
   Subtract line 8 from line 5. Enter the result here and if there are no amounts converted to Roth IRAs, **stop here** and enter the result on line 15a of Form 8606 .... **9.** _____

10. Enter the amount included on line 9 that is allocable to amounts converted to Roth IRAs by December 31, 2008. (See *Note* at the end of this worksheet.) Enter here and on line 18 of Form 8606 .... **10.** _____

11. **Taxable portion of the distribution (after adjustments for conversions).**
    Subtract line 10 from line 9. Enter the result here and on line 15a of Form 8606 ..... **11.** _____

Note. If the amount on line 5 of this worksheet includes an amount converted to a Roth IRA by December 31, 2008, you must determine the percentage of the distribution allocable to the conversion. To figure the percentage, divide the amount converted (from line 16 of Form 8606) by the total distributions shown on line 5. To figure the amounts to include on line 10 of this worksheet and on line 18, Part II of Form 8606, multiply line 9 of the worksheet by the percentage you figured.

 If code D, J, P, or S appears on your Form 1099-R, you are probably subject to a penalty or additional tax. If code D appears, see Excess Contributions, *later. If code J appears, see* Early Distributions, *later. If code P appears, see* Excess Contributions, *later. If code S appears, see* Additional Tax on Early Distributions *in chapter 3.*

Withholding. Federal income tax is withheld from distributions from traditional IRAs unless you choose not to have tax withheld.

The amount of tax withheld from an annuity or a similar periodic payment is based on your marital status and the number of withholding allowances you claim on your withholding certificate (Form W-4P). If you have not filed a certificate, tax will be withheld as if you are a married individual claiming three withholding allowances.

Generally, tax will be withheld at a 10% rate on nonperiodic distributions.

IRA distributions delivered outside the United States. In general, if you are a U.S. citizen or resident

Worksheet for Taxation of Regular IRAs Used for IRAs with some nondeductible contributions.

Can You Contribute to a Roth IRA?

Generally, you can contribute to a Roth IRA if you have taxable compensation (defined later) and your modified AGI (defined later) is less than:

- $169,000 for married filing jointly or qualifying widow(er),

- $116,000 for single, head of household, or married filing separately and you did not live with your spouse at any time during the year, and

- $10,000 for married filing separately and you lived with your spouse at any time during the year.

 You may be eligible to claim a credit for contributions to your Roth IRA. For more information, see chapter 5.

Is there an age limit for contributions? Contributions can be made to your Roth IRA regardless of your age.

Table 2-1. **Effect of Modified AGI on Roth IRA Contribution**
This table shows whether your contribution to a Roth IRA is affected by the amount of your modified adjusted gross income (modified AGI).

IF you have taxable compensation and your filing status is ...	AND your modified AGI is ...	THEN ...
married filing jointly or **qualifying widow(er)**	less than $159,000	you can contribute up to $5,000 ($6,000 if you are age 50 or older) as explained under *How Much Can Be Contributed.*
	at least $159,000 but less than $169,000	the amount you can contribute is reduced as explained under *Contribution limit reduced.*
	$169,000 or more	you cannot contribute to a Roth IRA.
married filing separately and you lived with your spouse at any time during the year	zero (-0-)	you can contribute up to $5,000 ($6,000 if you are age 50 or older) as explained under *How Much Can Be Contributed.*
	more than zero (-0-) but less than $10,000	the amount you can contribute is reduced as explained under *Contribution limit reduced.*
	$10,000 or more	you cannot contribute to a Roth IRA.
single, **head of household,** or **married filing separately** and you did not live with your spouse at any time during the year	less than $101,000	you can contribute up to $5,000 ($6,000 if you are age 50 or older) as explained under *How Much Can Be Contributed.*
	at least $101,000 but less than $116,000	the amount you can contribute is reduced as explained under *Contribution limit reduced.*
	$116,000 or more	you cannot contribute to a Roth IRA.

Note. You may be able to contribute up to $8,000 if you participated in a 401(k) plan maintained by an employer who went into bankruptcy in an earlier year. See *Catch-up contributions in certain employer bankruptcies,* later.

For 2009, the amounts in Table 2-1 increase. For 2009, your Roth IRA contribution limit is reduced (phased out) in the following situations.

- Your filing status is married filing jointly or qualifying widow(er) and your modified AGI is at least $166,000. You cannot make a Roth IRA contribution if your modified AGI is $176,000 or more.
- Your filing status is married filing separately, you lived with your spouse at any time during the year, and your modified AGI is more than -0-. You cannot make a Roth IRA contribution if your modified AGI is $10,000 or more.
- Your filing status is different than either of those described above and your modified AGI is at least $105,000. You cannot make a Roth IRA contribution if your modified AGI is $120,000 or more.

Roth IRA Contribution Eligibility

- The employer (or any other person) must have been subject to indictment or conviction based on business transactions related to the bankruptcy.

 If you choose to make these catch-up contributions, the higher contribution limits for individuals who are age 50 or older do not apply. The most that can be contributed to your Roth IRA is the smaller of $8,000 or your taxable compensation for the year.

Repayment of reservist, hurricane, disaster recovery assistance, and recovery assistance distributions. You can repay qualified reservist, qualified hurricane, qualified disaster recovery assistance, and qualified recovery assistance distributions even if the repayments would cause your total contributions to the Roth IRA to be more than the general limit on contributions. However, the total repayments cannot be more than the amount of your distribution.

Worksheet 2-1. Modified Adjusted Gross Income for Roth IRA Purposes
Use this worksheet to figure your modified adjusted gross income for Roth IRA purposes.

1. Enter your adjusted gross income from Form 1040, line 38; Form 1040A, line 22; or Form 1040NR, line 36	**1.** _____
2. Enter any income resulting from the conversion of an IRA (other than a Roth IRA) to a Roth IRA, a rollover from a qualified retirement plan to a Roth IRA, and a minimum required distribution from an IRA (for conversions and rollovers from qualified retirement plans only)	**2.** _____
3. Subtract line 2 from line 1	**3.** _____
4. Enter any traditional IRA deduction from Form 1040, line 32; Form 1040A, line 17; or Form 1040NR, line 31	**4.** _____
5. Enter any student loan interest deduction from Form 1040, line 33; Form 1040A, line 18; or Form 1040NR, line 32	**5.** _____
6. Enter any tuition and fees deduction from Form 1040, line 34 or Form 1040A, line 19 ..	**6.** _____
7. Enter any domestic production activities deduction from Form 1040, line 35, or Form 1040NR, line 33	**7.** _____
8. Enter any foreign earned income exclusion and/or housing exclusion from Form 2555, line 45, or Form 2555-EZ, line 18	**8.** _____
9. Enter any foreign housing deduction from Form 2555, line 50	**9.** _____
10. Enter any excludable qualified savings bond interest from Form 8815, line 14	**10.** _____
11. Enter any excluded employer-provided adoption benefits from Form 8839, line 30	**11.** _____
12. Add the amounts on lines 3 through 11	**12.** _____
13. Enter: • $169,000 if married filing jointly or qualifying widow(er), • $10,000 if married filing separately and you lived with your spouse at any time during the year, or • $116,000 for all others	**13.** _____

Is the amount on line 12 more than the amount on line 13?
If yes, see the note below.
If no, the amount on line 12 is your ***modified adjusted gross income*** for Roth IRA purposes.

Note. If the amount on line 12 is more than the amount on line 13 and you have other income or loss items, such as social security income or passive activity losses, that are subject to AGI-based phaseouts, you can refigure your AGI solely for the purpose of figuring your modified AGI for Roth IRA purposes. When figuring your modified AGI for conversion purposes, refigure your AGI without taking into account any income from conversions or minimum required distributions from IRAs. (If you receive social security benefits, use *Worksheet 1* in *Appendix B* to refigure your AGI.) Then go to list item 2 under *Modified AGI* earlier or line 3 above in *Worksheet 2-1* to refigure your modified AGI. If you do not have other income or loss items subject to AGI-based phaseouts, your modified adjusted gross income for Roth IRA purposes is the amount on line 12 above.

Roth MAGI Contribution Worksheet

Note. If you make repayments of qualified reservist distributions to a Roth IRA, increase your basis in the Roth IRA by the amount of the repayment. If you make repayments of qualified hurricane, qualified disaster recovery assistance, or qualified recovery assistance distributions to a Roth IRA, the repayment is first considered to be a repayment of earnings. Any repayments of qualified hurricane, qualified disaster recovery assistance, or qualified recovery assistance distributions in excess of earnings will increase your basis in the Roth IRA by the amount of the repayment in excess of earnings. For more information, see *Qualified reservist repayments* under *How Much Can Be Contributed?* in chapter 1 and chapter 4, *Disaster-Related Relief.*

Contribution limit reduced. If your modified AGI is above a certain amount, your contribution limit is gradually reduced. Use Table 2-1 to determine if this reduction applies to you.

Figuring the reduction. If the amount you can contribute must be reduced, figure your reduced contribution limit as follows.

1. Start with your modified AGI.

2. Subtract from the amount in (1):

   a. $159,000 if filing a joint return or qualifying widow(er),

   b. $-0- if married filing a separate return, and you lived with your spouse at any time during the year, or

   c. $101,000 for all other individuals.

3. Divide the result in (2) by $15,000 ($10,000 if filing a joint return, qualifying widow(er), or married filing a separate return and you lived with your spouse at any time during the year).

4. Multiply the maximum contribution limit (before reduction by this adjustment and before reduction for any contributions to traditional IRAs) by the result in (3).

5. Subtract the result in (4) from the maximum contribution limit before this reduction. The result is your reduced contribution limit.

You can use Worksheet 2-2 to figure the reduction.

Worksheet 2-2. **Determining Your Reduced Roth IRA Contribution Limit**

Before using this worksheet, check Table 2-1 *to determine whether or not your Roth IRA contribution limit is reduced. If it is, use this worksheet to determine how much it is reduced.*

1. Enter your modified AGI for Roth IRA purposes	1. _____
2. Enter: • $159,000 if filing a joint return or qualifying widow(er), • $-0- if married filing a separate return and you lived with your spouse at any time in 2008, or • $101,000 for all others	2. _____
3. Subtract line 2 from line 1	3. _____
4. Enter: • $10,000 if filing a joint return or qualifying widow(er) or married filing a separate return and you lived with your spouse at any time during the year, or • $15,000 for all others	4. _____
5. Divide line 3 by line 4 and enter the result as a decimal (rounded to at least three places). If the result is 1.000 or more, enter 1.000	5. _____
6. Enter the lesser of: • $5,000 ($6,000 if you are age 50 or older, or $8,000 for certain employer bankruptcies), or • Your taxable compensation . . .	6. _____
7. Multiply line 5 by line 6	7. _____
8. Subtract line 7 from line 6. Round the result up to the nearest $10. If the result is less than $200, enter $200	8. _____
9. Enter contributions for the year to other IRAs	9. _____
10. Subtract line 9 from line 6	10. _____
11. Enter the lesser of line 8 or line 10. This is your **reduced Roth IRA contribution limit**	11. _____

Round your reduced contribution limit up to the nearest $10. If your reduced contribution limit is more than $0, but less than $200, increase the limit to $200.

Example. You are a 45-year-old, single individual with taxable compensation of $113,000. You want to make the maximum allowable contribution to your Roth IRA for 2008. Your modified AGI for 2008 is $102,000. You have not

Roth IRA Reduced Contribution Worksheet

Figure 2-1. **Is the Distribution From Your Roth IRA a Qualified Distribution?**

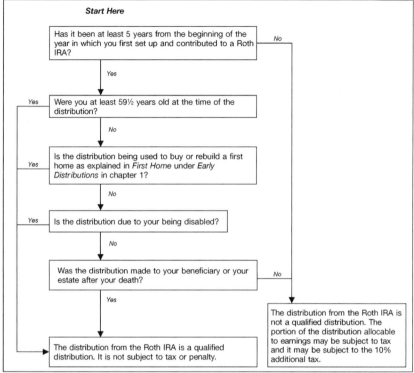

- The distribution is a qualified reservist distribution.
- The distribution is a qualified disaster recovery assistance distribution.
- The distribution is a qualified recovery assistance distribution.

Most of these exceptions are discussed earlier in chapter 1 under *Early Distributions*.

Roth Distribution Qualification Flowchart

How Do You Figure the Taxable Part?

To figure the taxable part of a distribution that is not a qualified distribution, complete Worksheet 2-3.

Worksheet 2-3. **Figuring the Taxable Part of a Distribution (Other Than a Qualified Distribution) From a Roth IRA**

1. Enter the total of all distributions made from your Roth IRA(s) (other than qualified charitable distributions or a one-time distribution to fund an HSA) during the year . . . .   1. _____

2. Enter the amount of qualified distributions made during the year   2. _____

3. Subtract line 2 from line 1 . . . . . .   3. _____

4. Enter the amount of distributions made during the year to correct excess contributions made during the year. (Do not include earnings.)   4. _____

5. Subtract line 4 from line 3 . . . . . .   5. _____

6. Enter the amount of distributions made during the year that were contributed to another Roth IRA in a qualified rollover contribution (other than a repayment of a qualified disaster recovery assistance or recovery assistance distribution) . . . .   6. _____

7. Subtract line 6 from line 5 . . . . . .   7. _____

8. Enter the amount of *all* prior distributions from your Roth IRA(s) (other than qualified charitable distributions or a one-time distribution to fund an HSA) whether or not they were qualified distributions . . . .   8. _____

9. Add lines 3 and 8 . . . .   9. _____

10. Enter the amount of the distributions included on line 8 that were previously includible in your income . . . .   10. _____

11. Subtract line 10 from line 9 . . . . .   11. _____

12. Enter the total of all your contributions to all of your Roth IRAs . . . .   12. _____

13. Enter the total of all distributions made (this year and in prior years) to correct excess contributions. (Include earnings.) . . . .   13. _____

14. Subtract line 13 from line 12. (If the result is less than 0, enter 0.) . . . .   14. _____

15. Subtract line 14 from line 11. (If the result is less than 0, enter 0.) . . . .   15. _____

16. Enter the smaller of the amount on line 7 or the amount on line 15. This is the **taxable part of your distribution** . . . .   16. _____

Must You Withdraw or Use Assets?

You are not required to take distributions from your Roth IRA at any age. The minimum distribution rules that apply to traditional IRAs do not apply to Roth IRAs while the owner is alive. However, after the death of a Roth IRA owner, certain of the minimum distribution rules that apply to traditional IRAs also apply to Roth IRAs as explained later under *Distributions After Owner's Death*.

Minimum distributions. You cannot use your Roth IRA to satisfy minimum distribution requirements for your traditional IRA. Nor can you use distributions from traditional IRAs for required distributions from Roth IRAs. See *Distributions to beneficiaries*, later.

Recognizing Losses on Investments

If you have a loss on your Roth IRA investment, you can recognize the loss on your income tax return, but only when all the amounts in all of your Roth IRA accounts have been distributed to you and the total distributions are less than your unrecovered basis.

Your basis is the total amount of contributions in your Roth IRAs.

You claim the loss as a miscellaneous itemized deduction, subject to the 2%-of-adjusted-gross-income limit that applies to certain miscellaneous itemized deductions on Schedule A, Form 1040. Any such losses are added back to taxable income for purposes of calculating the alternative minimum tax.

Distributions After Owner's Death

If a Roth IRA owner dies, the minimum distribution rules that apply to traditional IRAs apply to Roth IRAs as though the Roth IRA owner died before his or her required beginning date. See *When Can You Withdraw or Use Assets?* in chapter 1.

Distributions to beneficiaries. Generally, the entire interest in the Roth IRA must be distributed by the end of the fifth calendar year after the year of the owner's death unless the interest is payable to a designated beneficiary over the life or life expectancy of the designated beneficiary. (See *When Must You Withdraw Assets? (Required Minimum Distributions)* in chapter 1.) If you are a beneficiary receiving distributions over a 5-year period, you can waive the distribution for 2009, effectively taking distributions over a 6-year rather than a 5-year period.

Taxable Worksheet for Premature Roth IRA Withdrawals

Appendix A. Summary Record of Traditional IRA(s) for 2008

Keep for Your Records

Name _____

I was ☐ covered ☐ not covered by my employer's retirement plan during the year.

I became 59½ on _____ (month) (day) (year)

I became 70½ on _____ (month) (day) (year)

Contributions

Name of traditional IRA	Date	Amount contributed for 2008	Check if rollover contribution	Fair Market Value of IRA as of December 31, 2008, from Form 5498
1.				
2.				
3.				
4.				
5.				
6.				
7.				
8.				
Total				

Total contributions deducted on tax return . . . . $ _____

Total contributions treated as nondeductible on Form 8606 . . . . $ _____

Distributions

Name of traditional IRA	Date	Amount of Distribution	Reason (for example, retirement, rollover, conversion, withdrawal of excess contributions)	Income earned on IRA	Taxable amount reported on income tax return	Nontaxable amount from Form 8606, line 13
1.						
2.						
3.						
4.						
5.						
6.						
7.						
8.						
Total						

Basis of all traditional IRAs for 2008 and earlier years (from Form 8606, line 14) . . . . $ _____

Note. *You should keep copies of your income tax return, and Forms W-2, 8606, and 5498.*

Publication 590 (2008)

Record of IRA Distributions

Appendix A. (Continued) Worksheet for Determining Required Minimum Distributions

Keep for Your Records

1. Age	70½	71½	72½	73½	74½
2. Year age was reached					
3. Value of IRA at the close of business on December 31 of the year immediately prior to the year on line 2[1]					
4. Distribution period from Table III or life expectancy from Life Expectancy Table I or Table II[2]					
5. Required distribution (divide line 3 by line 4)[3]					

1. Age	75½	76½	77½	78½	79½
2. Year age was reached					
3. Value of IRA at the close of business on December 31 of the year immediately prior to the year on line 2[1]					
4. Distribution period from Table III or life expectancy from Life Expectancy Table I or Table II[2]					
5. Required distribution (divide line 3 by line 4)[3]					

1. Age	80½	81½	82½	83½	84½
2. Year age was reached					
3. Value of IRA at the close of business on December 31 of the year immediately prior to the year on line 2[1]					
4. Distribution period from Table III or life expectancy from Life Expectancy Table I or Table II[2]					
5. Required distribution (divide line 3 by line 4)[3]					

1. Age	85½	86½	87½	88½	89½
2. Year age was reached					
3. Value of IRA at the close of business on December 31 of the year immediately prior to the year on line 2[1]					
4. Distribution period from Table III or life expectancy from Life Expectancy Table I or Table II[2]					
5. Required distribution (divide line 3 by line 4)[3]					

[1]If you have more than one IRA, you must figure the required distribution separately for each IRA.
[2]Use the appropriate life expectancy or distribution period for each year and for each IRA.
[3]If you have more than one IRA, you must withdraw an amount equal to the total of the required distributions figured for each IRA. You can, however, withdraw the total from one IRA or from more than one IRA.
Note. For 2009, you are not required to take a minimum distribution.

Worksheet for Regular IRA Required Distributions

Appendix B. Worksheets for Social Security Recipients Who Contribute to a Traditional IRA

If you receive social security benefits, have taxable compensation, contribute to your traditional IRA, and you or your spouse is covered by an employer retirement plan, complete the following worksheets. (See *Are You Covered by an Employer Plan?* in chapter 1.)

Use Worksheet 1 to figure your modified adjusted gross income. This amount is needed in the computation of your IRA deduction, if any, which is figured using Worksheet 2.

The IRA deduction figured using Worksheet 2 is entered on your tax return.

Worksheet 1
Computation of Modified AGI
(For use only by taxpayers who receive social security benefits)

Filing Status — Check only one box:
☐ **A.** Married filing jointly
☐ **B.** Single, Head of Household, Qualifying Widow(er), or Married filing separately and *lived apart* from your spouse during the *entire year*
☐ **C.** Married filing separately and *lived with* your spouse at *any time* during the year

1. Adjusted gross income (AGI) from Form 1040 or Form 1040A (not taking into account any social security benefits from Form SSA-1099 or RRB-1099, any deduction for contributions to a traditional IRA, any student loan interest deduction, any tuition and fees deduction, any domestic production activities deduction, or any exclusion of interest from savings bonds to be reported on Form 8815) . . . . 1. _____

2. Enter the amount in box 5 of all Forms SSA-1099 and Forms RRB-1099 . . . . 2. _____

3. Enter one-half of line 2 . . . . 3. _____

4. Enter the amount of any foreign earned income exclusion, foreign housing exclusion, U.S. possessions income exclusion, exclusion of income from Puerto Rico you claimed as a bona fide resident of Puerto Rico, or exclusion of employer-provided adoption benefits . . . . 4. _____

5. Enter the amount of any tax-exempt interest reported on line 8b of Form 1040 or 1040A 5. _____

6. Add lines 1, 3, 4, and 5 . . . . 6. _____

7. Enter the amount listed below for your filing status.
   - **$32,000** if you checked box **A** above.
   - **$25,000** if you checked box **B** above.
   - **$0** if you checked box **C** above. . . . . 7. _____

8. Subtract line 7 from line 6. If zero or less, enter 0 on this line . . . . 8. _____

9. If line 8 is zero, **stop here**. None of your social security benefits are taxable.
   If line 8 is more than 0, enter the amount listed below for your filing status.
   - **$12,000** if you checked box **A** above.
   - **$9,000** if you checked box **B** above.
   - **$0** if you checked box **C** above. . . . . 9. _____

10. Subtract line 9 from line 8. If zero or less, enter 0 . . . . 10. _____

11. Enter the smaller of line 8 or line 9 . . . . 11. _____

12. Enter one-half of line 11 . . . . 12. _____

13. Enter the smaller of line 3 or line 12 . . . . 13. _____

14. Multiply line 10 by .85. If line 10 is zero, enter 0 . . . . 14. _____

15. Add lines 13 and 14 . . . . 15. _____

16. Multiply line 2 by .85 . . . . 16. _____

17. **Taxable benefits** to be included in modified AGI for traditional IRA deduction purposes. Enter the smaller of line 15 or line 16 . . . . 17. _____

18. Enter the amount of any employer-provided adoption benefits exclusion and any foreign earned income exclusion and foreign housing exclusion or deduction that you claimed . . 18. _____

19. **Modified AGI** for determining your reduced traditional IRA deduction — add lines 1, 17, and 18. Enter here and on line 2 of Worksheet 2, next . . . . 19. _____

Worksheet for Social Security Recipients Contributing to Regular IRAs (page 1).

Appendix B. (Continued)

Worksheet 2
Computation of Traditional IRA Deduction For 2008
(For use only by taxpayers who receive social security benefits)

IF your filing status is ...	AND your modified AGI is over ...	THEN enter on line 1 below ...
married filing jointly or qualifying widow(er)	$85,000*	$105,000
married filing jointly (you are not covered by an employer plan but your spouse is)	$159,000*	$169,000
single, or head of household	$53,000*	$63,000
married filing separately**	$0*	$10,000

*If your modified AGI is **not** over this amount, you can take an IRA deduction for your contributions of up to the lesser of $5,000 ($6,000 if you are age 50 or older or $8,000 for certain employer bankruptcies) or your taxable compensation. Skip this worksheet, proceed to Worksheet 3, and enter your IRA deduction on line 2 of Worksheet 3.
If you did **not live with your spouse **at any time** during the year, consider your filing status as single.
Note. If you were married and you or your spouse worked and you both contributed to IRAs, figure the deduction for each of you separately.
Certain employer bankruptcies. See *Catch-up contributions in certain employer bankruptcies* in chapter 1 for instructions to complete lines 4 and 6 of this worksheet.

1. Enter the applicable amount from above . . . . 1. _____
2. Enter your **modified AGI** from Worksheet 1, line 19 . . . . 2. _____
   Note. If line 2 is equal to or more than the amount on line 1, **stop here;** your traditional IRA contributions are not deductible. Proceed to Worksheet 3.
3. Subtract line 2 from line 1 . . . . 3. _____
4. Multiply line 3 by the percentage below that applies to you. If the result is not a multiple of $10, round it to the next highest multiple of $10. (For example, $611.40 is rounded to $620.) However, if the result is less than $200, enter $200.
   - Married filing jointly or qualifying widow(er) **and** you are covered by an employer plan, multiply line 3 by 25% (.25) (by 30% (.30) if you are age 50 or older). . . . . 4. _____
   - All others, multiply line 3 by 50% (.50) (by 60% (.60) if you are age 50 or older).
5. Enter your compensation minus any deductions on Form 1040, line 27 (one-half of self-employment tax) and line 28 (self-employed SEP, SIMPLE, and qualified plans). If you are the lower-income spouse, include your spouse's compensation reduced by his or her traditional IRA and Roth IRA contributions for this year . . . . 5. _____
6. Enter contributions you made, or plan to make, to your traditional IRA for 2008, but do not enter more than $5,000 ($6,000 if you are age 50 or older) . . . . 6. _____
7. **Deduction.** Compare lines 4, 5, and 6. Enter the smallest amount here (or a smaller amount if you choose). Enter this amount on the Form 1040 or 1040A line for your IRA. (If the amount on line 6 is more than the amount on line 7, complete line 8.) . . . 7. _____
8. **Nondeductible contributions.** Subtract line 7 from line 5 or 6, whichever is smaller. Enter the result here and on line 1 of your Form 8606, *Nondeductible IRAs.* . . . . 8. _____

Worksheet for Social Security Recipients Contributing to Regular IRAs (page 2).

Appendix B. (Continued)

Worksheet 3
Computation of Taxable Social Security Benefits
(For use by taxpayers who receive social security benefits and take a traditional IRA deduction)

Filing Status — Check only one box:

☐ **A.** Married filing jointly

☐ **B.** Single, Head of Household, Qualifying Widow(er), or Married filing separately and *lived apart* from your spouse during the *entire year*

☐ **C.** Married filing separately and *lived with* your spouse at *any time* during the year

1. Adjusted gross income (AGI) from Form 1040 or Form 1040A (not taking into account any IRA deduction, any student loan interest deduction, any tuition and fees deduction, any domestic production activities deduction, any social security benefits from Form SSA-1099 or RRB-1099, or any exclusion of interest from savings bonds to be reported on Form 8815) . . . . **1.** _____
2. Deduction(s) from line 7 of Worksheet(s) 2 . . . . **2.** _____
3. Subtract line 2 from line 1 . . . . **3.** _____
4. Enter amount in box 5 of all Forms SSA-1099 and Forms RRB-1099 . . . . **4.** _____
5. Enter one-half of line 4 . . . . **5.** _____
6. Enter the amount of any foreign earned income exclusion, foreign housing exclusion, exclusion of income from U.S. possessions, exclusion of income from Puerto Rico you claimed as a bona fide resident of Puerto Rico, or exclusion of employer-provided adoption benefits . . . . **6.** _____
7. Enter the amount of any tax-exempt interest reported on line 8b of Form 1040 or 1040A . . . . **7.** _____
8. Add lines 3, 5, 6, and 7 . . . . **8.** _____
9. Enter the amount listed below for your filing status.
    - **$32,000** if you checked box **A** above.
    - **$25,000** if you checked box **B** above.
    - **$0** if you checked box **C** above. . . . . **9.** _____
10. Subtract line 9 from line 8. If zero or less, enter 0 on this line. . . . . **10.** _____
11. If line 10 is zero, **stop here**. None of your social security benefits are taxable. If line 10 is more than 0, enter the amount listed below for your filing status.
    - **$12,000** if you checked box **A** above.
    - **$9,000** if you checked box **B** above.
    - **$0** if you checked box **C** above. . . . . **11.** _____
12. Subtract line 11 from line 10. If zero or less, enter 0 . . . . **12.** _____
13. Enter the smaller of line 10 or line 11 . . . . **13.** _____
14. Enter one-half of line 13 . . . . **14.** _____
15. Enter the smaller of line 5 or line 14 . . . . **15.** _____
16. Multiply line 12 by .85. If line 12 is zero, enter 0 . . . . **16.** _____
17. Add lines 15 and 16 . . . . **17.** _____
18. Multiply line 4 by .85 . . . . **18.** _____
19. **Taxable social security benefits.** Enter the smaller of line 17 or line 18 . . . . **19.** _____

Worksheet for Social Security Recipients Contributing to Regular IRAs (page 3).

TEN IRA
COMMANDMENTS

1. Thou shalt divide up thy IRA (and other retirement accounts) and convert them all to separate Roth IRAs on January 4, 2010 at 9:57AM. Leave the favored Roth IRAs converted and unconvert selected less favorable Roths before the deadline and repeat every year.

2. Thou shalt pay income tax with outside funds.

3. Thou shalt always maximize retirement plans to the matching point.

4. Thou shalt maximize non-deductible IRAs then convert immediately to a Roth IRA every year.

5. If not in the maximum income tax brackets thou shalt convert some IRAs every year enjoying the lower tax brackets.

6. If money needed, spend from everything else first. Roth last.

7. Use a special IRA inheritance trust as the beneficiary of the Roth IRA.

8. Thou shalt not die with regular IRA but with Roth IRA.

9. Thou shalt not ever commingle IRAs that came from retirement plans with contributory IRAs.

10. Thou shalt not incur penalties.

GLOSSARY

Adjusted Gross Income (AGI) An amount used in the calculation of an individual's income tax liability. AGI is calculated on the IRS Form 1040 by taking gross income and subtracting certain deductions. AGI is the last number on page 1 of the IRS Form 1040 and repeated on the top of page 2 of the same form.

Age Requirements Age 70½ is the starting point for mandatory distributions from regular IRAs and certain retirement plans. Age 59½ is the minimum age you can take distributions from regular IRAs without a penalty unless you qualify for an exception.

Aggregation Considered as a whole or in aggregate. When money is withdrawn from regular IRAs or Roth IRAs it does not matter what specific account it is taken from because the IRS has aggregation rules that defines the character of the money removed. This rule also applies to mandatory IRA distributions meaning the distribution can be taken out of any one IRA to satisfy the minimum for all of them. Aggregation is Yoga like ... it is as if they are one.

Annuity An investment vehicle sold by an insurance company that offers deferral of income tax on the earnings until money is withdrawn. Annuities can have underlying investment choices that are similar to CDs (fixed) or mutual funds (variable). An annuity may offer income from the inception (immediate), or the income may be delayed or deferred.

Asset Allocation Picking and combining asset classes to diversify your investments among a broad spectrum of choices to manage risk and increase overall long-term results.

Asset Class A group of investments or securities that have similar attributes and behave in a similar way in the marketplace. Stocks and CDs are two different asset classes. You can narrow down asset classes like stocks to one specific type and size of business with the idea that the asset class holding will rise and fall in a similar way.

Basis or **Cost Basis** The nondeductible or after-tax amount put into a regular IRA or Roth IRA. The excess balance over the cost basis is the gain or income.

Beneficiary A beneficiary or primary beneficiary is the person or entity to inherit a certain asset like an IRA at the holder's death. The beneficiary is named with the IRA paperwork and supersedes whatever the will or living trust says.

Bubble Brackets A bubble bracket is an income tax bracket that taxes some income above a certain amount at a higher than normal rate serving to eliminate the lower tax brackets.

Catch Up Provision The increased annual contribution limit for regular or Roth IRAs for those age 50 or older. For 2010, the maximum IRA contribution limit is $6,000 for those age 50 and over, but only $5,000 for others. The only requirement for this provision is age.

Compensation Payment received for work done.

Contributions Annual deposits that may be made to regular and Roth IRAs and retirement plans subject to certain limits. Contributions are different from rollovers or conversions.

Contingent Beneficiary A contingent beneficiary is the backup or next in line to receive an inheritance if the primary beneficiary is not alive or disclaims the inheritance.

Earned Income Wages, commissions, tips, salaries, and self-employed income. You must have this to contribute to an IRA.

Efficient Frontier The concept of investment returns having a direct relationship to risk. The less risk of loss that an investment has, the lower the return, and conversely the greater the risk the potential for greater returns. The efficient frontier also measures and ranks investments by their risk versus reward attributes.

First In, First Out (FIFO) A method for establishing the order of assets removed from a certain investment or account for potential penalties or taxation. This method of calculation is usually favorable because the basis, or original conversion amount, is considered to be withdrawn first. After the basis is withdrawn, the balance is considered to be from earnings. Roth IRAs use the FIFO method.

Inherited IRA An IRA received by the IRA's beneficiary after the death of the IRA holder. Inherited IRAs remain in the name of the original owner; however, if the beneficiary is a spouse, the spouse can rename the inherited IRA as his or her own.

IRA Custodian or **Trustee** The administrator of an IRA account. Every IRA or retirement plan must have a custodian or trustee. Often the bank, investment company, or insurance company providing the IRA investments also serves as the custodian. The custodian is responsible for sending out the required statements and notices to the participant and the IRS.

IRA Inheritance Trust A specialized trust created to be the beneficiary of IRA and retirement accounts. If properly implemented, it can add flexibility and protection for the beneficiaries for a long time after the IRA holder's death.

IRC 72(t) The specific Internal Revenue Code reference to one of the penalty exceptions for pre-59½ IRA distributions. Also known as "substantially equal periodic payments for life," this exception is a form of annuitization where equal distributions are taken from the IRA every year. To use this exception, you must continue the exact same annual distribution for at least five years and also be age 59½ or older before stopping. The annual payments are based on life expectancy tables.

Last In, First Out (LIFO) A method for establishing the order of assets removed from a certain investment or account for potential penalties or taxation. This method considers the earnings or income to be withdrawn first and the basis to be withdrawn last.

Modified Adjusted Gross Income (MAGI) A measurement used by the IRS to determine if a person qualifies to use certain types of retirement accounts. It is based on your adjusted gross income (AGI) number that appears on the income tax return with the addition of some other items.

Nondeductible IRA A regular IRA that does not receive a deduction for its annual contribution. Anyone with income, no matter how high, may contribute to a nondeductible IRA, even with a retirement plan at work. Nondeductible IRAs are reported on IRS Form 8606 each year as a part of an individual's tax return.

Payable on Death (POD) An investment or bank account that upon the death of the owner is paid to the beneficiary without probate.

Penalty Punishment from the IRS in the form of dollars for not meeting specific tax rules. Tax penalties are generally not tax deductible.

Private Letter Ruling A specific IRS judgment about a certain situation where a taxpayer spells out the exact details in advance of a transaction and the IRS determines the way that it will treat the transaction. These rulings are not really private because we can see the way other rulings have worked; the private part is that the IRS only guarantees that specific result for the person getting the letter ruling. If considering a transaction in an untested or grey area, these are worth the time and money for the assurance.

Qualified Charitable Distribution (QCD) Direct gifts from IRAs to charities up to $100,000 per year only for people over age 70½. Scheduled to end in 2009 but has been extended before.

Qualified Domestic Relations Order (QDRO) A legal order subsequent to a divorce or legal separation that splits and changes ownership of an IRA or retirement plan to give the divorced spouse his or her share of the IRA or pension plan.

Ratability When TIPRA allows for the tax triggered by 2010 Roth IRA conversions to be delayed, ratability until 2011 and 2012, it means that half of the 2010 conversion would be counted as income in 2011 and half in 2012 if the deferral is chosen.

Recharacterization Reversing or undoing a Roth IRA conversion back to the original regular IRA or retirement plan status. Also referred to as *unconverting*. When you recharacterize a Roth IRA conversion, it is as if it was never converted.

Regular IRAs Receive an income tax deduction for annual contributions and grow tax-deferred. When distributions from regular (or traditional) IRAs are made, income taxes are paid on the entire distribution. After age 70½, regular IRAs must begin distributions with annual increases.

Required Beginning Date (RBD) April 1 of the year following the IRA holder reaching age 70½. The first RMD from a regular IRA must be made by the RBD. Subsequent RMDs must be made by each December 31.

Required Minimum Distribution (RMD) The mandatory post-age 70½ distributions from regular IRAs and retirement plans. If an RMD is not distributed in time, the IRS penalty is 50 percent of the RMD. Roth IRAs have no RMDs as long as the owner is alive.

Rollover A deposit into an IRA or retirement plan from another IRA or retirement plan.

Roth Conversion Advantage (RCA) The calculation of the increase in total spendable dollars (after tax) in a specific future year by making a Roth IRA conversion versus not making the conversion. For example, if in 10 years a regular IRA would have $100,000 in spendable money and the Roth IRA conversion would have $120,000, the RCA would be $20,000 for year 10. If there are RMDs or the use of non-IRA money to pay the conversion tax, it is included in this calculation to get an exact comparison.

Roth Conversion Advantage Percentage The percentage increase of spendable dollars made available in future years as a result of the Roth IRA Conversion. If in year 10, the RCA was $20,000 as a result of the regular IRA having $100,000 after taxes and the Roth having $120,000, the RCA would be 20 percent. This is an important measurement of the potential increase in spendable dollars that a Roth IRA conversion might yield as a future result.

Roth Conversion Option (RCO) A strategy for converting all regular IRAs into Roth IRAs first and not deciding to actually commit to any of the Roth conversions until later. The RCO is performed in three steps:

1. Convert all regular IRAs (and available retirement plans) into several separate Roth IRAs by asset class as early in the year as possible.

2. Decide before the recharacterization deadline of October 15 the year after the conversion which Roth accounts are to remain converted. This decision is based on all information known before the deadline including the Roth account performance after conversion and other important factors.

3. Repeat the RCO every year you have regular IRAs or available retirement plans.

Roth IRA A special IRA that receives no deduction for contributions. Qualified Roth distributions are received tax-free. When regular IRAs or retirement plans are converted to Roth IRAs, income taxes are triggered. Unlike regular IRAs, Roth IRAs have no mandatory lifetime distributions.

Rule of 72 The time in which an investment will double in size can be determined by the formula found in the Rule of 72. The formula is 72/(interest or growth rate)=(number of years to double). Therefore at 7.2 percent interest or growth, an account doubles in 10 years. At 10 percent interest or growth, the account doubles in 7.2 years.

Savers These people are always Type 1. They save a certain percentage of money first and spend only what is left over. Savers tend to delay spending gratification and are usually debt free as a result. Savers usually do not want to be forced to take distributions from their regular IRAs at age 70½ but want to have the money available in case of a rainy day.

SIMPLE IRA Employer provided retirement plan that has lower costs to set up and maintain than certain types of retirement plans. SIMPLE stands for Savings Incentive Match Plan for Employees.

Spenders Type 2 people who spend their money as it comes in on "necessities" and plan to save any money that is left over. As a result of this approach, spenders rarely have substantial savings. Spenders are fun to be around.

Tax Bracket The level of a person's income tax, as indicated by the amount of taxes that person pays on his last dollar of taxable income. This is also called the *marginable tax bracket* or *tax rate*. Primary use is for bragging about at parties.

Tax Credit A dollar-for-dollar savings in income tax. If you had a $1,000 tax credit, you would pay $1,000 less in income tax than without the tax credit.

Tax Deduction Generally lowers your taxable income by this amount. Tax deductions may lower your income tax based on your tax bracket. For example, if you made a deductible IRA contribution for $5,000 and were in the 35 percent income tax bracket your income tax reduction would be 35 percent of $5,000 or $1,750.

Tax Increase Prevention and Reconciliation Act of 2005 (TIPRA) The law that allows Roth conversions for everyone starting in 2010. Before 2010, you could only convert if your MAGI was $100,000 or less.

Trust An entity that can hold assets with certain rules and provisions. Trusts may have the same or different trustees and beneficiaries. The control is in the hands of the trustee within the rules of the trust. An individual may be a trustee, or an institution may be utilized. *See* **IRA Inheritance Trust.**

Turnover Portfolio turnover is a measurement of investment activity (buying and selling) within an account. The higher the turnover rate, the more buying and selling that takes place within an investment or a fund.

Type 1 People who have the access and availability of non-IRA or outside funds that could be used to pay the income tax triggered by a Roth IRA conversion.

Type 2 People who have no other sources to pay the income tax if they converted to a Roth IRA except the IRA or retirement plans.

ACKNOWLEDGMENTS

BERNARD OF CHARTRES USED TO say "that we are like dwarfs on the shoulders of giants, so that we can see more than they, and things at a greater distance, not by virtue of any sharpness of sight on our part, or any physical distinction, but because we are carried high and raised up by their giant size." I have had a great deal of assistance with this project from so many people. My sincerest thanks to each of you who helped me during this journey. The good stuff came from the following giants...

Doug Barnes	Natalie Choate
Rick Benzel	Trey Cousins
Beverly Bledsoe	Ken Dickerson
Jack Bledsoe	Guerdon Ely
Lesa Bledsoe	Les Frieden
Nancy Bledsoe	Chuck Friley
Wilson Bledsoe	David Fuller
Sal Capizzi	Don Harris

Dave Hoffman
Dale Irvin
Doug Jacobs
Keith Johnson
Larry Johnson
Bob Keebler
Paul Kolander
Greg Kolojeski
Jim Lacamp
Matthew Land
Nancy Land
Jim Lange
Laurin Levine
Terry Lustig
Rob Messett
Jonathan Mintz

Jim Mixtacki
Alex Nakos
Randy Pennington
Barry Picker
Dan Poynter
Pat Reddell
Ryan Rogers
Ray Rutherford
Chris Seidman
Frank Sloan
Ed Slott
Bobby Stover
Maria Umbach
Joyce Wilson
Larry Winget

Any flaws or bad jokes were unassisted and I accept sole responsibility.

INDEX